Naked, And You Clothed Me
HOMILIES AND REFLECTIONS FOR CYCLE A

Naked, And You Clothed Me
HOMILIES AND REFLECTIONS FOR CYCLE A

EDITED BY DEACON JIM KNIPPER

Published by:
Clear Faith Publishing LLC
Princeton, New Jersey
2013

Published by Clear Faith Publishing LLC
22 Lafayette Road
Princeton, NJ 08540

ISBN 978-1-940414-00-3

First Printing November, 2013

Cover & Interior Design by Doug Cordes
Illustrations by Brother Mickey O'Neill McGrath

Naked, And You Clothed Me is printed on 60# Glatfelter Natural and the text is set in Fairfield and Scala Sans.

Printed in the United States of America

CONTRIBUTING AUTHORS

Rev. William J. Bausch

Rob Bell

Joel Blunk

Fr. Greg Boyle, SJ

Sr. Simone Campbell, SSS

Rev. Dr. David A. Davis

Msgr. Michael Doyle

Michelle Francl-Donnay

Fr. Jim Greenfield, OSFS

Rev. Paul A. Holmes

Fr. Dan Horan, OFM

Deacon Greg Kandra

Deacon Jim Knipper

Michael Leach

Fr. Richard G. Malloy, SJ

Fr. James Martin, SJ

Rev Carol Howard Merritt

Rev. Penny Nash

Msgr. Walter E. Nolan

Christine Valters Paintner, PhD

Jan Richardson

Fr. Richard Rohr, OFM

Mary Elizabeth Sperry

Fran Rossi Szpylczyn

Patrick Wenrick

The opinions in each homily/reflection do not necessarily
represent the views of the other contributors.

DEDICATION

For my wife,
Teresa Poloney Knipper
Whose constant love, care, support and blessing
gives life to our family.

And for all who are naked in body, mind or soul.

Since many of you do not belong to the Catholic Church and others are non-believers, from the bottom of my heart I give this silent blessing to each and every one of you, respecting the conscience of each one of you but knowing that each one of you is a child of God.

Pope Francis

We are the Bibles the world is reading;
we are the creeds the world is needing;
we are the sermons the world is heeding.

Rev. Billy Graham

I simply taught, preached, and wrote God's Word; otherwise I did nothing.

Martin Luther

"Prayer is the raising of the mind to God.
We must always remember this.
The actual words matter less."

Pope John XXIII

"Faith comes from hearing the message, and the message is heard through the word of Christ."

Romans 10:17

CONTENTS

FOREWORD   1
PREFACE   3

ADVENT SEASON

1ST SUNDAY OF ADVENT   7
REV. DR. DAVID A. DAVIS

2ND SUNDAY OF ADVENT   13
FR. BILL BAUSCH

3RD SUNDAY OF ADVENT   19
JAN L. RICHARDSON

4TH SUNDAY OF ADVENT   23
DEACON GREG KANDRA

CHRISTMAS SEASON

NATIVITY OF THE LORD: VIGIL   29
ROB BELL

NATIVITY OF THE LORD: DAY   33
MSGR. WALTER NOLAN

HOLY FAMILY OF JESUS, MARY AND
JOSEPH   37
FRAN ROSSI SZPYLCZYN

MARY MOTHER OF GOD   41
DEACON GREG KANDRA

THE EPIPHANY OF THE LORD   45
MSGR. WALTER NOLAN

BAPTISM OF THE LORD   51
CHRISTINE VALTERS PAINTNER

LENT

ASH WEDNESDAY   57
CHRISTINE VALTERS PAINTNER

1ST SUNDAY OF LENT   63
REV. DR. DAVID A. DAVIS

2ND SUNDAY OF LENT   69
MICHELLE FRANCL-DONNAY

3RD SUNDAY OF LENT   73
FR. JAMES J. GREENFIELD, OSFS

4TH SUNDAY IN LENT   77
REV. PENNY NASH

5TH SUNDAY OF LENT   81
FR. BILL BAUSCH

PALM SUNDAY   87
RICHARD ROHR, OFM

HOLY THURSDAY   91
DEACON GREG KANDRA

GOOD FRIDAY   95
FR. PAUL HOLMES

EASTER SEASON

EASTER VIGIL   101
FR. RICHARD G. MALLOY, SJ

EASTER SUNDAY   105
REV. DR. DAVID A. DAVIS

2ND SUNDAY OF EASTER   111
FR. RICHARD ROHR, OFM

3RD SUNDAY OF EASTER   115
PATRICK WENRICK

4TH SUNDAY OF EASTER   119
MARY ELIZABETH SPERRY

5TH SUNDAY OF EASTER   123
FR. DANIEL P. HORAN, OFM

6TH SUNDAY OF EASTER   129
FRAN ROSSI SZPYLCZYN

7TH SUNDAY OF EASTER 133
MICHELLE FRANCL-DONNAY

ASCENSION OF THE LORD 137
FR. PAUL HOLMES

PENTECOST 139
FR. BILL BAUSCH

ORDINARY TIME

2ND SUNDAY IN ORDINARY TIME 147
DEACON JIM KNIPPER

3RD SUNDAY IN ORDINARY TIME 151
PATRICK WENRICK

4TH SUNDAY IN ORDINARY TIME 155
ROB BELL

5TH SUNDAY IN ORDINARY TIME 161
SISTER SIMONE CAMPBELL, SSS

6TH SUNDAY IN ORDINARY TIME 165
ROB BELL

7TH SUNDAY IN ORDINARY TIME 169
FR. JAMES MARTIN, SJ

8TH SUNDAY IN ORDINARY TIME 175
JOEL BLUNK

9TH SUNDAY IN ORDINARY TIME 181
FR. DANIEL P. HORAN, OFM

10TH SUNDAY IN ORDINARY TIME 185
REV. CAROL HOWARD MERRITT

11TH SUNDAY IN ORDINARY TIME 189
DEACON JIM KNIPPER

12TH SUNDAY IN ORDINARY TIME 193
MSGR. MICHAEL DOYLE

13TH SUNDAY IN ORDINARY TIME 199
MARY ELIZABETH SPERRY

14TH SUNDAY IN ORDINARY TIME 203
DEACON GREG KANDRA

15TH SUNDAY IN ORDINARY TIME 207
FR. PAUL HOLMES

16TH SUNDAY IN ORDINARY TIME 209
DEACON JIM KNIPPER

17TH SUNDAY IN ORDINARY TIME 215
FR. JAMES MARTIN, SJ

18TH SUNDAY IN ORDINARY TIME 221
JOEL BLUNK

19TH SUNDAY IN ORDINARY TIME 227
FR. BILL BAUSCH

20TH SUNDAY IN ORDINARY TIME 231
REV. CAROL HOWARD MERRITT

21ST SUNDAY IN ORDINARY TIME 235
DEACON JIM KNIPPER

22ND SUNDAY IN ORDINARY TIME 241
FR. RICHARD ROHR, OFM

23RD SUNDAY IN ORDINARY TIME 245
REV. PENNY NASH

24TH SUNDAY IN ORDINARY TIME 249
FR. RICHARD ROHR, OFM

25TH SUNDAY IN ORDINARY TIME 253
FR. PAUL HOLMES

26TH SUNDAY IN ORDINARY TIME 255
JAN L. RICHARDSON

27TH SUNDAY OF ORDINARY TIME 261
FR. JAMES J. GREENFIELD, OSFS

28TH SUNDAY IN ORDINARY TIME 265
REV. PENNY NASH

29TH SUNDAY IN ORDINARY TIME 269
MICHAEL LEACH

30TH SUNDAY IN ORDINARY   273
FR. RICHARD G. MALLOY, SJ

31ST SUNDAY IN ORDINARY TIME   277
FRAN ROSSI SZPYLCZYN

32ND SUNDAY IN ORDINARY TIME   281
REV. DR. DAVID A. DAVIS

33RD SUNDAY IN ORDINARY TIME   285
FR. JAMES MARTIN, SJ

FEAST DAYS

MOST HOLY TRINITY   293
FR. DANIEL P. HORAN, OFM

MOST HOLY BODY AND BLOOD OF
CHRIST   299
FR. JAMES J. GREENFIELD, OSFS

FEAST OF ALL SAINTS   303
JAN L. RICHARDSON

ALL SOULS DAY   309
MSGR. MICHAEL DOYLE

CHRIST THE KING   315
FR. GREG BOYLE, SJ

THEMATIC CROSS REFERENCE   319

THE CONRTIBUTORS   321

THE CHARITIES   335

ACKNOWLEDGEMENTS   339

FOREWORD

The words that inspired the title of this volume come from the extraordinary text in the Gospel of Matthew where Jesus describes the hidden key to salvation: "I was hungry and you fed me, naked and you clothed me, a stranger and you welcomed me…"

I had probably heard these words many times before I left college long ago to join the Catholic Worker movement. It was there, in the movement begun by Dorothy Day, that I first realized that the works of mercy enumerated in this passage could describe a way of life. Day built her life around the simple but astonishing message that Jesus left us: "Insofar as you have done these things to the least of my brothers and sisters, you have done them to me."

Everyday I fall short of living out the practical implications of this teaching: that the most direct way of showing love for Jesus is in my response to those in need. Perhaps that is why Jesus could state, "The poor you will have with you always." He wasn't justifying the persistence of poverty, but acknowledging my own failures, as he did with Peter, when he said, "Before the cock crows you will have betrayed me three times."

The sermons collected in this volume are like bells of awareness. There is nothing here that has not been said before, whether by the authors of scripture, the saints throughout history, or the many preachers who have gone before. But we need reminding. The mysteries of our faith can become worn smooth with too much handling. A good sermon can surprise us, wake us up, set a trap in which we are suddenly caught. We hear the cock crowing and know it cries for us. And we remember anew what Jesus taught us.

It is easy to become preoccupied by the externals of faith and religious practice. This is no less true for us than it was for people during Jesus' time. The message Jesus spread then is no less relevant for us today. We too must be constantly renewed and surprised by the astonishing news that love is at the heart of everything: God's love for us, and the importance of returning that love through forgiveness, compassion, and service toward others, especially those who suffer.

This one sentence from Dorothy Day was the best sermon I ever heard: "The mystery of the poor is this: that they are Jesus, and what we do for them, we do for him." It was nothing original. But because of the way she lived, and the way she said it, I believed.

Robert Ellsberg

PREFACE

---

*W*hen *I launched this series* with *Hungry, And You Fed Me*, I never expected that book would be received with such enthusiasm. In June 2013 it received awards from the Catholic Press Association (http://www.catholicpress.org) in categories for Liturgy (2nd place) and Best Book by a Small Publisher (2nd place). Currently, nearly 1,000 people follow us on Facebook (www.facebook.com/Homilists). Many have asked, "Will there be a book for Cycle A?"

Yes…and here it is.

I am most grateful to all fifteen contributors who returned to provide, once again, gifted homilies. In addition, we're pleased to add ten more contributors from a range of Christian backgrounds. (See page 321 for more information.)

Like the first volume, our goal with this series of homiletic books is two-fold. First, we wish to provide a resource that "breaks open" the Lectionary readings so our eyes, lips, and hearts become more Christ-centered.

Second, thanks to the generosity of our contributors, we're able to donate proceeds from each book to charity. For *Naked and You Clothed Me*, we've selected charities that focus on providing clothing for men, women, children, and infants in the greater Trenton, NJ area who are homeless or are in need. (See page 335 for more information.)

Over the past year, the world has welcomed Pope Francis, a new pope who continues to emphasize the core Gospel imperative to serve the poor and who preaches Christ's call for simplicity.

Pope Francis has said, "Bringing the Gospel is bringing God's power to pluck down evil and violence, to destroy and overthrow the barriers and selfishness, intolerance and hatred so as to build a new world." While I know this book will not, in itself, build a new world, I do hope one or more of these homilies will inspire you to renew your Christian commitment to aid the hungry, the naked, and the sick, for that is what we are called to do.

May the words of these gifted homilists do exactly that and bring blessings to you and yours.

Jim Knipper
21 September 2013
Feast of St. Matthew the Evangelist

we are to name him Jesus.

ADVENT SEASON

Isaiah 2:1-5
Rom. 13:11-14
Matt. 24:37-44

"In days to come..."

The Word of the Lord. An oracle of Isaiah. In days to come. In prophet's voice. In days to come. "In days to come the mountain of the Lord's house shall be established as the highest of all the mountains, and shall be raised above the hills; all the nations shall stream to it." A word of the Lord that emanates from deep within the history of God's people. In days to come. "Many peoples shall come and say, 'Let us go up to the mountain of the Lord, to the house of the God of Jacob.'" That the Lord may teach. That we may walk in the Lord's paths. In days to come. A prophetic voice that echoes, that repeats, that never fades.

In days to come. It comes not just from Isaiah, but from Micah, too. You remember what made Micah famous: "What does the Lord require of you but to do justice and to love kindness and to walk humbly with your God?" In days to come. Micah proclaimed it as well. In prophets' voice. That's plural. In days to come. That teaching shall go forth from Zion and the Word of the Lord from Jerusalem. It's not a piercing prophetic refrain, not a glorious trumpet sound, but more of a guttural groan. In days to come. "The Lord shall judge between the nations, and shall arbitrate for many peoples; they shall beat their swords into plowshares, and their spears into pruning hooks." Isaiah's oracle. Constant. Rhythmic. Played into every period of history. Bass notes plucked forever over there in the prophets' section of the orchestra. In days to come. In days to come. In days to come. "Nation shall not lift up sword against nation, neither shall they learn war anymore." I guess we're not there yet. So play on, Isaiah. We're not there yet. We're still walking. We're walking still. So play on.

Wreath. Candle. Purple. Calendars sent home. "Come, Thou Long Expected Jesus." "O Come, O Come, Emmanuel." It must be Advent. The beginning of the church's holiday season. Advent is happy new year. The beginning of a new year in terms of the church's liturgical calendar. As we begin in terms of the life cycle of Jesus and the gestation in Mary's belly and the birth of a baby. And Advent is John the Baptist and preparing the way. Sermon after sermon in pulpit after pulpit in the weeks to come. Sermons about the difference between preparing and just waiting. I've preached more than my share. Preparing for the advent of the Christ Child again and again and again. That's Advent. And Advent is living that in-between, that grey area between the *already* and the *not yet*. Indeed, the Lord has come and we want at least to appear as though we are eager and ready and willing for Christ to come again! And Advent is the end of Thanksgiving and the beginning of Christmas. Those weeks when anticipation builds and the room gradually fills with color, and the children start to beam, and some of us demand Christmas carols while others of us hold out for some good Advent singing still this side of Bethlehem! "Rejoice, Rejoice, Immanuel..." It must be Advent. Pick any of the above for your Advent theme of the day, or the week, or the season. Four candles. Four weeks. Advent. A kind of comfort food for the regular worshiper for whom church feels like home.

Just the other day, a church member introduced me to a longtime Princeton resident. He retired when I was about ten. I think he mentioned that he was 85, though I would never have guessed. Our conversation was light fare, like the lunch we shared. It was only later, when he and I had a moment to ourselves, when just the two of us found ourselves away from the others, it was only then that he followed up on the introduction that had identified me as pastor of Nassau Presbyterian Church. "So what do you say to people who worry about the state of the world?" I hesitated trying to wrap my head around the sudden shift from just talking about the weather. He went on, "More than thousands of years and we're still fighting each other and killing each other. It makes no sense. All the death and destruction. It's not getting any better. How can there be a God?" Wishing we were still talking about what Princeton used to be like, I tried a bit of Calvinism. "I'm not sure God is the one to blame here. Don't you think it's more humanity's utter failure, humankind's total depravity?" My effort was a bit weak. He got a bit defensive. "I'm not depraved," he said with some bristle. And then he thought some more, "Well, it's not my problem; I'm not going to be around much more. But what about your generation, or the next?"

What about the days to come? That's what he was asking. It was only later that I decided his question was less intellectual, less theological. It wasn't about theodicy or philosophy. I don't think he was looking for debate, or was expecting some magic answer from me. In hindsight, I think it was an opportunity for pastoral care. An opportunity that I mostly missed. This no-longer stranger, I think he just wanted some care and companionship in his angst. He was looking for some comfort when reading the morning newspaper. He was yearning for some assurance when looking out at the world. His only expectation was a little bit a hope for his grandchildren. Without wading into politics or foreign policy at all, he was shrugging his shoulders and throwing up his arms. "How about a little peace?" In days to come.

I think he was asking me about Advent. No, he certainly wasn't inquiring as to the calendar or the babe in a manger. He wasn't wanting to talk about "prepare ye the way of the Lord" or the delay of the parousia (that

Second Coming of Christ). And though just a week or so prior to Thanksgiving, we shared no holiday chat at all! But he was asking me about Advent, about the days to come. In days to come. In days to come. Swords into plowshares. Spears into pruning hooks. Learning war no more. In days to come. That's Advent. Because there's this prophet's voice that just won't quit!

We must still be walking, because we're clearly not there yet. That prophets' voice, the prophets' plural voice, the prophet's oracle includes an appeal, a reminder, an affirmation for those of us who find ourselves no longer strangers along this worn pathway of life and faith, those of us yet trying to make some sense of what we see, trying to name some purpose, those of us who pray with more than a hint of urgency, "Is a little more peace out of the question?" In days to come? What about now? And the Word of the Lord plays on. "But we will walk in the name of the Lord our God forever and ever!" That's Micah. Isaiah is just as clear. "O house of Jacob, come, let us walk in the light of the Lord!" Yes, we're walking still. It must be Advent.

A long time. ago I organized a weekend work trip to our cabin in the Endless Mountains of Pennsylvania. The plan for this "men's retreat" called for the interior of the cabin to be finished with tongue and groove cedar. Not being particularly sure of my ability to complete such a task, nor being too proud to ask for help, I had invited about five or six guys who had the skill. Late one night, as all were safely snuggled into sleeping bags after a long day of work, the lights were turned off and the darkness of the woods settled all around there inside the cabin. After some silence, which was clearly long enough for some important thoughts and bedtime prayers, one of the men made the following observation. "You're not going to believe this," he said, as if sharing a new discovery, "but it is darker with my eyes open than it is with my eyes shut!"

Wreath. Candle. Purple. New Year. Weeks to go before Christmas. Prepare ye the way. Yes, of course. But when it is darker when your eyes are opened, when it is so uncomfortably frighteningly, overwhelmingly dark, when the reality of the world simply magnifies the darkness that comes in broken relationships, or conversations with doctors about diagnoses, or parents that won't listen, or the worry for one of your children, or caring for a dying parent, or the stress at work, or the urgency of no work, or the terrifying prospects of college admission, or the unrelenting power of depression, or the exhaustion that comes long before the end of the week, or the helpless feeling of losing your independence, or when you are totally convinced that everyone in your sixth period class hates you, or when any sense that there is a God seems laughable, or the feeling that the notion of resurrection and life eternal has long since been lost on you, when it seems darker when your eyes are wide open, even then—this prophets' voice, it just won't quit. In days to come. In days to come.

And together, you and I, we will be walking still, walking in the light of the Lord. Finding comfort in God's grace. Hearing assurance by God's mercy. Sensing hope in God's promise. While basking in God's presence, still crying out for more peace. That's Advent.

Walking God's paths. Teaching shall go forth. Plowshares. Pruning hooks. Learning war no more. Come, even if for just a taste! The table is set for days to come!

Isa. 11:1-10
Rom. 15:4-9
Luke 3:1–12

"Prepare the way of the Lord"

In the fifteenth year of Tiberius Caesar
when Pilate was governor of Judea
Herod, tetrarch of Galilee
Philip, tetrarch of Ituraea
Annas and Caiaphas, high priests of the Temple
the word of God came to a desert prophet.

Did you listen to the cadence of this gospel opening, catch its rhythm? Did you sense a kind of drum roll? It's like a metronome. It is gospel writer Luke's way of playing an overture, fanfaring what's to come. It's the blaring graphics and loud music that introduce the six o'clock news or *The O'Reilly Factor* or *Larry King Live*. So, likewise, with this drum roll, Luke is saying, "Here he comes! Get ready for the Messiah!" But note that, in the process, Luke makes two points that will mark the Messiah's story and our story.

First, those names at the beginning: Tiberius Caesar, Pontius Pilate, King Herod, High Priest Annas; yes, psychotic Tiberius, vacillating Pilate, quisling Herod, corrupt Annas—they will be back later at the passion of Jesus. The mention of their names are dark hints of the outcome of Christ's life before he is even born.

Second, when Rome held all the power, when Rome's heel was firmly on Israel's neck, God's word came forth in the wilderness. That is to say, God's word did not stop at war rooms, palaces, and temples. Rather, it searched out a minor priest's son who is dressed in a camel skin and finds him in the desert of an occupied country. Yes, the word of the Lord came to this little speck in the empire who was to prepare the way of One who would straighten broken moral paths, fill valleys of despair, level mountains of trouble, and smooth out the rough ways of wickedness and sin. The word of the Lord had indeed bypassed the high and the mighty and fallen upon a nobody in the unlikeliest of desert places.

Interestingly, unbeknownst to John, the same thing had already happened years earlier to a young illiterate girl in a backwater village called Nazareth. She had a mystical experience and said yes to a vision and the word to her became a living Word *inside* her. The Word was beyond spoken. It was made flesh. That was some thirty years before. Now Mary's child was grown up and here was John preparing his way. All that had been set in motion was converging at this moment, and a darkened world saw the glimmer of light and took hope.

What a gospel for our times, for this gospel's Good News is that we should seek hope in our world as well, for the truth is, if you think about it, our world is not much different from John's. The world today is still symbolically the Rome of the Caesars. That is to say, in many parts of the world today the heel of repression and tyranny still grinds firmly upon the necks of its people. There is China with its imprisonments and executions without trials. There are countries in Africa and South America where political and religious freedom do not exist or are brutally repressed. There is Russia which, amidst dire poverty, boasts of 25 newly oil-rich billionaires and 88,000 millionaires who are living luxuriously while the majority are barely eking out a living.

Here in our own country, though blessedly freer and far less overtly brutal, the gap is just as wide. The high and the mighty, often through legal corruption, siphon off our public money and determine our lives. Last year lobbyists spent a record 2.4 billion to get their way, not our way, with the government. The record shows that the richest 300,000 Americans have had their incomes more than triple since 1970 while the real income of the working poor fell. War, crime, broken families abound. Rome lives.

Yet, the gospel news is that, as in the days of Rome, as in the days of John the Baptist, it still happens. What happens? The word of God still comes, and it comes, as it did then, to the small folk and in the unlikeliest of places. In every age it bypasses the boardrooms, complexes, and mega-mansions to lodge in the hearts of the little ones who become pinpoints of light and harbingers of hope. Think of worldly, carefree Francis from Assisi. Think of an ignorant, illiterate girl, Bernadette, from Lourdes. Think of a life-of-the-party playboy, Tom Merton, from Greenwich Village, and an unwed mother, Dorothy Day, from Staten Island, and, yes, even a streetcar conductor named Barney Casey from Milwaukee. All these nobodies received God's word, sometimes reluctantly, and they gave us light and hope. They remain a firm sign of God's presence and power.

Barney Casey? Did you hear me right? Who's he? I know you've heard of the others, so let me tell you about him and God's word and about his being a pinpoint of light. A nondescript kid from Milwaukee at the turn of the last century, a teenager who was the mainstay of his family, Barney Casey worked as a farmhand, lumberjack, brick maker, prison guard, and finally a streetcar conductor. Then one day he witnessed a tragedy that set him on a new course in life.

On a cold rainy afternoon as he guided his streetcar around a curve in a rough part of town, he saw a lot of people gathered on the tracks. He stopped the car, pushed through the crowd to see a young drunken sailor standing over a woman he had assaulted and stabbed repeatedly. He couldn't get the brutal incident out of his mind. He began to pray for the sailor. He prayed for the woman and gradually he felt he must pray for the whole world.

So eventually he quit his job and applied to the seminary. But Barney was not that bright. So the seminary brass dismissed him and told him to go become a brother where the studies were not as rigorous. But Barney, frustrated but not defeated, applied and joined the Capuchin order at St. Bonaventure in Detroit where he got his religious name of Solanus, after St. Francis Solanus: Solanus Casey. Still he really wasn't that sharp and some seminary professors opposed his ordination, but an old priest spoke up for him and he was ordained in 1904. However, the doubts about the intelligence and the abilities of this underachiever still lingered, so the seminary would ordain him only under one condition, that he would remain what is called a "simplex priest," that is, he could celebrate Mass but that's all. He could not hear confessions, preach, or wear the Capuchin hood.

So for forty-three years Father Solanus Casey never heard a confession or gave a retreat or preached a mission. What did he do? He was assigned as a lowly doorkeeper, answering the door and greeting visitors, a no-brainer. He spent his first fifteen years answering the door in Yonkers and in Manhattan and then in 1921 was transferred to Our Lady of the Angels in Harlem.

But in this desert of the ordinary, the word of God bypassed the local bishop and the chancery officials and the abbot and came to Barney, because people were discovering something about this doorkeeper. It was that this simple doorkeeper, having listened so intently to the word of God, turned out to be a wonderful listener to them and an insightful counselor. Word spread and soon many would come, bypass the prior and abbot, and ask to speak with the doorkeeper, Father Solanus. But that wasn't all. Father Solanus—Barney Casey—was also put in charge of the Capuchin Prayer Association, but no sooner did he take charge then ~~miracles began to happen. People were being healed of all sorts of ail-ments: pneumonia, heart disease, blindness.~~ This doorkeeper turned out to be ~~also a wonder-worker.~~

His superiors soon transferred him back to St. Bonaventure in Detroit, where they could keep an eye and a lid on him. But there he attracted an even larger following and so for the next two decades people trekked literally from all over the world, like the crowds that came to John in the desert, to receive the simple doorkeeper's ministry and hear his words.

Father Solanus—Barney Casey—worked twelve hours a day helping and counseling others. At night he was found praying in the chapel and often sound asleep before the altar. This streetcar driver turned simple priest, not trusted with anything important, died in 1957 and his cause is now up for canonization. Who would have thought, in the car capital of the world, the word of God would come to somebody who answers the door and a light would shine forth?

My point in telling you all this during Advent is precisely the old Christo-pher point: *Better to light one candle than to curse the darkness.* Times are threatening, times are bloody and dark, but let the word of God lodge in your heart. Pray the prayer, do the good deed, be holy, put yourself in the hands of God. Have a sense of calling.

Be a candle, be a Francis, be a Bernadette, be a John the Baptist, be a simple doorkeeper who lets out the light. And then, lo and behold, you will become today's voice of hope, of one crying out in the desert of our times, "Prepare the way of the Lord, for he is near."

Reprinted from Once Upon a Gospel: Inspiring Homilies and Insightful Reflections *by William J. Bausch,* ©2008. *Twenty-Third Publications. Used with permission. All rights reserved.*

Isa. 35: 1-6, 10	
James 5:7-10	*"When John heard in prison what the Messiah was doing…"*
Matt 11:2-11	

John in prison, thrown there by Herod because he dared tell the king that it was unlawful for him to have married his brother's wife.

John, locust-and-honey-eating prophet of the wilderness, confined to a cell.

John the Way-Maker, his own way ending in captivity and, shortly, a brutal death.

When John heard in prison what the Messiah was doing…

This is the John of whom we read in Luke 1, where his mother, Elizabeth, says to her kinswoman Mary, "For as soon as I heard the sound of your greeting, the child in my womb leaped for joy." A leap of recognition, Luke means us to see: even in his mother's womb, John the Way-Maker, John the Messenger, is able to discern and recognize the One for whom the world has longed.

It is a far different enclosure that John finds himself in now. He will not emerge from this one into life, as when he left the safe confines of his mother's womb. This enclosure will lead instead to his death at a gruesome dinner party.

When John heard in prison what the Messiah was doing...

Even here, John's powers of discernment are at full force. Enclosed within his cell, John has not closed in on himself. This one whom Jesus calls a messenger is still receiving messages. Is still keeping his ears and eyes open. Is still able to turn his attention beyond himself.

In his confinement, John refuses to stop looking, stop listening, stop preparing. In his enforced and final enclosure, John persists in turning an eye toward the Messiah. Seeks him. Inquires after him. When John's disciples return to him with news of the blind who see, the lame who walk, the lepers made whole, he knows. Recognizes once again. Leaps, perhaps, for joy.

When John heard in prison what the Messiah was doing...

I keep wondering what it must have been like for John, imprisoned, to receive word of the Messiah, the one for whom John had made a way. I wonder what wedge of hope, freedom, possibility the news must have stirred in John. I suspect he well knew he would never leave his physical captivity, but when this preparer of Jesus's path receives word of what the Messiah is up to, what chains must have fallen away? What light must have gathered there in his cell?

When John heard in prison what the Messiah was doing...

John's story that we hear on this Advent day draws me to contemplate the word of Christ that comes to those in captivity. I think of how, lately, I have felt drawn to pray for those who live in bondage of body or soul or both: those in prison, those who have been kidnapped, those in slavery, those living with addictions that have bent and broken them. I think of, and pray for, those who live within systems of oppression, as well as those who create their own systems and situations that rob them of power. I think of those who, for reasons of fear or ignorance or an illusion of security, have given away their freedom little by little, in such small increments that they hardly notice until it's gone. In John's company today, I find myself wondering where these prayers might lead me, what path they might be preparing, what call I might have to work for freedom and healing and release.

When John heard in prison what the Messiah was doing...

This reading invites me also to ponder whether there are any places of bondage within myself, any part of my being that lives with less freedom, less fullness, less wholeness than God intends. I think of occasions when I have struggled within an institutional system, or times when I gave away my power. I recall seasons when I became entangled in situations that exhausted me. And I celebrate the times when I resisted the urge to settle for less, to trade my autonomy for something that looked like safety.

John challenges me to ask: Whatever my circumstance, how does God call me to live with freedom, with hope, with trust in the One who came to proclaim release to the captives?

When John heard in prison what the Messiah was doing...

On this Advent day, is there any place of unfreedom within you? Is there some part of your soul, your spirit, your mind that lives in confinement? To what, or to whom, are you giving power and control these days? Why?

What news of Christ, what word of hope, is God offering in that place of confinement? What is one tiny step that would lead to greater freedom?

In this season of expectation and incarnation, how might God call you to enter into places where others live in bondage and captivity, and to speak the news of liberation there?

I Cannot Say What Shape
A Blessing

I cannot say what shape
this blessing will take for you,
what form by which
it will find you
in the place
where you need it
most.

It cannot be pinned down,
this blessing that
inscribes itself
on prison walls,
works its way
between the bars,
comes as a word
in the ear
that has never heard,
a brilliance in the eye
that has not seen.

But you can trust
that a blessing
that comes as healing
in the body broken
will know how
to reach you.

You can be sure
that a blessing
that returns the dead
to life
will know
with exquisite precision
how to bring you back
from your bondage
from your captivity
from your exile
from your pain.

Whatever holds you,
this blessing will loose.
Whatever confines you,
this blessing will overcome.

A glimmer of light
in the darkness,
an outstretched hand
in the shadows:
who knows how it
will show up,
or what it will bear?

Just watch for it.
Wait for it.
This blessing is
on its way.

4ᵀᴴ SUNDAY OF ADVENT

DEACON GREG KANDRA

Isa. 7:10-14
Rom. 1:1-7
Matt. 1:18-24

"Do not be afraid."

In the late 19th century, one of the most sought-after portrait painters was a Frenchman by the name of James Tissot. He made his reputation painting society women and the wealthy in and around Paris. But at one point in his life, while doing research for a painting, he stepped into a church. While there, he had a profound religious experience. He left a changed man, and devoted the rest of his life to spiritual and religious themes—including hundreds of paintings depicting scenes from the Bible, most famously the life of Christ. The Brooklyn Museum has many of these sketches and watercolors, and they had an exhibit last year. They are beautiful, and moving.

They are also deeply human—none more so than a work that has direct bearing on this Sunday's gospel. It is a surprising portrait of St. Joseph.

Joseph is shown at his carpenter's table, with tools scattered around him. His shop is small and cramped, planks and pieces of wood everywhere, shavings piled up on the floor. The windows look out onto the bustling streets of Nazareth, where townspeople are going about their business. But in the middle of all that stands Joseph, bent over his table, his bearded chin in his hand, deep in thought.

The painting's title says it all: "The Anxiety of Joseph".

We rarely think of him that way. But Tissot, as he often does, penetrated to the heart of his subject.

Maybe Tissot was showing Joseph the morning before he has the dream we just heard in Matthew's gospel. Or maybe it is the morning after—and he is coming to terms with what the angel has said, and what he must do. Maybe it was even later, and this new father is concerned with the worries that every father has.

But what we see in Tissot's picture—and what is hinted at in this gospel today—is a man more like us than we realize.

We tend to think of Joseph the way we see him in the manger scene outside our church, or on the cards we send, or the pageants that are staged. He is strong, stoic, patient—"righteous," as Matthew describes him.

But Tissot understood that the man betrothed to Mary was a man of worries, and apprehension, and even fear. This morning, I'd like to suggest that Joseph is also a man who speaks to our own time.

He is a man for our age—an Age of Anxiety.

He must have known economic uncertainty—wondering how he would support and sustain his family, running his own small business. He had to pay taxes—to "render unto Caesar." Like many people today, shortly after his son was born, Joseph and his family became refugees, immigrants in a foreign land—the land that had held his people as slaves. Joseph also lived with the threat of terror—a ruthless king bent on murdering children.

On a more personal level, Joseph knew the anxiety of any man about to become a father. He must have asked himself: Am I ready for this? Am I good enough, strong enough, wise enough? And then, confronting the very real possibility of scandal, Joseph must have had more than a few sleepless nights. How, he must have wondered, could he protect and spare the woman he loved?

And—like Mary, the woman he loved—he also must have thought at some point: This is not what I had planned. Everything is suddenly different.

How many of us have said that about our own lives? How many of us have had to face, like Joseph, a confusing world with uncertainty, and doubt, and anxiety, and fear?

How many of us have felt like the man in that Tissot drawing, frozen in place, while the world moves on around us, and we stand there and worry and wonder: What do I do? How will I get through this?

But into all that, in Joseph's complicated life, comes a voice in a dream.

"Do not be afraid. God is with us."

And his world—and ours—is changed.

In the middle of "the anxiety of Joseph" comes blessed reassurance—and a reminder that God's will sees beyond our fears, beyond our limitations.

When our lives can seem a nightmare, we cannot forget to dream. When every demon seems to be making our lives hell, we cannot forget to listen for angels.

When our world has been turned upside down, we cannot forget to trust that God will make it right.

Again and again, the words come to us from the gospels, in times of confusion and doubt and anxiety.

"Do not be afraid."

That is the message to Joseph, to Mary, to the shepherds, to the apostles— and to us.

And in these last days of Advent, that is the great message the gospels leave us with as we light the last candle and sing "O Come, O Come Emmanuel." The light is brighter. God's presence is closer.

If you have any doubts about that, just think of Joseph, the great silent partner of the Holy Family, the man who doesn't utter a word in the gospels—but whose ability to trust, and to dream, and to listen speaks volumes.

In the end, the words of the angel echo down to us as the great defining message of Advent hope—banishing all fear, easing all anxiety.

"Do not be afraid. God is with us."

CHRISTMAS SEASON

NATIVITY OF THE LORD: VIGIL

ROB BELL

Isa. 62:1-5
Acts 13:16-17, 22-25
Matt. 1:1-25
Luke 2:1-14

"The time came for her to have her child"

This evening we celebrate the birth of Jesus. God has not abandoned the world, but comes into the world to save it, redeem it, renew it, restore it, and reconcile everything through this child, Jesus. Here in these passages from Matthew and Luke, we find the stunning, electric announcement of the birth of this child whom people have been waiting for years and years and years for…here we find the Christmas story.

Luke, interestingly enough, does not begin the Christmas story with the birth of Jesus. He begins with the birth of a relative of Jesus named John the Baptist. But he begins even before that with John the Baptist's parents, who have been longing for a child but have been unable to conceive. And an angel appears to Zechariah and says, "Now, I know you've been longing for a child, and you're going to have a child. And your child's name is going to be John. And John is going to prepare the way for another child who will be the Messiah, who will save the world."

And the angel says to him, "I stand in the presence of God, and I've been sent to speak to you and to tell you this good news. And now you will be silent and not be able to speak until the day this happens, because you did not believe my words, which will come true at their appointed time. God has not abandoned human history, but God has been at work all along, and some really, really big things are about to go down. But you, Zechariah, you didn't believe me. So you aren't going to be able to speak until it happens." And these things are going to happen at the appointed times.

Remember that phrase: "the appointed time."

So Zechariah was told all sorts of things that were going to happen at the appointed time. And then it happens. And throughout the many stories surrounding the birth of Jesus we find many people had been waiting for this baby year after year after year after year. Angels, Zechariah, Simeon, Mary, and Joseph all filled with this anticipation of a child that will be born at the appointed time. And then the baby is born, and there is celebration.

Now, here's what I find fascinating. Zechariah is told, "God is going to send a Messiah. A Savior is going to be born, and it will happen at the appointed time." There is a word in the Greek language for "time". It is the word *"chronos."* It's where we get the word "chronograph" or "chronological". The word refers to time that moves forward in a sequential fashion.

There was yesterday. There was today. There is tomorrow. There is the day after that, when you return the things that don't fit. There is the day after that, when you go take a long walk, and there is the day after that, when you might have to go back to work. There is the day after that, when you might get the day off. There is *chronos*, sequential time; last Christmas, the Christmas before that one, next week, three months ago, seven years from now. Chronos, where you get a watch that measures time in quantifiable units forward.

When Zechariah is told all this is going to happen in time, the angel does not use the word *chronos*. He uses a different word, which we have no English equivalent of. He uses the word *kairos*.

Kairos refers to an opportune moment. It's an undetermined period in which something special happens. He says, "Listen, you're living in *chronos*, but when God shows up, it's not ordinary time. God is not going to move in chronos. God is going to move in *kairos*." There is your calendar, your watch, your beeper, your timer, your alarm. That kind of time. And then there is that other time when things happen. And the angel says, "God is about to invade *chronos* with some *kairos*." Are you with me?

In our *chronos* we long for things. Jesus is the prince of peace, and yet there isn't fully peace on earth. Jesus is the great healer, and yet this Christmas everything is not healed. Jesus saves us, but yet this Christmas everything and everybody isn't saved. And so we celebrate, and yet we also long for all that which hasn't been fixed, which hasn't been healed, which hasn't been repaired. We lived in *chronos*, but we long for *kairos*.

The challenge when you're in *chronos* waiting for the *kairos* is not to get bitter or disillusioned, but to allow God to shape and form you so when *kairos* hits, you're ready and you can celebrate.

Are you celebrating this Christmas with things in your life that are un-healed, unresolved, unreconciled? And so you're celebrating the birth, and yet at the same time, there is a longing.

In God's time, God sent Jesus and said, "I'm sending him to save the world. You're going to be okay. Trust him. Listen to him. Do what he says." And so Jesus came and he opened up a whole new world. He offers forgiveness. He offers hope. He offers liberation. He offers healing. He offers peace. And you can trust him.

This Christmas, you can trust him. You can trust him with your past. You can trust him with your present. You can trust him with your future. You can trust him with your hopes. You can trust him with your sins. You can trust him with your sexuality. You can trust him with your checkbook. You can trust him with your family members. You can trust him with the awkward relationships where you don't know what to do next. You can trust him with your infertility and you can trust him with the chaos of way too many kids.

You can trust this Jesus because in the fullness of time, God said, "I'm sending my son to heal the world and he can be trusted." And so in the meantime, when everything isn't fixed, and when there isn't peace, and when the healing hasn't yet come and you're in *chronos* and you're longing for *kairos*, you can trust him then too. You can celebrate this Jesus at Christmas and you can beat your chest and sob over the things that aren't yet healed, fixed, or whole.

And you can have all of that because God says, "Give it to Me all. Give Me the celebration. Give Me the good. Give Me the ugly. Give Me the bad. Give Me your yesterday. Give Me your today. Give Me your tomorrow. I sent My son and he's going to clean up the whole thing. Trust him."

Is there any way in which you are operating in your time, and things aren't happening like they're supposed to, and your prayer has been, "God, show up. I need some *kairos* in the midst of this *chronos*"? And God is saying to you, "Be patient. Hold on. I haven't forgotten about you." Lots of people waited lots of years for Jesus. "I'll show up. Trust me. Trust me with it. Trust me with it. Trust me. Trust me. You can trust me."

A baby has been born.

NATIVITY OF THE LORD: DAY

MSGR. WALTER NOLAN

Isa. 52: 7-10
Heb. 1:1-6
John 1:1-18

"From his fullness we have all received grace in place of grace."

Merry Christmas. All during Advent, we pray that the love of Christ has filled us with joy as we prepare to celebrate his birth, so that when he comes he may find us watching in prayer with our hearts filled with wonder and praise. Wonder and praise—why? Why wonder? Why praise? Christ is born. Christ is God made man. The earth forever bears his imprint. You and I are graced to walk on it. Each step that we take on our journey is an adventure in faith, hope, and love. Incredible, so incredible. How could we not love this earth? It is so incredible that the stars speak of it. And the moon and the sun behold his glory on earth from his birth until death. So incredible that a piece of bread and a cup of wine becomes his body and blood that you receive.

So incredible that "Happy Holidays" just doesn't do it. So we pray, we shout, we sing the songs of Christmas: Silent Night, Holy Night, O Come All Ye Faithful. Kindness and truth shall meet. Justice and peace shall kiss. And so we say "Merry Christmas!" When you pass another or shake someone's hand, be proud to say "Merry Christmas!" This is a time to increase our faith, not the hype. The Lord himself will give us this sign— the Virgin shall be with child and bear a son and she'll name him Emmanuel, God with us. That's what we believe, that's what we live, that's what we share and so we sing with great joy. So many songs. What song to sing?

Allow me to offer you the Twelve Days of Christmas. Why? Because it's a very, very religious song that was given to us when Catholics could not even dare say who they were. In England, a long time ago, when Catholics were persecuted, two priests wrote the song and they put it together. They put it together so that the children would learn the doctrine of their faith. The days between Christmas and the Feast of the Epiphany are twelve.

On the first and all the days they say, "My true love gave to me..." Some people would say that must be some little boy or little girl winking at each other. Maybe so, but our true love is our God and all love is based on that true love or it's not love at all.

So on the first day our true love gave us a partridge in a pear tree, which is a code name for the Christ. The reason is that partridges, especially mother partridges, take care of their young. When their young are attacked, the mother will actually lead the aggressor away and even give up her life to save the life of her own little chicks. So this partridge, this Christ-bearer, is willing to give his own life so that we children will have life. And the pear tree is the sign of the Cross. Christ on his Cross, the ultimate gift given to us.

On the second day our true love gave two turtle doves, the doves representing peace and truth...as well as the Old Testament and the New Testament.

On the third day, three French hens. French hens were very rare and very costly and only the very rich kings could be served these kinds of hens. Symbolically, we talk about Christ the King and the gifts that would come to him in three: gold, frankincense, and myrrh.

On the fourth day our true love gave four calling birds, which represent the Gospels. The birds could be called Matthew, Mark, Luke, and John. Stories that we can never, never forget and we need to tell them over and over and over again.

NATIVITY OF THE LORD: DAY   **35**

The gift of five gold rings represents the first five books in the Old Testament—the Pentateuch, which tells of the Exodus, our flight to freedom. These are the books that remind us of our Covenant of God—that this God will always be our God and we would always be His people.

The egg is a symbol of new life, new birth. So on the sixth day of Christmas our true love gave six golden geese. This is to remind us that God created the world in six days and that all life and all creation is holy and blessed because our God made it holy and blessed.

On the seventh day our true love gave seven swans-a-swimming. St. Paul writes to us about the Seven Gifts of the Holy Spirit. You and I know very well the great signs that Christ left to us, the seven Sacraments of our grace.

The eighth day is a gift of eight maids-a-milking. Many would say they are the beatitudes, but I would also say maybe something deeper. Back then, a maid milking was considered a very lowly job—a job that would give not much worth at all. Thus, this verse reminds us that all people are worthy of God's love.

On the ninth day of Christmas my true love gave to me nine ladies dancing. The nine fruits of the Holy Spirit: love, joy, peace, patience, kindness, goodness, faithfulness, gentleness, and self control.

On the next day, my true love gave ten lords-a-leaping to represent our Ten Commandments, the pathway of all love to God, filled with Grace.

Eleven pipers piping is the next gift given. They represent the eleven apostles who remained loyal and would always take the message of Christ to the world.

And on the twelfth day of Christmas our true love gave twelve drummers drumming. The twelve elements in the Apostles' Creed, that creed that you and I learned as children. It is the creed that we'll never forget, and we continue to say over and over and over again.

I would dare say on this Christmas Day that these 12 gifts are gifts to be wrapped up in that one precious gift, that gift of Eucharist, that gift that we hold precious. It is a gift that we will receive often. For it is a gift that allows us to know the mercy of God because it is a gift of forgiveness. It is a gift of memory of times back when our eyes were filled with the wonder and the joy. But we also remember, as Christ said to us, "Do this in memory of me." And so we remember and dare never to forget the gift of thanksgiving, to be able to say on this day, "Thank You God for my love, thank You for my life, thank You God that we can be instruments of peace as You asked us to be."

We live in wonderful times. We live in times that test us. Maybe the time is the same. Maybe the song that we sing to our loving Christ is the song of the Twelve Days of Christmas, to renew our faith and to remind us of God's love. And this time, when so many of us are very happy, we remember that there is always sadness at Christmastime. There's sadness because some are lonely, there's sadness because some have lost loved ones. There's sadness because there's a war and every day we look at the paper or the television and every day we know that some men and women will never be able to love and never be able to share.

So, as we sing the songs and we laugh with Christmas joy, we also know that there is pain in some people's hearts, and so as I pray this day, I pray of my joy because I love my God. I pray with you because I love you dearly. I pray with my family and I pray with my friends and I pray for peace on Earth and goodwill to all people.

Merry Christmas!

HOLY FAMILY OF JESUS, MARY AND JOSEPH

FRAN ROSSI SZPYLCZYN

Sɪʀ.3:2-6, 12-14 Cᴏʟ. 3:12-21 Mᴀᴛᴛ. 2:13-15, 19-23	*"Out of Egypt, I called my son."*

*F*amily. *Now there's a loaded* word. For some of us, the word "family" conjures happiness, support, love, connection, and community. For others it can mean pain, rejection, and despair. Yet, we are often obsessed with this word, this unit, and this group of people. What is a family? And how do we get to the place where "family" lives?

The word "family" has a powerful meaning in our faith, and that meaning is more painful for some of us. Perhaps it reminds us of who and what we are *not*. Or it may remind us that we might not be as safe or as welcomed as we hoped.

Today, we celebrate the Holy Family, awash in thoughts of Christmas. Families are meant to be places of refuge and goodness, sources of love, but family life can also be challenging. Family is an invitation from God that can bring us to many places we would rather not go.

Luke's Gospel tells us Joseph has a dream and hears that he must take his family and flee. Can you imagine having this dream and acting on it immediately? I can't. Yet this is exactly what Joseph does.

Like any good father, Joseph wanted to provide safety and security for Mary and Jesus; to that end, he did what he had to in order to provide those things. It would be easy to stay in the most literal territory here, and think of a father protecting his family from harm by physically moving them. But what if the dream asks us not to go out into the world, but rather to go more deeply into God's invitation?

Hold that thought as we head into more challenging ideas from the second reading, from Colossians. Some of the words from Saint Paul's letter run like a fault line through ideological lands, causing some of us to turn away and not listen. If we are too literal, are there any worse words than what Paul writes? *"Wives, be subordinate to your husbands, as is proper in the Lord."*

What?

It is easy to get stuck here. But if we go back to the call to travel more deeply into God's invitation, we might find something. This is an invitation to be part of God's family. What happens when we respond to the call of *that* dream?

Consider today's texts with some words from that letter to the Colossians that are not heard today, words in the prior verses:

> But now you must put them all away: anger, fury, malice, slander, and obscene language out of your mouths. Stop lying to one another, since you have taken off the old self with its practices and have put on the new self, which is being renewed, for knowledge, in the image of its creator. Here there is not Greek and Jew, circumcision and uncircumcision, barbarian, Scythian, slave, free; but Christ is all and in all.

Did you hear that? *"Christ is all and in all."* Being submissive creates a vertical power structure that may be a challenge—causing others to either submit or dominate. With Christ, everything changes! Through the dynamism of the Trinity, we are called to live in mutuality. The old model no longer functions. When we think about being submissive in this context, we might be able to see a way in which we submit to one another, finding the freedom of faithful surrender to the common good.

It does seem like a stretch, but so does waking up and taking your entire family to Egypt after a dream. In fact, doesn't pretty much everything about Jesus seem like a stretch? It does if we live in our rational heads alone.

So, now what?

God sends us dreams that challenge us to surrender. Surrendering to God takes us to new and unknown places, places that may be difficult. Kind of like family life, or most relationships, for that matter! If we can let go and follow, we may understand that we are free. It is a mutuality that demands we surrender our need for power and give that to God. This is the dream that asks us to drop everything and go to a place of love.

How do we do this? And what kind of family does God ask us to dream into reality in our world?

First, let us examine our own families. Every family is burdened with some kind of division. What can we do to heal the strife? If we have fled, is it time to return? Do we come back to our original place or allow God to lead us new places? Can we surrender to one another in the love of Christ? Can we dream and find the courage to journey with our families? It is only through our trust in God that we have freedom along with our belief in Christ Jesus. This, along with the movement of the Spirit, helps us find our way.

Second, what about our faith communities? Every worship community that I have ever been a part of has had some divisions. Whether it is over the music, the priest, and/or gossip—divisions exist. In Catholic parishes there is the ever-popular pre- and post- Vatican II split. If you notice, all of these tussles fall into vertical power structures, even if they are well-intended and meant to serve the Lord. If we are the mystical Body of Christ, are we willing to be that Body in the world? And be called forth to journey to places that we never imagined we would go to, but where God invites us?

Third, our world. Big or small government, open or closed borders, love stranger or fear them, war, peace, weapons, torture, hunger, climate change, justice, and more. What if God's dream says that we need to reposition our hearts and minds? Can we surrender, seeing all as one in Christ? Or at least trying to do this? Can we call "outsiders" our Christian family? Global family? If God created everyone, we *are* family. This can't simply be a happy-clappy wake up and love the world moment. It is the transformation that comes from our relationship with God, and through the journeys on which God leads us.

Now, that's a tall order, and God knows that. We have to start small and work outward. If we begin with the dream to take the journey, we begin first with ourselves, and then our families. The world? If we say yes to the dream, God can mold us into a family, but we must say "yes", even if it terrifies us to do so. God is with us in each moment.

What will you dream tonight? What will you do in response to your dream? May we all find the courage in Christ to hear God and listen—to go where we are called to go, forever changed in and by love. The journey is a risk; the decision to not undertake it is a greater risk. What will you dream tonight? And what will you do when you awaken?

MARY MOTHER OF GOD

<table>
<tr><td>

NUM. 6:22-27
GAL. 4:4-7
LUKE 2:16-21

</td><td>

"God sent his Son, born of a woman."

</td></tr>
</table>

Every year, at the end of the year, the *New York Times* runs a series of articles on notable people who have died during the previous 12 months. A few years ago, one of the most notable was a woman most people have never heard of. But her story, I think, gives particular meaning to this first day of the new year.

Her name was Martha Mason, of Lattimore, North Carolina. She was born in 1937, and when she was just 11 years old, she and her 13-year-old brother were stricken with polio. Her brother died in a matter of days.

But Martha lived.

Within a few months, however, she became a helpless cripple. The disease left her a quadriplegic. After spending a year in the hospital, she was sent home in an iron lung, a massive machine that resembled a coffin, but which was equipped with pumps that made her lungs work. The doctors told her mother to keep the girl comfortable and happy. She would probably be dead by the end of that year.

But—confounding every expectation—Martha lived.

She lived not just that year, but the next, and the next, and the next. Her high school teachers brought her lessons every afternoon. She studied hard, got good grades, and graduated. After she graduated, her parents moved with her to a nearby junior college, and then to Wake Forest University, where she attended class by intercom. Martha dreamed of being a writer. When she could, she would dictate feature stories to her mother, who would type them up for publication in the local paper.

Against all odds, Martha lived an astonishingly productive life. She gave dinner parties at her parents' home, with the iron lung pulled up to the table. She read books with an electronic page-turner and watched videotapes. In the 1990s, she was able, through computers, to use a phone, turn on lights—and finally, to write. She poured her life story into a memoir called *Breath: Life in the Rhythm of an Iron Lung*. Around this time, her mother became sick after a series of strokes. Martha Mason managed her mother's care, remembering how much her mother had cared for her.

By the time she died, Martha ended up spending 61 years in an iron lung—possibly a world record. Yet she considered her life to be one of great joy. "I live in a stable of nightmares," she once wrote, "but hope keeps them in harness."

On this first day of a new year, I think Martha Mason's story is a profoundly beautiful testament to living—to confronting challenges and pain. But also to living a life of possibility. And hope.

And possibility and hope lie at the heart of this feast day. The church, in her wisdom, has chosen this particular day to celebrate Mary as the Mother of God—the New Eve who gave birth to possibility and brought forth our great hope. Through her, the human race was reborn, revived, redeemed. Through her, we are all able to begin again.

And isn't that what New Year's is all about?

Of course, we've reduced this day to hangovers and resolutions. It's the day for sweeping up the confetti and watching football games and promising to walk a mile on that treadmill that you found under the Christmas tree last week. By the end of the month, the treadmill will be a display case for potted plants. So much for resolutions.

But if you want to make resolutions, the great model for us all is, in fact, the woman we honor today. If we want to truly transform our lives, we can do no better than to resolve to live more like Mary, the Mother of God.

Resolve to accept angels when they come into our lives, announcing the impossible.

Then, resolve to remember that nothing is impossible with God.

Resolve to welcome strangers—the shepherds of our own world who show up unexpectedly in our lives.

Resolve to live in wonder, and humility, and trust.

Resolve to keep all things, and reflect on them in your heart.

And resolve, my friends, to live in possibility, and in hope.

That is what it means to live like Mary, really. It is to embrace the divine and welcome it, and not be afraid of what is to come.

And that is what this first day of a new year represents. It is an opportunity to begin again—to cherish more deeply the life we have been given, by honoring the one who gave life to our salvation.

The fact is: when we honor the Mother of God, we honor as well the gift of life. At a time when that gift is increasingly under attack, my hope and my prayer is that we can each strive to defend that gift, to protect it, to cherish it. And the best place to start is with ourselves.

Let us resolve, on this first day of a new year, to make our lives matter.

Let us resolve, like Martha Mason, to make every breath count.

THE EPIPHANY OF THE LORD

MSGR. WALTER NOLAN

Isa. 60:1-6
Eph. 3:2-6
Matt. 2:1-12

"Opening their treasures, they offered him gifts, gold and frankincense and myrrh"

When there is so much turmoil, so many wars, so much unrest in our world and in our lives, many will ask, "What is this epiphany, this manifestation of the Lord?"

The blessings of God that we hear in our scriptures went out to the whole world—not just to our Jewish brothers and sisters, but to all. So why does God allow so much chaos in the world? Even at the birth of Jesus, as the scriptures tell us, there was no peace. King Herod stayed in power by taking the lives of others. Scripture tells us that after the Magi left, he decreed that the lives of all the young boys would be taken. So what does this epiphany tell us? What did the wise men see? What did they learn? What happened to their gifts of gold, frankincense, and myrrh? What kind of king did they see in a baby lying in a manger? Were their eyes opened, and did they begin to realize what would come forth from a feeding trough?

This Jesus who would become Christ would feed us, sustain us, and invite us with Eucharist. So that, from being fed from the feeding trough to being fed at the altar in Eucharist, the two come together and can never be separated. Is that what they saw? For it's the way God invites you and me to be. He invites us to be Eucharistic people—to regain what is lost.

I think the wise men saw a new life, new joy, a new family, but they also knew death. But they knew that the child could bring it all to resurrection. That's what the wise men saw. When they peered down and looked at the infant, did they see the God in him? Maybe one eye, so to speak, peered out into the eternal graciousness of the Father and maybe the other eye peered into the created world. Both eyes of this young child focused on the coming-together of eternity and our time in Kingdom here on earth.

The wise men were learning a new wisdom that they could see with both eyes into their own soul. That's the same gift of wisdom that comes to you and me. We can see through both of our eyes; the eyes of eternity and the eyes of the Kingdom on earth. For they come together in the oneness of the Christ child feeding us from the manger to the altar. So, I wonder what the wise men did and what they said on the way home. Perhaps Balthazar told the following story:

> You know, my good brothers, I left my gift of gold, but I received the gift of the knowledge of God. I would like to tell you this little story. One day, a son said to his father, "Have you ever asked for the kind of knowledge whereby you can hear what cannot be heard and see what cannot be seen and know what cannot be known? If so, please tell me how."
>
> The father replied, "So be it, my son. Put some salt in the water and come back tomorrow."
>
> And the son did so, and returned the next morning. His father said, "Please return to me the salt you placed in the water."
>
> The son looked but could not find it. The son said, "Sir, the salt has been dissolved."
>
> His father asked, "How does the water on the top taste, my son?"

The son replied, "Like salt."

Then the father asked, "How does the water taste in the middle, my son?"

The son replied, "Like salt."

Finally the father asked, "How does the water on the bottom taste, my son?"

The son replied, "Like salt."

The father said, "You see, son, the salt remains in the water even though you do not see it. And though you do not see Him, your God is fully present in you and everywhere else. Our God alone is the essence of all. Our God is the soul of the world, the eternal truth, the supreme self. My son, that's the gift that I give to you."

And perhaps Melchior smiled and said, "Thank you, Balthazar. My brothers, I left the gift of frankincense. I started to realize the grace of God in its fullness. I would like to tell you this story, my brothers. A holy man gave a woman a sieve and a cup. They went to the nearby seashore, where they stood on a rock with the waves breaking all around them.

"Show me how you fill the sieve with water," he said.

The woman bent down and held the sieve in one hand and scooped water into it with a cup, where it barely appeared at the bottom of the sieve and it was gone. "It's just like that with spiritual practice," the holy man said. "While one stands on a rock and tries to ladle the divine realization into it, that's not the way to fill the sieve with water. Nor is it the way of the self of the divine life. So he took the sieve from her hand and threw it out far into the sea, where it floated momentarily and then sank. The man said, "Now it's full of water, and it will remain so. That's the way to fill it with water—that's the way to a spiritual life. It's not ladling little cupfuls of divine life into yourself, but it is throwing yourself far out into the sea of divine life."

Gaspar would say, "Thank you, my brothers, thank you for your gifts. May I share with you, my gift of that of a housewife?"

Befana the Housewife, scrubbing her pane,
Saw three old sages ride down the lane,
Saw three gray travelers pass her door—
Gaspar, Balthazar, Melchior.

"Where journey you, sirs?" she asked of them.

Balthazar answered, "To Bethlehem,
For we have news of a marvelous thing.
Born in a stable is Christ the King."

"Give Him my welcome!"

Then Gaspar smiled,
"Come with us, mistress, to greet the Child."

"Oh, happily, happily would I fare,
Were my dusting through and I'd polish
"Then send but a gift to the small Newborn."

"Oh, gladly, gladly I'd send Him one,
Were the hearthstone swept and my weaving done.
"As soon as ever I've baked my bread,
I'll fetch Him a pillow for His head,
And a coverlet too," Befana said.
"When the rooms are aired and the linen dry,
I'll look at the Babe."

But the Three rode by.

She worked for a day and a night and a day,
Then, gifts in her hands, took up her way.
But she never could find where the Christ Child lay.

And still she wanders at Christmastide,
Houseless, whose house was all her pride,
Whose heart was tardy, whose gifts were late;
Wanders, and knocks at every gate,

Crying, "Good people, the bells begin!
Put off your toiling and let love in."

PHYLLIS MCGINLEY

During this New Year, maybe it's time to learn from our wise men. Maybe it's our time to let love in. We must live together and love together. When disasters occur, wars take place, and there is unrest in our lives, maybe God is asking all of us to realize that we are all one family. It is His created family. The wise men looked into the manger and they left their gifts. So, too, we are to bring the gift of feeding, the gift of Eucharist—the gift that binds us together as a family of God. I hope we start to realize that we are one family, that we are one people. And that we are God's family and that we all belong to God. If that happens, we know that this little baby in a manger, from the feeding trough in Bethlehem, will always feed us and bring us all to resurrection. This is truly our story.

BAPTISM OF THE LORD

CHRISTINE VALTERS PAINTNER

ISA. 42:1-4, 6-7
ACTS 10:34-38
MATT 3:13-17

"The heavens were opened to him."

A year ago, my husband and I heard a call to embark on a grand adventure and pilgrimage. We moved from Seattle in the United States, first to Vienna, Austria for six months, and then to Galway, Ireland, where we currently live.

Galway called to me because of the sea and because it was on the west coast of Ireland. I was captivated by imagining the ancient monks wandering out to the wild edges of life to encounter God.

We moved here in January, and while I had lived for nine years in the Pacific Northwest, an area known for its rain, nothing had really prepared me for the regular deluges I experienced in the first couple of months we lived in Galway. "Galway takes her rain much more seriously," I found myself often saying to old Seattle friends. "Lashing" and "bucketing" is how the locals describe it.

Next to our apartment, the River Corrib rushes out into the wide expanse of Galway Bay. We walk its shores almost daily, while staying present to the call of the tides. And so my time here has already been keenly shaped by the element of water and its power to shape my imagination.

Water shapes the biblical imagination as well. Flowing through the scriptures are stories about the waters of Creation, parting the Red Sea, the great Flood, the well of Jacob, Jesus walking along the Sea of Galilee, and healing by the Pool of Bethesda, among others. These stories of water are each about thresholds; they invite the characters, and us as readers, to powerful crossings and a new awareness or way of being.

The story of Jesus's baptism in the Jordan River is a threshold story as well. Jesus's baptism precedes his forty-day journey into the desert, where he wrestles with demons. It initiates him into a depth journey and marks the beginning of his public ministry. This is the first time we see the adult Jesus in Matthew's gospel. He has been readying himself, but first needs this ritual, in this river of his ancestors, where the Israelites generations before finally crossed into the Promised Land. It is the river which King David crosses as he prepares for battle.

Baptism is an act of humility for Jesus, of bowing down to enter into and become one with the community of those baptized. He recognizes how this ritual ushers him into a new landscape of his life. Jesus surrenders himself, yields to John and to the path that is calling him. He is not resigned, but active in his "yes" to this new path. This kind of assent to a holy call requires courage. Baptism became a sacred "yes".

With baptism, "the heavens were opened to him." Jesus has an encounter with God and is given the name "Beloved" as he steps forth into his ministry of healing and challenging the dominant powers of his day.

The gospel text for today invites us to consider the power of water in our own lives. To remember that we were each baptized and called to participate in God's unfolding work.

Over time, we forget. We become cynical and jaded. We lose faith in new possibilities. But the prophet Isaiah reminds us: "New things I now declare, before they spring forth, I tell you of them." There are things we cannot know in this moment. God's imagination is so much greater than ours. Our call is to continue yielding to the expansiveness.

As human beings, we forget, we fall asleep, repeatedly. Which is why we listen to these stories over and over. We require the impetus to action. We need to awaken to the call to always begin our commitment again.

There is a quiet kind of justice happening in the first reading. The prophet says: "He will not cry or lift up his voice, or make it heard in the street. …He will not grow faint or be crushed until he has established justice in the earth." There is a steady patience, a commitment to continue on even when hope seems feeble. The prophet goes on to name this call: "I have given you as a covenant" where eyes are opened and prisoners are freed. The letter from Acts proclaims that God anointed Jesus "with the Holy Spirit and with power," which Jesus uses for healing and good work.

As we remember the baptism of Jesus, how do we remember our own sharing in those threshold waters, which initiated us into a community on behalf of justice, and ushered us toward our own calling? What have we forgotten that needs to be reclaimed? How might we yield to God's great vision and freedom?

In much of the medieval art depicting Jesus's baptism, we see the river rising up to meet him. Sometimes our lives rise up to baptize us anew, to offer us a ritual of renewal, and send us forth once again. As we hear these stories once again, we remember the call to bring holy justice.

We must do the work, even in the face of it meaning nothing. We must act anyway, daily. This is all that matters.

So when our resolve weakens, we can be baptized again into the vast imagination of God. We must remember that we, too, are beloved, called to quiet justice, anointed with power, and offered holy courage again and again to say our own sacred "yes".

Each day, as I gaze upon my own ancestral waters—the Atlantic Ocean, which my ancestors crossed in their search for a new life generations ago, and which I crossed back again last year over my own threshold into newness—I am called to this wild edge to remember my calling, my encounter with holy possibility, to recommit and offer vision and freedom in the ways I can. And the Great Beloved continues to sing out to us, to all those immersed in the waters, asking only that we say "yes" once again.

LENT

ASH WEDNESDAY

CHRISTINE VALTERS PAINTNER

JOEL 2:12-18
2 COR. 5:20-6:2
MATT. 6:1-6, 16-18

"When you pray, do not be like the hypocrites."

Today we leave Ordinary Time to enter into the journey of Lent through the desert. The desert is that uncharted terrain beyond the edges of our seemingly secure and structured world, where things begin to crack.

We begin this desert journey marked with ashes, the sign of our mortality. There is wisdom in these ashes. If you have ever been near death or had a loved one die, you know the clarity that an awareness of our bodily limits can bring. How suddenly what is most important in life rises to the surface. This is the invitation of Lent, to realign our priorities. In remembering that we will die, we are called to remember God who is the source of our life.

When we are marked with ash on our foreheads we hear the invitation to "repent and believe the good news." One of the Hebrew words for "repent" is *nacham*. The root of this word means "to draw a deep breath," as well as to be deeply moved to a feeling of sorrow. The Greek word for "repent" is *metanoia*, which means "to reconsider." But it is also a compound word made up of the words "meta" and "nous". "Meta" means "transformation" and "nous" means "soul". So, as we begin this journey, we are invited to nothing less than a "transformation of the soul".

But how are we to be transformed and believe the good news? How are we to have hope when our lives are faced with the struggle of trying to make our way in the world, when loved ones face illness, when we are *still* at war with other countries and with ourselves? Certainly, our journey through Lent is toward the season of Easter, a season of resurrection, but how do we get from here to there?

The prophet Joel offers some insight in our first reading. "Even now, says the Lord, return to me with your whole heart, with fasting and weeping and mourning." Even now, in the midst of death and destruction, loss and pain, God calls to us. Not for a half-hearted acknowledgement, but to return to God with our whole heart, with the fullness of who we are. Return with fasting and weeping and mourning. This is a call to the practice of lament.

Each one of us carries grief, sorrow that has perhaps gone unexpressed or been stifled or numbed. Each of us has been touched by pain and suffering at some time. Yet we live in a culture that tells us to move on, to get over it, or to shop or drink our way through sorrow. Or to fill our moments with the chatter of TV and radio and internet so that we never have to face the silent desert of our hearts. It is the same kind of attitude that forces us to answer "fine" when others ask how we are, when we really aren't. Even our churches often try to move us too quickly to a place of hope without fully experiencing the sorrow that pierces us.

Why do we work so hard to resist our tears? Jesus wept. We see him in John's gospel shedding tears over the death of his friend Lazarus; in Luke we see him weeping over the whole city of Jerusalem because of their indifference.

What is the sorrow you carry with you today? Is it because of personal loss? A death, a job lost, a broken relationship, or an illness? Is it sorrow over the wars that rage on, thousands of miles from us? Is it because of the thousands of children who will die today because of preventable hunger? Is it the ongoing racism that devastates communities, or the religious hostilities that divide nations?

I invite you to take just a moment to be in touch with the grief that you carry with you.

We resist feeling our pain because our society discourages it. Even without the absence of permission to feel sorrow, how many of us have the time and space it requires to adequately mourn our losses? Beyond the brief sound bites we receive in the news each night, where is the space and the resources we need to process our sorrow?

This is where the profound wisdom in our tradition of lament enters. The Hebrew Scriptures are filled with this prayer of crying out to God. Lament gives form and voice to our grief, a space to wail and name what is not right in the world in the context of prayer.

The Protestant theologian Walter Brueggemann writes about the need for lament in his book *The Prophetic Imagination*. He says that people can only dare to envision a new reality when they've been able to grieve, to scream out, to let loose the cry that has been stuck in their throats for so long. That cry, the expression of that grief, says Brueggemann, "is the most visceral announcement that things are not right." Only then can we begin to "to nurture, nourish, and evoke a new consciousness," a new vision. We so desperately need a new way of seeing the world.

The prayer of lament is first and foremost truth-telling. It begins by challenging the way things are. Lament names that something is not right in the world. *This* pain, *this* suffering should not be. It helps us to name the lies we have been living and participating in.

Lament opens us up to a new vision of how God is present to our suffering. We call on the God who weeps with us, whose groans are our own, and we express our hope in God's tender care.

Lament is a form of resistance. We allow ourselves to be present to God in our brokenness and resist the cultural imperative to be strong and hold it all together. We resist cultural practices of denying death through our worship of eternal youth. We stop pretending everything is okay and put an end to worshipping the status quo.

Lament puts us in solidarity with those who are suffering and schools us in compassion. Only when we have become familiar with the landscape of our own pain can we then enter into the suffering of another. Lament moves us beyond our own narrow perspectives.

In the prayer of lament we help give voice to the oppressed, to hidden suffering, the suffering in silence that happens because pain takes our language away. The prophet Joel says to blow the trumpet and call the assembly, because lament is the work of the community. Gathered together, we say that the pain is being heard, that it is valid. Our community votes with its tears that there is suffering worth weeping over.

Finally, lament is the release of power, God's power. The power that is the soul-transforming call of repentance. The paradox of our faith is that we must first surrender fully to these ashes, into the desert places of brokenness, before Easter and its promise of resurrection can fully enter and fill us. In the second reading for today, Paul invites us to be ambassadors of reconciliation. Lament invites in God's reconciling and healing power.

During Lent, my practice will be truth-telling. I will inhabit my places of grief, the sorrows I have resisted up until now, and allow my unspoken lament to rise up in me like fire. I will turn off the endless noise and chatter that distract me from those places where my heart has hardened. I will be in solidarity with those who have no voice, and listen for their silent groans. I will trust, along with our spiritual ancestors who wrote and sang the Psalms in the assembly, that when I go to the rawest, most vulnerable places, my soul is then transformed and I can answer the call to repentance with my whole heart.

In today's Gospel, Jesus warns us against practices that are done for their visibility. He calls us to examine the integrity and intention of our actions. Lent is not a second chance at New Year's resolutions, so I encourage you to consider continuing to eat chocolate, but make intentional space for your grief. Give permission for others in your life to express their sorrows. Help to create an atmosphere in your communities that encourages prayer of lament. Think of a friend or acquaintance who has experienced a loss in the last few months and make time to ask them about their stories and let them know they will be heard. Examine the subtle ways that your own actions participate in and perpetuate the pain of the world. Cry out in public ways, express your lament perhaps in letters to the newspaper and those in power. Refuse to say that everything is fine. *Practice truth-telling.*

Is our image of God big enough to imagine that God can embrace all of our pain? Can we trust that the God who cries out alongside us, whose cry is our own, will also transform us in that space of darkness?

1ˢᵗ **SUNDAY OF LENT**

REV. DR. DAVID A. DAVIS

GEN. 2:7-9; 3:1-7
ROM. 5:12-19
MATTHEW 4:1-11

"Take wisdom every time"

Jesus and the devil and their wilderness exchange—trying to outdo each other by dropping Bible verses. From Jesus: "One does not live by bread alone, but by every word that comes from the mouth of God"; "Do not put the Lord your God to the test"; "Worship the Lord your God and serve only him." It's all from Deuteronomy—all from just a few chapters in Deuteronomy. Hardly an expansive or exhaustive reference list offered by the Lord. But everyone knows that even the devil can quote Scripture. The devil can proof text with the best of them. The Devil can memorize Scripture. For it is written: "He will command his angels concerning you. On their hands they will bear you up so that you will not dash your foot against a stone." Psalm 91. If the conversation between Jesus and Satan there in the wilderness was an argument over Scripture, if it was little more than a game of bible trivia, they'd still be going at it. Or at least there would be a whole lot more annotations, footnotes, verses. No, it's more than a Scripture contest.

The literary tradition has labeled seven sins as deadly: pride, envy, anger, sloth, greed, gluttony, and lust. Those seven sins don't seem to have much play here when Jesus was led up by the Spirit to the wilderness. If one was hoping to find a recipe in the gospels to withstand sin, or a description of a practical approach to right living, this account of the tempter coming to Jesus leaves something to be desired. When Jesus was led by the Spirit up to the wilderness, it was not his morality that was being tested. The trials tossed his way have little to do with the fleshy side of life—the seedier side of being human, the steamier side of our existence. No, it's more than a morality play here in the wilderness.

But for those who have ears to ear, there is a profound wisdom on display when Jesus is up in the wilderness. For those who have ears to hear... forty, forty, forty. Forty days and forty nights. Forty rings a bell. Wilderness, when you have the ears to hear, isn't all that new either. The trial of hunger in the wilderness, putting God to the test in the wilderness, falling down to worship something, someone other than God in the wilderness. The ears perk and the memory kicks in of the people of Israel in the wilderness after Moses brought them out of Egypt. The people of God and their season of complaint in the wilderness—with manna from heaven, and water from a rock, pillar of cloud by day, fire by night, tablets, golden calf, forty years.

Of course Jesus quoted Deuteronomy and the godly wisdom about life in the wilderness. "One does not live by bread alone, but by every word that comes from the mouth of God"—Dt. 8:3. "Do not put the Lord your God to the test"—Dt: 6:16. "Worship the Lord your God and serve only him"—Dt. 6:13. Jesus pointing to the wilderness wisdom of God. And the devil not really tracking that part of the argument at all, that Jesus was referring to the post-Exodus encounter between God and God's people, the devil missing that reference all together. Satan, nonetheless wanting to keep up, tosses in some Scripture. Uh, Bible, verse, yes, Psalm 91. Yeah, that's it! Let the angels come save you. Throw yourself down. You toss yourself down and let the angels come. The devil missing the Lord's reference to the Exodus, yet foreshadowing those who yelled up from the foot of the cross...You save yourself, and come down from that cross!

The temptation of Jesus in the wilderness was about him saving himself. The Scripture references, the language, the images, the trials, they all point to a bigger picture; THE picture. The whole temptation scene conjures up God and God's people. Jesus in the wilderness revealing, pointing to, and living what it means to be in relationship with God. The temptation of Jesus in the wilderness strikes at the very heart of the identity of God's people. The allure, the trial, the struggle, the battle, what's at stake….is the wisdom it takes to be the people of God when you are in the wilderness. Jesus as prophet there in the wilderness embodying the wisdom of God. A wisdom that forever shapes, informs, guides, and sends the people of God. A wisdom that nurtures, builds, and creates the Kingdom of God. A wisdom that forever offers praise to God, and reflects the will of God, and basks in the glory of God.

Jesus and his trifold trial in the wilderness: turning stones into bread, leaping from the highest steeple into the arms of angels, kneeling before false gods. It's not about our temptations, as real as they are, as powerless as we may be. It's about us learning from his temptations. That up in the wilderness, life for the people of God is not all about meeting your own needs, satisfying your own cravings, quenching your own thirst. In the wilderness, the work of the Kingdom doesn't happen only on the highest pinnacles, where spotlights shine and heroes abide with daring leaps, or bold claims, or predictions of divine intervention—all that put God to the test. Up in the wilderness, it's a daily grind for God's people, who live with the powerful, never-ending temptation to bow down over and over again not to the Living God but to the splendors of this world.

The temptation of Jesus. It's not about our morality, or our piety, or our doing battle with the devil. It is about claiming our identity as God's people here in the wilderness and soaking in Christ's wisdom, taking his wisdom every time. For us as God's people, it is a wisdom that teaches that any concern for my own self-interest ought to be outmatched by the concern for my neighbor, for the stranger, for the widow, for the orphan, for the other. Here, for us as God's people, it is a wisdom that affirms that ultimatums and pronouncements and doctrinal litmus tests are nothing compared to caring for the sick, and serving the poor, and comforting the grieving, and speaking for the long-silenced. Here, among God's people, this wilderness wisdom of Christ questions the worship of Mammon and the lust for power and the faith statement of winning at all costs. The wisdom of Christ is a wisdom that challenges when ivory towers become sacred and corporate ladders divine and extreme wealth a divine right of the few. Worship the Lord your God, and God alone. Do not put the Lord your God to the test. One does not live by bread alone, but by every word that comes from the mouth of the God. The mouth of God. The wisdom of Christ.

Our life in Christ requires a daily reaffirmation of our baptism and the turning away from evil and sin. Daily forgiveness. Hitting the refresh button on confession, forgiveness, and discipleship—it's part of the experience of Lent, isn't it? But Lent can be uncomfortably individualistic. My life. My sin. My relationship with God. My confession. My prayer. My devotion. My discipline. My Jesus. Jesus and me. Uncomfortably individualistic in this world of wilderness, where a greater threat might just be to our identity as the people of God, our corporate witness as God's people, our collective servanthood in the kingdom of God, our life as the Body of Christ.

In the wilderness, you are expected to look for a church where everyone agrees with you, sings the songs you like, and makes you feel good week in and week out, helping you turn your stones into bread. But in the wilderness, God's people yearn for every Gospel word, and God's people sing for the one in the pew who can't sing today, whose heart is broken, and God's people look to bear the mission of God into the world rather than making sure this or that church survives. In the wilderness, you are expected to put God to the test, thinking you're always right, or you should always win, or you should pay less, or you should have more, or you should always be happy. But in the wilderness, God's people settle for living the Gospel in very ordinary yet sacred ways, like advocating for one immigrant at a time, helping one refugee family at a time, working to free the wrongly imprisoned one at a time. The Kingdom of God, not at the pinnacle of power and might, but in the wilderness, one by one by one. In the wilderness, you are expected to bow down, pay homage, kneel before, devote yourself to someone—to a job, a family, a hobby, an education, success, a political party, your alma mater, a nonprofit passion, a nation, heritage, values, status, legacy, the past, religion, the church…. but in the wilderness, God's people worship the Lord your God, and God alone. God alone.

Here in the wilderness, the biggest threat might just be to our collective witness as the people of God. Temptation and trial not just impacting you or me, our life with Jesus—but together, here, our life together as servants of the kingdom of God.

Here in the wilderness, what's at stake is our life as God's people.

2ᴺᴰ SUNDAY OF LENT

MICHELLE FRANCL-DONNAY

GEN 12:1-4
2 TIM 1:8-10
MATT 17:1-9

"The Lord said to Abram…"

Forgive me. I realize our feet are firmly set on Lenten roads, but I cannot listen to this first reading from Genesis without hearing the faint whispers of Christmas past.

Last Christmas Eve, in the dimness just before Midnight Mass began, I stood at the ambo in my parish church and broke Advent's silence, chanting the Roman Martyrology—the Great Proclamation of Christmas. The proclamation cascades through salvation history, literally counting off the "ages beyond numbers from the creation of the world" through the twenty-one centuries "since Abraham, our father in faith, came out of Ur of the Chaldees," to the birth of Christ.

In that long list of years, Abram's departure from Ur is the first event we can place firmly in time. It begins here. With the events recounted in these bare four lines of Genesis, God's plan for our salvation begins to unfurl in human history. The Church is conceived now, in the desert with Abraham and Sarah, to be brought to birth on the other side of Easter, twenty-one centuries later at Pentecost.

The author of this passage in Genesis is terse and matter-of-fact, opening with the bald statement: "The Lord said to Abram…" It is easy to let the eye and ear slide past these words, to consider them a mere frame for what God actually had to say to Abram. Instead, I invite you to stop for a moment and imagine what the experience summed up in that line might have been like for Abram. God *spoke* to Abram.

Was it a gentle breathing of God's Spirit, like the small, still voice Elijah heard at the mouth of the cave in the silence after the whirlwind? The barest prompting wafting under the tent flaps in the cool clarity of a desert night. Or was it more like Peter, James, and John's experience on the mountaintop? The ordinary became dazzling, time collapsed, prophets from the past appeared, and the voice of God left him trembling and prostrate on the ground.

Savor these few, perfectly ordinary words that hold out to us a dazzling gift: in whatever way He chose, God spoke to Abram; indeed, at any moment, and in many different ways, God may choose to speak to us.

Regardless of what the experience was like for Abram, it was transformative. It was, dare I say it, transfiguring. He packed up kith, kin, and kine and at age 75 went sojourning in the desert to claim a people and a nation for God, to seed the future with descendants more numerous than the stars, to become a new figure for us—our father in faith.

In both these pivotal encounters, God not only speaks to Abram and the disciples words of instruction—Go. Listen. Don't tell anyone (yet).—but He offers them words of blessing as well. Jesus lays hands on the disciples, assuring them they are safe. In graceful poetic form, God promises Abram many things, among them, as one translation puts it, that he will be "blessed to be a blessing."

Poet and priest John O'Donohue writes in his *Book of Blessings* that unlike poems, which can wrap tightly into themselves, even the most poetic of blessings simultaneously keeps one hand on the listener and one door open to the sacred. Blessings enrich our perception of the divine that surrounds us (though I imagine the disciples on Mount Tabor needed no such reminder of the sacredness of those grounds!); through them, the infinite touches the quotidian.

Blessings usher us across thresholds, literal and metaphorical. They are invitations into new realities—transfigurations. Two weeks ago, we marked the entrance to Lent with a blessing, ashes streaked across our forehead inviting us to a time of prayer, fasting and almsgiving. A time of transformation, a reminder of the transfiguration we await at the end of time, and of the threshold we stand on, our arms outstretched between heaven and this earth.

But God's blessing of Abram went beyond an invitation to cross into a new place, beyond an assurance of safety and God's everlasting favor. Through this blessing, Abram was to become a blessing. Like rosary beads and holy water, ordinary things, once blessed, become vehicles of grace, tiny sanctuaries which point to immense mysteries.

What then, might happen to our ordinary selves, as God's blessing of Abram pours forth onto us? What threshold is God inviting us to cross? What sanctuary of grace is He expecting us to become this Lent? What are we blessed to become?

Listen to the psalm. We ask for God's blessing, that His kindness may be upon us, that we may be righteous. And who are the righteous, but those who are the light to the nations that Abram was promised to become. Those who are the wellsprings of peace and justice and mercy that the psalmist sings of. Those who are the hands that, as Christ's, reach out to those who are anxious and in need. Hear in the psalm our call, sounding clearly across the centuries we so dutifully counted up at Christmas, to *be* the blessings we have been blessed with.

This is the reality we stand on the threshold of in Lent, to know who we are as the people of God, as daughters and sons of Abraham and Sarah. It begins here. Blessed so that we might be blessings. It begins with us.

Transformed—transfigured—so that others might be the Light of Christ to all the world, so that we might be the Body of Christ—the Church. God spoke to Abram, and we are blessed to be.

3RD SUNDAY OF LENT

FR. JAMES J. GREENFIELD, OSFS

Exo. 17:3-7
Rom. 5:1-2, 5-8
John 4:5-42

"My food is to do the will of the one who sent me"

We are privileged to eavesdrop into the longest recorded conversation Jesus ever had, with a Samaritan woman, and we do not even know her name! It has been said that anytime someone significant in the Scriptures remains nameless, that person acts as the universal person—standing in for each of us! So, as we listen to the conversation between Jesus and the Samaritan woman, let's imagine ourselves sitting there at the well, too.

We discover a sullied, compromised, and heterodox personality emerging from the dialogue, but we quickly learn that Jesus sees beyond these. And, since we are right there at that well, too, Jesus describes our plight perfectly when he says to the woman, "Everyone who drinks of this water will thirst again, but whoever drinks of the water that I shall give will never thirst."

Continuing on our Lenten journey, we hear our readings today invite us to name and consider the many wells from which we are we drinking. As the chosen people complained to Moses about not having water to drink in the desert, as the Samaritan woman carried her heavy water jar to Jacob's well, we also have needs deeper than the various wells from which we draw our daily sustenance.

Do we drink from the well of self-pity? How often do we not see the larger picture, and live from our own reference point only? On a recent trip to Cité Soleil, the poorest slum in Port-au-Prince, Haiti, I met a woman who was waiting her turn in a food-line that had queued up hours before. Only exchanging glances for a couple of seconds, I have memorized her smile as she received the simplest provisions of rice, beans, and canned fish made available to her through the work of Hands Together and Mary's Meals. Her smile appears prominently in my mind when I play the "woe is me" game at my desk with too many emails, letters, phone calls, deadlines, and appointments.

Perhaps we drink from the well of self-absorption. I recall a sermon in another church when the minister shared how his staff was instructed to answer the phones: "We are here to serve our congregation." Can we imagine Jesus saying, "I am here to serve the disciples"? Jesus came to save the world, not just his colleagues in ministry. He came to serve the beggars and the blind, the oppressed and oppressor, the marginalized and ostracized. We are here to serve the world, not ourselves.

Or, maybe we drink from the wells of excessive self-care? How many of us worry more about how fit we make our bodies so that we look good, rather than out of a concern for good health? How do we listen to the deep yearning of our souls for meaning, depth, and authenticity?

I heard a minister share about a dad drinking from the well of net worth. That parent (regretted spending more time managing his mutual funds than managing his child's development.) Do we spend as much time creating family priorities as we do social and business ones?

While considering these questions, let's return to Jacob's well—notice the time of day is noon, the moment of peak intensity of the scorching rays of the sun. This woman, who went to draw water at noon, exposing herself at this hour because she drank of other wells, leading her to feel shame, is about to learn her most important lesson. The man she meets at that well will never leave her vulnerable and ashamed, as he himself, at high noon, will transform all vulnerability and shame when he is lifted high on the cross, pulled from death by his Father.

This unnamed woman calls Jesus by many names—prophet, Messiah, Lord—as she recognizes and accepts the gift he offers. In her openness to the good news she receives in this life-changing conversation, she leaves her water jar, the symbol of what she thought needed to be filled, at the well, and goes back into town. She now desires that others be filled to the brim with the same transforming experience she had with Jesus. This woman, who gathers the townsfolk at the well to experience Jesus, stands in bold contrast to the disciples, whose names we do know, who simply return with lunch! How often those of us who are known by name, pillars of the community, and fully initiated from the cradle, happen to be the ones who are more concerned with the next meal than evangelization?

Spending time at that well with Jesus, we can see his ministry as sitting with tax collectors and prostitutes, the impoverished and destitute, and those emotionally and mentally unstable. As Pope Francis remarked at his first Chrism Mass as Bishop of Rome: "The ministers need to smell like the sheep." Jesus is the Good Shepherd who smells like his sheep, and he likes it this way.

We see Jesus reaching beyond the borders, the places not just anyone would go. Too many of us are afraid to reach beyond borders, beyond our comfort zones. I read where Sr. Mary Scullion, co-founder of Project Home in Philadelphia, speaking at a Notre Dame commencement, challenged the graduates to find their comfort zones and then stay as far away as possible from them for the rest of their lives! That's good advice for all of us as we consider the wells from which we draw vitality. Staying in our comfort zones, we engage only a small fragment of what life has to

offer. But, like Jesus, when we reach out and across borders we are able
to drink from so many other wells that life has to offer.
We are more thirsty than we can possibly imagine, and Jesus desires to
meet us at the wells of our lives. He wants us, in the words of the poet
Rumi, to close both eyes and see with the other eye everything around us.
As with his encounter with the woman at the well when he broke down
all barriers of tradition, culture, and religiosity, the Lord wants to speak a
word to us. "If only you knew who it is that is speaking to you …. If you
only knew!" God ventures into everything all around us, into our development, our history, our woundedness, our family, and our world. And he is
no stranger in any of those places.

From what wells do you and I drink?

1 SAM. 16:1, 6-7, 10-13
EPH 5:8-14
JOHN 9:1-41

"I have come into this world, so that the blind will see."

This is one of the funniest stories in the Bible. It sounds like the script for a skit featuring the Keystone Kops—those incompetent policemen from the silent film era who ran around with great energy and enthusiasm, but were so unseeing and inept they were never able to solve any of the cases set before them.

The story goes like this: A man who was born blind is healed by Jesus, and the people around him seem not to be happy about this wonderful thing. Some don't want to believe it—they say that the healed man is not the same guy who was a blind beggar. Others demand, skeptically, that the formerly blind man tell them exactly how Jesus healed him. The Pharisees then jump in to say that Jesus couldn't have healed the man because Jesus is a sinner.

And why was Jesus a sinner? Because he healed someone on the Sabbath, and everybody knows one can't work on the Sabbath. Right!

The Pharisees then go after the man's parents. The nervous parents decide they don't want to be embroiled in this controversy, as it might result in a negative outcome for them, even though surely they must have been happy to see their son restored of his sight. So they toss the hot potato back to the formerly blind man, who has to tell the story once again about how Jesus healed him. People continue to refute him: Jesus is a sinner, so he couldn't have done this wonderful thing. Plus, nobody knows who Jesus is or where he is from, and so he couldn't be going around healing people. Only the right kind of people can do that. Right?

Finally, in frustration, the formerly blind man basically tells his interlocutors off, and in return they tell him off, and they drive him out of the synagogue, where Jesus comes to find and reassure him.

So why is this funny? What's so funny about healing and fighting and throwing people out of the house of worship?

Well, of course, healing is not funny, and neither is throwing people out of the house of worship. That is rather serious stuff.

And yet, the Pharisees and their antics, their posturing, their assumptions and assertions, even in the face of contradictory evidence, their going over and over the same territory again and again expecting a different answer, their stomping and flailing around because a poor blind man has been made whole, well, that is pretty funny in a really, really sad kind of way.

Jesus spent a lot of his time breaking down barriers. He broke the religious rules and the social and cultural rules, not because he was a "bad boy", but because he wanted to heal people so they would experience the love of God firsthand. He wanted to restore the outcast and lonely. He wanted everyone to know God's love for them, despite their shortcomings. He said that he came so that people would have life and have it abundantly and that all who wanted it should have everlasting life. This, Jesus said, comes straight from God, and woe to those who put stumbling blocks in front of others to keep them from participating in that abundant life.

Meanwhile, we all, in our fear and shortsightedness, go around like the frenetic Kops, like the Pharisees, trying to re-erect those barriers and stumbling blocks as quickly as Jesus tears them down. Jesus heals a blind man: barrier down. Pharisees' response: deny that it happened. Next response: Even if it did happen, it couldn't have actually happened because Jesus is a sinner. That healing couldn't be from God. Further response: Jesus is a sinner because he breaks the rules.

And, ta-da! The barrier is back up and the "same old rules" continue to rule.

None of us want to be "the Pharisees," but we often resemble them nonetheless. Life is constantly shifting, and we want certainty and order. Change is hard, and most of us just don't like it. So if we have always held an assumption that something or someone is "wrong," then we'd rather stick with our assumption than face our fears and prejudices. We unreflectively buy in to the idea, for example, that people who need assistance are lazy, rather than look at the larger picture to see where the barriers to their wholeness are, from poverty to mental illness to discrimination.

We rarely look for barriers, but when we see them being broken, our impulse is to rush to put them back up. We think they keep us safe, I guess, and we imagine that somehow we will always be on the "right" side of the barrier anyway. We imagine that those people on the "wrong" side of barriers deserve to be there. That helps us hold fast to the understandable but misguided belief that because we are "good" or "hard-working" or "blessed", we will never be in the situation of finding ourselves on the "wrong" side of the barrier.

But if we look to Jesus, we see that *this whole idea of barriers itself* is where we keep getting it wrong. The life of a faithful person is not about being on the "right" side of the barrier instead of the "wrong" side, but about working along with Jesus to break down the barriers altogether. Being faithful means looking at the bigger picture to see where people are broken and hurt and hungry and naked—and doing something to help heal them because they are (like us) beloved children of God.

Those on the other side of whatever barrier we support or have erected are beloved children of God!

No, that's not funny either.

But I think we can make good use of the ridiculous aspect of the story. Perhaps if we cannot see how wrongheaded we can be through a serious discussion, then maybe we can see it through humor. Imagining Jesus, with all of God's love and power and might, breaking down barriers— followed by our tiny flailing frantic efforts to put them back up—*is* like the Keystone Kops.

Perhaps if we can truly see how bumbling and silly we can be, if we can see how much God loves those whom the world does not love, then we can truly see what we could not see before, and we can change our ways.

5ᵀᴴ SUNDAY OF LENT

FR. BILL BAUSCH

EZEK. 37:12-14
ROM. 8:8-11
JOHN 11:1–45

"Untie him and set him free."

A little boy was afraid of the dark. One night his mother told him to go out to the back porch and bring her the broom. The little boy turned to the mother and said, "Mama, I don't want to go out there. It's dark." The mother smiled reassuringly at her son. "You don't have to be afraid of the dark, dear," she explained. "Jesus is out there. He'll look after you and protect you." The little boy looked at the mother real hard and asked, "Are you sure he's out there? "Yes, I'm sure. He is everywhere, and he is always ready to help you when you need him," she said. The little boy thought about that for a minute and then went to the back door and cracked it a little. "Jesus? If you're out there, would you please hand me the broom?"

In two weeks we will recall the death of Jesus, but today we are confronted with the death of Lazarus. It seems we're being asked to think about what we would prefer not to think about: death. And to ponder the little boy's question, "Jesus, are you out there in the dark?" Really?

In answer, let me offer some suggestive images for you that indicate that Jesus is out there in the dark. Years ago, I had the opportunity to make a trip to Washington, D.C., with some friends. Part of our itinerary was to visit the Vietnam Memorial Wall. As you may know, the monument is a long black granite wall with thousands of names of those who lost their lives in the war. As I walked the grounds of the memorial, a couple of things stood out.

The first thing I noticed was the silence. As crowded as it was, there was a hush of reverence over the whole setting. The next thing that caught my eye was how different people approached the wall. Some were obviously just there as spectators. They could touch lots of names on the wall, pass them over quickly, and have no reaction whatsoever. To them, the names were just letters carved in a granite wall.

But to others, those names, or rather, *this* name, was a reason to pause, to cry. They moved very slowly as if approaching something sacred and then touched the name. Some wept, others were just still, lost in grief or reverie. Some stood quietly as they ran their fingers gently over the letters. Some even knelt. As I watched this ritual unfold, I couldn't help but wonder what the relationship was between the living person and the name: husband, son, father, brother, friend. It had to be something special or it would not have solicited such a reaction.

Of course, the answer is that to those who knew the person behind the name, it represents all the memories, the history, the personality and intimacy created between these two people. It is the depth of the relationship that makes the connection, the investment of life one person made in another person. It represents someone who made a difference to the one who knew that person.

And so too, Jesus. He said, "I know mine and mine know me." "I no longer call you servants but friends." So we are not anonymous to him. He runs his fingers over our names and claims us as his own before and after our deaths. That is our hope.

Another image. In a cemetery in Hanover, Germany, is a grave on which were placed huge slabs of granite and marble cemented together and fastened with heavy steel clasps. Why? Because it belonged to a woman who vehemently did not believe in the resurrection of the dead. So she directed in her will that her grave be made so secure that if there *were* a resurrection, it could not reach her. On the marker were inscribed these words: "This burial place must never be opened."

Ah, but in time, you see, what happened was that a tiny, infinitesimal seed, covered over by the stones, began to grow. Slowly it pushed its way through the soil. As it grew and its trunk enlarged, the great slabs of the grave were gradually shifted so that eventually the steel clasps were wrenched from their sockets and then, one day, there it was: the grave was exposed. A tiny seed had pushed aside those enormous stones.

Faith says that if nature can move huge stones, God can move the huge stone at Jesus's grave. And ours as well. Such is the force of God's love.

A third image. The luminous paintings of the great artist Renoir, are, as you know, aglow with life and light and color. He seemed to put light inside the people he painted. Remarkably, as you may also know, for the last twenty years or so of his life—his most productive years—Renoir was terribly crippled with arthritis. His hands were twisted and gnarled. His wrists, his arms, even his spine were ravaged by the disease. He couldn't even stand as he worked.

He had to sit as he painted and be shifted about in his chair by assistants. At times the pain was so great as he worked that beads of perspiration would stand out on his face. On one occasion, one of his students said to him, "Why do go on and torture yourself like this?" Renoir looked at the canvas he was working on and replied, "The pain passes, but the beauty remains."

That is the promise we have. "Untie him and set him free." That is to say, after the ravages of sickness and death, the beauty of love and eternity remain.

A fourth image. A celebrity of his time, playboy, wit, editor of the famous British publication *Punch*, Malcolm Muggeridge, much to the chagrin of his worldly friends, became a Christian. In fact, he became the worst kind: he became Catholic. He did so because he was inspired by the presence and work of Mother Teresa. Anyway, elderly when he converted, he wrote many lovely things, including these words of imagery:

As I approach my end, I find Jesus's outrageous claim ever more captivating and meaningful. Quite often, waking up in the night as the old do, I feel myself to be half out of my body, hovering between life and death, with eternity rising in the distance. I see my ancient carcass, prone between the sheets, stained and worn like a scrap of paper dropped in the gutter and, hovering over it, myself, like a butterfly released from its chrysalis stage and ready to fly away. Are caterpillars told of their impending resurrection? How in dying they will be transformed from poor earth crawlers into creatures of the air with exquisitely painted wings? If told, do they believe it?

I imagine the wise old caterpillars shaking their heads—no, it can't be; it's a fantasy. Yet in the limbo between living and dying, as the night clocks tick remorselessly on, and the black sky implacably shows not one single scratch of gray, I hear those words: "I am the resurrection" and then I feel myself to be carried along on a great tide of joy and peace.

Faith asks, "If caterpillars, why not we?"

A final image. A long time ago there lived a little boy whose parents had died. He was taken in by an aunt who raised him as her own child. Years later, after he had grown up and left his aunt, he received a letter from her. She was in terminal illness and, from the tone of her letter, he knew she was afraid of death. This man, whom she had raised and touched, wrote her a letter in which he said:

It is now thirty-five years since I, a little boy of six, was left quite alone in the world. You sent me word that you would give me a home and be a mother to me. I've never forgotten the day when I made the long journey of ten miles to your house. I can still recall my disappointment when, instead of coming for me yourself, you sent your servant, Caesar, a dark man, to fetch me. I well remember my tears and my anxiety as, perched high on your horse and clinging tight to Caesar, I rode off to my new home.

Night fell before we finished the journey and as it grew dark, I became even more afraid. "Do you think she'll go to bed before I get there?" I asked Caesar anxiously. "Oh, no," said Caesar, "she'll be sure to stay up for you. When we get out of these woods, you'll see her light shining in the window."

Presently, we did ride out into the clearing and there was your light. I remember that you were waiting at the door; that you put your arms tight around me; that you lifted me—a tired, frightened little boy—down from the horse. You had a fire burning on the hearth; a hot supper waiting on the stove. After supper you took me to my new room. You heard me say my prayers. Then you sat with me until I fell asleep.

You probably realize why I am trying to recall this to your memory now. Very soon, God is going to send for you, and take you to a new home. I'm trying to tell you that you needn't be afraid of the summons or of the strange journey or of the dark messenger of death. God can be trusted. God can be trusted to do as much for you as you did for me so many years ago. At the end of the road you'll find love and a welcome waiting. And you'll be safe in God's care. I'm going to watch and pray for you until you're out of sight. And I shall wait for the day when I make the same journey myself and find you waiting at the end of the road to greet me.

Notice the symbols; Caesar, the dark figure, is death; the light at the end of the journey is Jesus, the light of the world; the house is the "many rooms" in the Father's house that Jesus promised; the supper is the heavenly banquet; God is the loving aunt. It's a homecoming story. It is gospel. It is hope. It is promise.

The little boy's question, "Jesus, are you out there?" must have been Lazarus' question. The Good News is that he was: for Lazarus, for you, and for me.

PALM SUNDAY

FR. RICHARD ROHR, OFM

MATT. 21:1-11

ISA. 50:4-7

PHIL. 2:6-11

MATT. 26:14-27:66

"Hosanna to the Son of David."

Of all the creatures that God created, the only one that apparently knows or foresees and therefore fears their own death is the human being. Animals and all of nature accept the natural cycle of death and life. Yet most of us fear it until the very end, because, of course, by dying we enter into the great unknown.

And yet in the Gospel today, as we begin Holy Week, we don't see Jesus marching out of the city to avoid what he knows is inevitable, but in fact, heading right into it, coming humbly as always, riding not a horse but a donkey. The First Reading from Isaiah says with great poetic clarity, "He set His face like flint, knowing He would not be put to shame."

Brothers and sisters, we have no ability to face our own deaths, or any death, without fear or shame unless we have a grand and great and deep experience of life. There has to be more than enough of life or we will always fear that death will be bigger and have the power to overcome it.

Some of the most exciting work being done with theology these days is coming from an unusual source—not by academics and universities but, of all things, from the hospice movement, largely emerging in the last 20-25 years. I'm sure many of you have benefited from hospice if you've accompanied a parent or a loved one in those last moments of life.

Many people who have companioned those at the threshold of death have written about it. What they recognize is rather consoling, but maybe somewhat surprising. As the person dying nears the end, he or she eventually (perhaps not until the last weeks, days, or even minutes) moves across a certain line. At the very end, most people are completely surrendered to the mystery and move into a kind of peace and freedom, so much so that many of them do not want to be called back.

It's we, the ones left to live, who are invariably doing all the crying and lamenting, but not the person who is dying. They come, it seems, to an awareness of what is real and what is unreal, what matters and what does not matter at all. Unfortunately, most of us push off that enlightenment—and that's what it is—until the last hours of life.

What religion is about, and what Jesus is exemplifying by going willingly to his death, is dying before you die. In fact, I would go so far as to say that the *only* function of religion is to teach you how to die before you die.

Why can't we get the message earlier, instead of waiting for enlightenment at gunpoint? We keep thinking that our very identity requires wealth, fame, and power until we know that they don't matter at all. They don't define us. In fact, we recognize that something much greater, much truer, and much deeper is given to all of us. But we fight it until the end.

Isn't it sad? Isn't it sad that we waste so much of our life in illusion? So scoot it up ahead of time. Learn what's real and what's unreal, what matters and what doesn't matter at all. And when you're tempted to get upset, ask yourself, "Will this really mean anything in the long run?"

Because at the end, death is the great equalizer. Kings and princes and popes and presidents and house cleaners die the same. And at the end, all these things that we've grasped onto and the things that we think make us important and significant will pass away. And then we have to say, "Who am I now? Who am I now? Who am I now?"

Jesus marches into this Holy Week, his face set like flint, seemingly without fear, knowing his death will come soon. As we celebrate with freedom and even joy on Palm Sunday, he marches right into it because he can trust there is a bigger life. Death is simply the other side of life and, in fact, apparently you don't really know what life means until you've faced your own death.

So let's truly follow Jesus this week and face death ahead of time. It's nothing morbid, tragic or sad. Everybody who's ever lived on this Earth for generation after generation has had to face this mystery. And our only work here is to tell you, "Face it now, and then, like Jesus, you will have nothing to be afraid of."

HOLY THURSDAY

DEACON GREG KANDRA

Exo. 12:1-8, 11-14
1 Cor. 11:23-26
John 13:1-15

"Do this in remembrance of me."

When I was growing up, my dad had one of those small, cheap Kodak Instamatic cameras. You used those flash bulbs that looked like ice cubes, and got these little square pictures back from the drug store when you had them developed. My dad must have taken hundreds, if not thousands, of pictures with that camera. I never appreciated them until years later, after I was grown, when my parents had died and we were going through their things and we found all these pictures. Boxes of them, curled and faded. But there they were—life, captured by Kodak. Memories you can put in a shoebox.

We need that. We want something of the person we love to outlast them, and stay with us.

We want to remember them.

Remembrance is at the very heart of what we celebrate this evening. But Jesus didn't leave us photographs in a shoebox.

He left us something better.

He left us himself.

Paul's letter to the people of Corinth is the earliest account ever written of the Last Supper. It pre-dates even the gospels. It is so close to the original event that its words are part of our Eucharistic prayer, spoken at every mass, at every altar, around the world. The words that created the Eucharist are the beating heart of our Catholic Christian belief.

And through it all, one word leaps out at us.

Remembrance.

Do this in remembrance of me.

Jesus is saying: This is how I want to be remembered.

In the gospel, John doesn't even mention the meal, or the institution of the Eucharist. But he finds something else for us to remember: Christ, the servant.

"You ought to wash one another's feet," Jesus says. "I have given you a model to follow, so that as I have done for you, you should also do."

In other words: remember what I have done. And do this, too, in remembrance of me. We are people of remembrance.

So were the Jews. It's there in the first reading, from Exodus, describing the institution of the Passover meal—the very meal that Christ was celebrating when he gave us the Eucharist.

One of the interesting aspects of this reading is that it the entire passage is, really, a monologue.

And the one who speaks…is God.

And He tells His people: "This day shall be a memorial feast for you, which all your generations shall celebrate with pilgrimage to the Lord, as a perpetual institution."

It is an occasion for calling to mind all that God has done for His people.

And he is calling on them, in a very particular way: "Do this in remembrance of me."

Do not forget.

It is no secret that the older you get, the more you forget. Every day is a battle for me to try and recall where I put my keys, or my glasses. I think my wife would like them to be clipped to my sleeves, the way kids do with their mittens.

It is easier to forget than to remember.

Which makes *tonight's* remembrance all the more remarkable.

For *five thousand years* mankind has re-enacted somehow the great Passover feast of Jesus and all those who came before him. The memorial feast has continued.

For *two thousand years* we have gathered around this table and repeated Paul's beautiful words—the words the Corinthians heard and took to heart.

For *uncounted generations* we have knelt and watched as the body and blood of Christ have been raised to God—and watched as we, too, have been raised with them, as offerings to God.

And down through history, we have knelt and washed one another's feet with a profound charity and sense of purpose that made Christian love the most powerful force on the planet. Even unbelievers were moved to say, "See how these Christians love one another."

See what we have done in remembrance of him.

They say a picture is worth a thousand words. All the pictures my father took over the years tell a story, and come with emotions attached—happiness, nostalgia, some sadness. I would suggest that the next few days will be worth a thousand *emotions*. From the wonder and gratitude of tonight, to the sorrow of Good Friday, and the loneliness of Saturday.

But then there is Sunday.

This night, our journey toward Calvary begins in earnest. But so does our journey toward Easter.

Holy Communion is often referred to as "viaticum," or food for the journey. Let us prepare to receive that food, so we can begin that journey. A journey of struggle. And of faith.

It is a journey that a billion others around the world are also undertaking with us on this sacred night.

We share it with them for one beautiful and hopeful reason:

We do this in remembrance of him.

GOOD FRIDAY

FR. PAUL HOLMES

Isa. 52:13-53:12
Heb. 4:14-16; 5:7-9
John 18:1- 19:42

"Are you the King of the Jews?"

*P*ontius *Pilate is the only* human being, other than Mary, to be named and remembered, for all time, in the Christian creed. We don't remember Judas, almost refusing to say his name. But we do say Pilate's name every Sunday, refusing to forget him and the role he played in crucifying our Savior.

What strikes me about Pilate on this Good Friday is that he asks so many questions...more questions than any other person in Scripture, Old Testament or New. Listen to how inquisitive Pilate is. Over a period of just a few hours, he asks eleven questions in all. It becomes clear soon enough, however, that Pilate doesn't really want to know the answers to any of these questions. But the last words of Jesus must have stung Pilate to the core.

When Pilate reminds Jesus of a procurator's power over life and death, Jesus simply reminds him *that he has no power*—no power of his own, anyway. And this certainly sealed our Savior's fate. To prove that he had power, Pilate almost *had* to hand Jesus over for crucifixion.

But I think it also sealed Pilate's fate. For from that moment on, Pilate had to go to bed each night, and wake up each morning, forced to face the fact that he had no real power whatsoever.

And, maybe, just maybe, Jesus wants to deliver that same message to us.

Our whole lives are spent deluding ourselves into thinking we have power. Power over ourselves. Power over our spouses and our children. Power at work. Power in the parish and the neighborhood.

But, if there's anything to learn from Pilate's many questions, and Jesus's answers, it might be the most important and the most difficult thing to learn in life: *That you and I don't have any real power.*

We're as powerless as Pontius Pilate.

And we hate that. We prefer to pretend. We walk into church on Good Friday as people who imagine ourselves as very, very powerful. And we often walk out feeling that none of that power is diminished one single bit.

It isn't until someone we love gets cancer. Or until someone we love loses his job. Or it isn't until someone we love loses their battle with alcohol, or lust, or drugs. Or until we turn on the television and look into the faces of tsunami victims or tornado victims or draught victims. It isn't until someone we know, or someone we've never met, has to give up in the face of something resistant to any real human remedies.

It isn't until *that moment* that our delusional thinking gets the Good Friday "reality check".

Because on one day a year, we listen to the story of our Savior. We listen to him reject authority of all kinds. We hear him surrender to all the pseudo-powers of this world. We witness the example of an all-powerful Savior simply surrendering and letting his all-powerful Father have his way.

For those of us who are really listening, we just have to walk out of the church today *different* from how we walked in.

God is more powerful than procurators. He is more powerful than presidents and kings. God is more powerful than cancer. He's more powerful than addictions. He's more powerful than human progress, human pride, and human sin and weakness.

Today is a veritable celebration of the *Number One Requirement* of Christian life: to set aside all our pretensions, all our delusions, and admit, on our knees, that we have no power whatsoever. When Jesus did it, he was nailed to a cross. And maybe that's why we're so terrified of giving up. Of surrendering. Of facing the truth.

Pilate's infamous question, "What is Truth?" is not answered with words. It is answered with a wordless *surrender*.

Maybe we resist surrender because we know where it leads. Today's Gospel ended with the simple words "the tomb was close by."

You and I have to let the tomb *be* close by. Close to our hearts. Close to our minds and souls. The closer we are to that tomb, the closer we'll be to the Resurrection. We have to remember that we can't rise from that tomb unless we enter it.

Let us enter *whatever* tomb is nearby. Today is a *Good* Friday only if we stop pretending.

If we insist on remembering Pontius Pilate in our creed, then let's remember the lesson he must have learned on that first Good Friday.

When we come up to kiss the Cross in a few minutes, let it be an act of true surrender. Give in, and give up. The only real power worth having comes from the wood of that Cross.

EASTER SEASON

EASTER VIGIL

FR. RICHARD G. MALLOY, S.J.

GEN. 1:1-2:2, 22:1-18
EXOD. 14:15-15:1
ISA. 54:5-14, 55:1-11
BAR. 3:9-15, 32-4:4
EZEK. 36:16-17A, 18-28
ROM. 6:3-11
MATT. 28:1-10

"…And they were utterly amazed"

There's an old joke about a guy walking in New York City. As he passes a manhole cover, all of a sudden there's a massive explosion underground. The earth trembles and the manhole cover flies straight up, flipping over and over. The New Yorker, not fazed in the least, looks up and observes the spinning 150 pound disc as it reaches its apex and starts flipping downward. He looks intently and, without missing a beat, pronounces, "Heads." Nothing amazes a real New Yorker. They've seen it all.

Too many of us today find it hard to be amazed. Life becomes routine. Marriage feels like a comfortable old coat. Nothing our spouses say can surprise us. Some feel they can predict what their better half will say before they say it. Notice I didn't take sides on which is the better half, the husband or the wife. After a few years in a Jesuit community, it's even worse. At least you only have to listen to your spouse tell the same old stories over and over. I live with twenty Jesuits who keep telling the same old stories over and over and over and over. And they can probably predict what I will say on most topics. And certainly nothing I say will amaze them.

The Gospel tonight tells us "they were amazed." This resurrection is a new story. This hasn't been told before. Nothing, I mean nothing, like this has ever happened before. It begins to dawn on the disciples that the crucified one has risen. The women are the first witnesses. They proclaim: The Lord Jesus lives! Hopes that had been dashed and broken reignite.

Can we allow ourselves to be amazed? Can we open our minds and hearts and let in the joyous news that what happens to Jesus happens to us? Can we believe it? Will we live it?

But the angel immediately tells them, "Don't be amazed!" Get going. He's heading to Galilee, the region where God among us began his annunciation of the new dawn, the reign of God breaking through into our time and space. Get going. It's time to begin to live the way of life he articulated. Don't be amazed. Be amazing. Start forming the Body of Christ. Be the Jesus who conquers death and gives us life and life eternal. Be the Jesus who calls us to love everyone, even our enemies. Get going and build with God the Kingdom of truth and trust, justice and joy, peace and prosperity, hope and healing, faith and freedom, love and life.

All the readings tonight speak the story of our God. From the opening words of Genesis to the call of Abraham, to the freedom song of Exodus through the consoling words of the prophets Isaiah, Baruch, and Ezekiel, we have a "Top Ten" of scripture readings. The Psalms are the actual greatest hits of Israel, King David having been the world's first rock star. St. Paul reminds us we have died with Christ. And Mark takes us back to the earliest accounts of the moment that changed all of human history, the resurrection of Jesus.

Let's allow ourselves to be amazed by all this. And let's get moving. Let's be amazing. Let's live as disciples of Jesus. When we see the equivalent of manhole covers flipping in the air like coins tossed by schoolchildren, let's realize that something awesome and magnificent is happening. When we see water poured on heads and lives transformed for eternity, let's be stunned and astonished. And then, let's get moving. Let's allow the

Holy Spirit to invigorate our lives and get us doing the deeds God needs done to make the reign of God real in our lives and in the lives of our contemporaries.

How? By responding to those hurt, suffering and crucified in our days. Sr. Linda Stilling, SSND, a great apostle to the people of Camden, NJ, for over twenty five years, used to say, "You have to stay with people in their pain, until you begin to feel the joy of resurrection."

Holy Saturday is the time between the cross and the resurrection. We wait for God's response to the crucifixion. Mary Magdalene, Mary, and Salome are responding to the horror of his murder. They want to prayer-fully anoint the body of the one they listened to and came to love, the one they had hoped would be the Messiah of Israel. They find an empty tomb and it begins to dawn on them the Lord of Life has risen. This Jesus, their Rabbi and Lord, has overcome death. They begin to hear again the words of the beatitudes and the parables. The teachings of the Beatitudes and Matthew 25—feed the hungry, visit those in prison—begin to amaze them. And they realize it's time to get moving, to tell the world we are to pray the Our Father, reconcile with those from whom we are estranged, and take up our cross and follow Christ.

The great Jesuit preacher John Kavanaugh, S.J., writes of Holy Saturday: "Jesus entered the deeps of death, a plunge he need not have made, had he not loved us in our sorry state. But he went to death with a 'yes,' with the utter trust of Abraham, the constancy of Moses, the bright reliance of Isaiah. In Easter's vigil, we plunge with him: "Are you not aware that we who were baptized into Christ Jesus were baptized into his death? Being like him through likeness to his death, so shall we be through a like resurrection."

Cardinal George tells a story of being in Africa visiting missionary priests of his order. Several African tribesmen came into the parish center to learn of Jesus. One man refused to enter. Cardinal George engaged him in conversation and gently asked him why he did not want to listen to the lessons about Jesus the others wanted to hear. The man replied, "I've decided that it makes no sense when I look at my life—that God would love us, that God would sacrifice himself for us, that God is stronger than the spirits who harm us. I don't believe it. It's too good to be true."

That guy is unable to be amazed. For him, the world is what it's always been.

For us who have been given the gift of faith and have opened our minds and hearts to the radical realities of our Triune God, the world changes again this night. The dawn brings the power of the love of God, the God we experience in the community of the church, the God we receive in the Eucharist. Let's allow ourselves to be amazed. Let's get going. And let us pray.

EASTER SUNDAY

REV. DR. DAVID A. DAVIS

<table>
<tr><td>ACTS 10:34, 37-43
1 COR. 5:6-8
JOHN 20:1-18</td><td>*"I don't know where they have laid him!"*</td></tr>
</table>

One Easter morning decades ago, William Sloane Coffin said this in an Easter sermon in the chapel at Yale University: "Too often" he preached, "Easter comes across very sentimentally, like a dessert wafer—airy and sweet. But there's nothing sentimental about Easter: Easter represents a demand as well as a promise, a demand not that we sympathize with the crucified Christ, but that we pledge our loyalty to the Risen One....I don't see how you can proclaim allegiance to the risen Lord and then allow life once again to lull you to sleep, to smother you in convention, to choke you with success."

That's William Sloane Coffin on the domesticated Gospel. A Gospel shaped to make you feel better, to achieve more, to increase your productivity, to assure purpose-driven success. A motivational tool. Gospel as a life coach. A domesticated Gospel is one where any hard edges are safely sanded down: edges of sacrifice, edges of discipleship that require investments of time and effort, edges that were formed by God's call for justice and righteousness, edges of discomfort that come when thinking about the plight of the world's poor. A gospel that never pushes you beyond your comfort zone, never challenges any opinion you hold about life, never questions how you view the other, never threatens the powerful. Easter with the domesticated Gospel is indeed all about sentimentality, and

familiar hymns, and a visit with family, and a nice crowd, and brunch—
or a dessert wafer, airy and sweet. The things we cling to on yet another
Easter when we find ourselves outside the empty tomb waiting to hear
once again of the resurrection.

Mary stood weeping. She had been the first to see the stone rolled away.
Convinced that someone had taken the body of Jesus, she ran to tell
the others. She remained unconvinced by their empty tomb conversion,
unmoved by linen clothes wadded up in a ball. After the two disciples
headed home, Mary stayed. She stood weeping outside the tomb. Every
now and then she must have bent over to look in to see. To see if the body
was still there—to see if this ongoing bad dream would end sometime.
Not even the angels could comfort her. "I don't know where they have laid
him!" Even her first sight of Jesus, her encounter with the one now raised
from the dead, even that didn't convince her. "Sir, if you have carried him
away, tell me where you have laid him." Mary's first brush with the Resurrection didn't seem to shake her from that grief.

That's when Jesus called her by name. She knew it was him. "Teacher,"
she said in response. And he said to her, "Do not hold on to me." Do not
grab hold here. Don't cling to me. "Because I have not yet ascended to
the Father." One preacher points out that it's not clear that Mary was
even reaching for a hug. She wonders if maybe Jesus heard it in her voice,
in what she called him, "Rabbouni." The preacher suggests that Mary
called him by his Friday name, "Teacher". But it's now Sunday. The Day
of Resurrection.

"Don't cling to me, for I have not yet ascended to the Father." Who knows
what on earth or in heaven Jesus meant by that? It would seem Mary,
in some fashion, simply wanted to hold on to the way things were; to
her relationship with the Teacher who healed the sick and touched the
outcasts and modeled for her and the others what a good and faith-filled

life should be like. Mary wanted to stop the weeping and hang on to her world. But resurrection power comes from the hand of God. The victory over the forces of death and darkness comes when this Jesus is seated at the right hand of God in all power and honor and glory. When the heavenly chorus gathered around the throne starts to sing, "Hallelujah... For the Lord God omnipotent reigneth."

Mary wants to cling, but Mary's world will never be the same. More than shaking off the grief that broke her heart and getting back to normal following in the Teacher's footsteps, yearning for a good and moral life—more than that, this resurrection life is about ushering in the kingdom of God. It's about toppling the powers and the principalities; it's about life conquering death, forgiveness stomping on hatred, generosity squelching greed, love overtaking success, the first being last, swords being smashed into plowshares, the hungry pushing away from the table now full, the poor being lifted up while the rich stoop down to help with the lifting. Mary's world will never be the same because, as Barbara Brown Taylor says, "Jesus was on his way back to God and taking the whole world with him."

Easter Sunday! It's not about Mary's world, or about your world; it's about God's world. Resurrection power is about the mighty act of God. God didn't just roll away the stone and raise a dead body to life; God raised this Jesus to redeem us and our world and all of creation. God is about the task of shattering every effort at domesticating the Gospel message of salvation that comes through the life, death, and resurrection of Jesus Christ, the Only Son of God. Stop clinging to an Easter morning that's airy and sweet—like a dessert wafer. Or, as William Sloan Coffin asked at the very end of that Easter sermon, "Are we going to continue the illusion of a Good Friday world, or start living the reality of an Easter one?"

In one of many mission trips years ago to the Gulf Coast after Hurricane Katrina, my wife Cathy was in a group working alongside a construction crew that had been all over down there. The foreman on the crew confessed that he was worn out with the tearing down and the hauling of debris. He really wanted to shift to rebuilding something. He described the moment he knew he had enough of hauling people's lives out to the curb. His crew was operating some heavy equipment and lifting pile after pile onto big trucks to be taken away. One pile at the curb, just down from the house, included an old piano. The homeowner told the construction guys about this warped, soaked, moldy piano. "My grandmother taught my mother to play on that piano. My mother taught me. And I taught my children," she told them with tears running down her cheeks. "Now look at it!" But then she asked them if they could leave it there. And as the crew moved to the next pile, she sat down and started to play it. Right there at the curb, surrounded by destruction, she sat and made some music. Maybe she was clinging to the way things used to be. Maybe, just maybe, she was searching for the strength to play a new song! She sat down in a Good Friday world, yearning to play for herself an Easter world. An Easter song.

Standing in a Good Friday world and daring to live into an Easter one. Yearning deep down to cling to that which you know, and yet being willing to point to that which God knows is yet to come. Standing there next to that tomb; the very threshold of death, and boldly announcing, "I have seen the Lord." Surrounded, indeed overwhelmed, by the grief and suffering and heartbreak that so mercilessly defines what it means to be human, and yet daring to live as Easter people who find the strength even at the grave to proclaim, "Thanks be to God who gives us the victory through our Lord Jesus Christ." To stand up in a Good Friday world, daring to live into Easter, by begging, pleading, even demanding, the "more excellent way." To live the reality of Easter, by singing a new song: "Christ has risen! He has risen indeed!" Children of God! Those who find the courage to stare a Good Friday world right in the face, and ignoring the sentimentality of Easter Lite, they're bold enough to say to you and to me, to the world, "No, there's another way."

Don't cling to the world as you want it to be; work for the promised Kingdom that God describes. Don't cling to the pressures of achievement and the stress of success, work for the promised Kingdom where kindness and humility and gentleness count for more. Don't cling to the hatred that resides so deep within, work for the promised Kingdom where there is neither Jew nor Greek, slave nor free, male nor female. Don't cling to the mentality of winner takes all or that charity begins at home or what's in it for me, work for the promised Kingdom where you rejoice with those who rejoice and weep with those who weep and if one member of the body suffers, we all suffer. Don't cling to the necessity of violence or the inevitability of a march to war, work for the promised Kingdom where strength comes to those who are weak and security and power and trust come from God alone.

Playing piano at the curb! That's not a bad image for the church at Easter. Teaching one generation after another what it means to be an Easter people, what it means to be the children of God! I know I'm not the only one worried that we are raising a generation of kids in this congregation who think Easter is nothing more than spring break. So let's stand at the curb of a world that would just as soon pass us by. Children of God! It's the Day of Resurrection! And so, right here at the curb, surrounded by the debris, with more than enough sentimentality to share, confronted day after day by this Good Friday world, God is calling you to live in the reality of Easter!

2ND SUNDAY OF EASTER

FR. RICHARD ROHR, OFM

ACTS 2:42-47
1 PETER 1:3-9
JOHN 20:19-31

"Do not be unbelieving, but believe."

Jesus showed them his hands and his side. Then the disciples rejoiced when they saw the Lord. Jesus said to them again, 'Peace be with you. As the Father has sent me, so I send you.' When he had said this, he breathed on them and said to them, 'Receive the Holy Spirit. If you forgive the sins of any, they are forgiven them; if you retain the sins of any, they are retained.'

JOHN 20:21 – 23

I've preached on this Gospel for many years, and still it has something new to teach me. Only with today's reading have I made the connection—Jesus is identifying forgiveness with breath, with the very air we breathe. The Holy Spirit is seemingly given with a breath. The Spirit is coexistent with life itself.

Why is Jesus's profound teaching on the union of Spirit and life immediately followed by the story of Thomas, the one we call Thomas the Doubter? Perhaps the reason Thomas could physically touch Jesus's wounds—to trust that Jesus was healed and transformed, that Jesus could be the same person and yet an utterly different person—is that he had been able to touch his own wounds.

And that's why Jesus talks about forgiveness—as available and as free and as given as the breath in front of his mouth.

If Thomas and all of us could touch our own wounds and know that God can transform them, then it would be easy to believe that God could do the same in the body of Jesus.

But if you've never experienced your own need for mercy, never had a need for the forgiveness of a friend or to apologize for something you've done wrong, you likely don't know that wounds can be turned into grace, that crucifixions can be turned into resurrection.

Unfortunately, the church has sometimes contributed to the limiting of forgiveness; we (Catholic priests) gave the impression that to have your sins forgiven, you had to go in the box and confess.

Looking closely at this Gospel, we see that Jesus doesn't say this to the Twelve. He tells the entire community of disciples that they have the power to forgive and to heal and to transform one another by letting each other off the hook once in a while, by overlooking offenses. However, they also have the terrible power to retain, to bind. Jesus makes the connection between what we do to one another and what God is able to do.

If you've never experienced a generous and gentle forgiveness from a friend or family member, someone who is willing to overlook your own offenses, I think that it is almost impossible to know how God could forgive you. How could you even imagine the forgiveness of God?

And so Jesus is saying to the entire community of Christians, to all of us, not just to a select group called priests, that we have the power to liberate one another. We have the power to bind one another up. The power is given to the entire community. And if we have not entered into that graceful releasing, healing, surrendering, and discovering that forgiveness always is, I don't think we can experience it from God.

The first part of Thomas's story was given last Sunday. In between then and the Gospel for this week, a week passed in Thomas's life. My guess is that during those seven days Thomas touched his own wounds, limitations, coldness, and unforgiveness. Only then was he ready, oh so ready, to experience the wounds of Jesus and to know that they were both filled with Spirit, with the breath of Life.

3RD SUNDAY OF EASTER

PATRICK WENRICK

ACTS 2:14; 22-33
1 PETER 1, 17-21
LUKE 24: 13-35

"He was made known to them in the breaking of the bread"

Often, along my travels to various cities and small towns, I take note of church marquees. There are some that are very "boring," as a friend of mine would say. Still others are very creative and unique. One such church marquee that I passed on my way home read: "God Allows U-Turns". I thought it strange only because where I was living at the time in New Jersey did not allow U-turns, no matter what. The glaring message of this church board went contradictory to my lived experience. It made a lasting impact, even though I now reside in Florida, where U-turns are not just allowed but encouraged with no penalties ascribed.

As I reflected on the Gospel story for today, I remembered the "U-Turn" message on that Church marquee. Cleopas and the other disciple (with no name mentioned) were walking away from Jerusalem, headed for Emmaus, about 7 miles away—quite a distance to walk. The distance and the manner of travel are not as relevant as why these two were on this road in the first place and what happened to these travelers as they walked.

It is intriguing to this writer that Cleopas is the only person of the two identified. Why is that? Did the Gospel writer deliberately leave it to the readers' imagination? Perhaps we are to put ourselves into the sandals of the one not identified.

Why were they leaving Jerusalem? What was in Emmaus that was of such importance? What happened that changed their minds and changed their plans? Emmaus stands as a place to get away to out of fear. Fear was cause of their departure. Fear and anxiety can do some devastating things to an individual. It can cause individuals to literally move away from that which threatens. Remember these were followers of Jesus, and yet they saw what the chief priests had done to their friend whom they believed was the Messiah. They were afraid for their lives. They were afraid that the same fate that was the demise of Jesus would be theirs if others discovered they were Jesus's followers.

Fear was part of their grief; their loss. They chose not to believe in the women that were part of the following, who returned to Jerusalem with statements that Jesus had been raised. Their loss, their grief, their rejection of faith in the message of Jesus, and their fear was as thick and heavy as the stone rolled in front of the tomb where Jesus was laid. Yet, as they walked, they talked about who this Jesus was for them.

Part of our experience of grief needs to be modeled on these two disciples on the road. Remember for the next few minutes a person whom you loved deeply who has died. This person could be a spouse, a parent, a sibling, a child, or a friend. Perhaps some of us are experiencing such a loss now. No matter when loss occurred or the nature of the loss, focus in on the feelings. There are feelings of fear, anger, loneliness, and guilt—and others that generate joy and gratitude. These feelings are like waves that come on strong and then diminish, like the waves on an ocean reaching the shore. These feelings come back on special events that recall your loved one's presence on this earth, such as Thanksgiving, Christmas, anniversaries, or birthdays. There can be no feelings if there were no memories and no memories unless you loved. As Rev. Martin Padovani states in his book, *Healing Wounded Relationships*, "Grieving is a feeling process, so we need to give ourselves permission to feel any emotion, and not allow unhealthy guilt or shame to prevent us from feeling." The power and intensity of the feelings become less threatening as you share these feelings with another or write them in a letter to your loved one that only you see. The two on the road did not believe the account of the women. Their sharing on the road helped a little, but it was when they invited the stranger, i.e. the outcasts, their eyes of faith were opened and they recognized Jesus, whereupon he vanished from their sight.

This sharing of feelings and memories that can happen when we experience loss is very similar to the experience of the Emmaus wayfarers. We, like them, do not want to listen or believe others who tell us platitudes that fail to move the rock of our hurt and pain. Things like "she is in a better place now," "time heals all wounds," "be a man, don't cry" and "he wouldn't want you to be sad" fail to move the stone that weighs heavy on our hearts. The two followers on the journey engaged in a process of listening and sharing with each other. In the process of listening and sharing they experienced a "Presence" between them that they couldn't recognize but felt good about. This "Presence" was a stranger to them. The stranger engaged them in sharing what they were talking about. So they shared with the stranger....then the stranger shared with them everything about himself.

I recall a true story that I read about years ago. The story took place in California and it involved a young 4-year-old girl whose father died at his own hands. The little girl doesn't understand why her Dad doesn't come home. She feels it is because she did something bad and he won't forgive her. Her mother and grandmother tried everything they knew to help her understand that Dad was in heaven but that did nothing to help her get unstuck from the ever deepening depression she was experiencing. Then one day, the grandmother, thought perhaps helping the little girl write a letter to her Dad in heaven would help. So the little girl, with the help of her mother and grandmother, wrote a letter that recalled how the little girl and her Dad would read the story of the Little Mermaid, her favorite story, before going to sleep every night, and how much she loved her Dad and missed him. Once the letter was written they tied it to a Little Mermaid Helium balloon and took it to the cemetery where her Dad was buried and mailed the letter by releasing the balloon. Weeks passed before a hunter residing in (you guessed it) Little Mermaid, Prince Edward Island discovered the letter and took it to his wife. Upon reading the letter, the family was moved to gather numerous books about the Little Mermaid and send it off in a letter to the Little Girl. They were strangers acting like angels for the little girl. Needless to say, the girl snapped out of her depression and was overjoyed because she believed her Dad was in heaven and it was just fine. A true story!

When they took the stranger in and shared bread at table, they recognized that it was Jesus….whereupon he vanished from their sight. When we share, when we show hospitality to the stranger or outcast as did Jesus, when we listen deeply, we will, like the two on the road to Emmaus, make a U-turn back to the origin. We will come to believe, like the women, in the resurrection of Jesus.

4ᵀᴴ SUNDAY OF EASTER

MARY ELIZABETH SPERRY

ACTS 2:14, 36-41
1 PETER 2:20-25
JOHN 10:1-10

"What are we to do?"

Do you own your stuff or does your stuff own you?

We live surrounded by *stuff*. On the way here today, you probably passed numerous stores, all selling *stuff*. You may have passed a storage facility or two—giving you a place to store your overflow *stuff*. Media, from television to Internet to newspapers and magazines, are filled with advertisements explaining why you need to buy more stuff. After all, it's new and improved! And—for a limited time—at a special price! In between the ads, you can watch any number of "reality" shows to help you learn how to organize, arrange, use, and display your *stuff*.

But the words of Scripture that we hear today break through this clutter of *stuff*. In the first reading, we hear the ending of Peter's great Pentecost sermon. His Spirit-filled witness to the power of the risen Christ compels his listeners to face the emptiness of their own lives, no matter how successful they might appear to the other members of their societies. In response, the listeners ask Peter and the apostles quite simply, "What are we to do?" Peter invites them to repent for their sins and to enter into a relationship with Jesus through baptism and the power of the Holy Spirit. In the second reading, the first letter of Peter details the nature of that relationship. In his love for us, Christ bore the weight of our sins and emptiness. He fills our lacks, and offers in their stead hope, strength, and healing. For our part, we must strive to follow in Jesus's footsteps, living righteously and doing good, even when it leads to suffering.

In the Gospel, Jesus identifies himself as the good shepherd, explaining his mission: "I came so that they might have life and have it more abundantly." But what abundance does Jesus offer us? Is it simply more of the stuff that already clutters our lives? Despite the popularity of some preachers and their so-called "prosperity gospel," the abundance of which Jesus speaks has nothing to do with economic success and material abundance. Material wealth is not a sign of God's favor, nor should it be our ultimate goal. If we pursue this abundance to the exclusion of all else, we will find ourselves, like Peter's listeners, forced to confront the paradox of empty lives filled with clutter.

We must be clear: Jesus does not come so that we might *possess* more, but that that we might live more fully. This new, abundant life is not the product of our own efforts, but the gracious gift of our loving God in baptism. Still, we must decide to accept the gift. As we now live *in* Christ, we must likewise live *for* him. We must follow in the footsteps of the shepherd who guards and guides us. Like Jesus, we must strive to "live in righteousness," bringing healing to the suffering and helping those in need.

The Scriptures do not pretend that accepting this gift will make our lives easy and comfortable. Rather, Peter reminds his readers that following Jesus means following his path to the cross. Rejecting the materialism that surrounds us and speaking out about the emptiness of values that make things more important than people will not make us popular. Advocating for those who lack even the basic necessities of life is, all too often, a thankless and discouraging task.

In the last decade, the disparity between the rich and the poor has grown more pronounced, both in the United States and internationally. Income inequality continues to grow as the rich get richer and the poor become ever more desperate. Domestically, social service agencies like food banks and organizations that assist with housing, utilities, and transportation costs report an ever-greater need for assistance as people who made donations in the past now come seeking aid for themselves. Assistance agencies are caught in a damaging cycle of decreasing donations and increasing requests for aid. Almost one in six people in the United States live in poverty. The numbers are even higher among children and seniors (when medical expenses are taken into consideration). Internationally, the numbers are even more alarming. Globally, almost half of all children live in poverty and too many die of easily preventable diseases. Many people lack even basic literacy. About eighty percent of all people on the planet live on less than ten dollars a day. Many of these, including children, work in abysmal conditions for almost no pay in service of our insatiable desire for more stuff at ever-lower prices.

These problems may seem overwhelming, as if no action on our part could ever make a real difference. And, truth be told, giving up a morning latte or even a new car won't bring an end to world poverty. But embracing the challenge presented by today's readings can make a difference. We can recognize that true abundance comes not from what we own, but from who we are and from our relationship with Christ. Our possessions are not symbols of our hard-earned success, but the gifts of a loving God, intended to be used for the common good and shared with those in need. We must place our time, treasure, and talent at the service of God and others. Living this way is not simply a matter of giving up luxuries so that we can contribute more to charity. It means considering how our purchases affect the well-being and livelihoods of those involved in its creation. Do the workers at all levels—from the gathering of raw materials to the sales floor—receive just wages? Do they work in conditions appropriate to human dignity, or are they treated as an expendable resource, just another raw material? Do we base our decisions at the cash register and in the voting booth on our pocketbooks or on the impact on the most vulnerable members of the global community?

Thinking and acting this way requires a radical reorientation of values in a world where material success determines status and profits are more important than people. Finding joy and abundant life in living with simplicity and valuing people above things will challenge those we encounter to examine their own values and way of life. Less time acquiring and caring for possessions will make more time available to aid those in need and to work toward social systems that help to break the cycle of poverty, both here and abroad.

In what do we find our abundance? Does the stuff we accumulate bring us closer to God and other people, or does it isolate us from them?

Do we own our stuff or does our stuff own us?

Acts 6:1-7
1 Peter 2:4-9
John 14:1-12

"I am the way, the truth and the life"

"Where were they going without ever knowing the way?"

This line, repeated at the end of each stanza of the rock band Fastball's 1998 number-one hit single, "The Way," haunts me like it does many other children of the '90s who hear Thomas's question to Jesus in today's Gospel. "Lord, we do not know where you are going," the disciple says. "How can we know the way?"

The Fastball song is catchy, upbeat, and memorable. Like so many songs of that decade, the music of "The Way" conveyed a spirit of optimism and enthusiasm; it communicated anticipation for the forthcoming turn of the century. When I was in high school, I loved this song (and, honestly, I still do). As someone who was getting closer to graduation and would then go off to college uncertain of what exactly I might find there, the repeated question—"Where were they going without ever knowing the way?"—resonated with my youthful insecurity and my lack of clarity about *where, exactly, I was going.*

And while this personal way of connecting with the lyrics of "The Way" is likely shared by millions of others who heard the song and liked it enough to keep it at the number one spot in the United States for seven weeks, the original inspiration for the lyrics are quite sad.

The true story centers on Lela and Raymond Howard, a couple in their mid and late eighties, respectively, who left their home on June 28, 1997 to attend a fiddling festival just 15 miles away. They got into their car and drove off. The next time they were seen was two weeks later, when their dead bodies were found in their car nearly 350 miles from their home. Their middle-aged children told reporters that the only consolation they had concerning the disappearance and the deaths of their parents was that they were together until the end.

The layers of meaning present in the song's lyrics, which were described by its composer, Tony Scalzo, as a romanticized take on what happened before he knew about the eventual deaths, can perhaps help us to consider today's Gospel in a new way.

What makes the song romantic is the sense of letting go, leaving all behind, and following one's dreams without knowing the way ahead. There is a sense in which we might place ourselves alongside Thomas, Philip, and the other disciples, grappling as we listen to Jesus with what it is that lies ahead. Like the romantic older couple in the song, the disciples might see themselves as having been overwhelmed by the encounter with God in Christ Jesus. They left everything behind—their expectations, livelihoods, hopes, and dreams—to follow him. And as they confess in response to Jesus's affirmation that "I will come again and will take you to myself, so that where I am, there you may be also. And you know the way to the place where I am going," the disciples pause and realize that *they don't actually know where they are going.*

How often is that the case in our own lives? We recognize that we've had an experience of God in Christ in our lives, but at some point we pause and think: "Wait a minute! I don't know where I'm going. How will I know the way?" My guess is that this experience of being unsure of the way, not knowing what's up ahead, arises from our desire to know about that path before us. It's a mini-crisis of planning and the sudden realization that we cannot know every detail about the future. Yet, Jesus's response is to challenge our default way of thinking about what is to come and to return to the experience of *knowing* God rather than *knowing about* some spelled-out plan.

This Gospel passage is all about living in the experience of one's relationship with God in Christ. Jesus begins this chapter in John's Gospel with this affirmation: "Do not let your hearts be troubled." How true is it that we spend so much of our lives worrying about what's to come, what's going to happen next, what about this and what about that? While we are all called to live as free and responsible human beings, women and men charged with duties of family, friendship, and work, we cannot reduce ourselves to a schedule or *curriculum vitae*, tracing what we've done, where we've been, and where we think we're going. No, if our hearts are troubled for that reason it is because we have forgotten that we already *know the way*.

"I am the way, and the truth, and the life," Jesus tells us. He didn't say, "I have told you the way and the truth and what is life," but instead affirms that "the way" is one of relationship—a relationship with God that is transformative, a relationship that *leads to relationship* with others. To recognize Jesus as the way is to, in a sense, still not know where one is going, in the most literal manifestation. Contrary to the belief of some, the Bible is not a guidebook or map for living, but the Word of God becomes a medium through which we come to recognize that Jesus is the way because of how he lived, what he did, how he spoke.

The early followers of Jesus did not refer to their belief in him and his teaching as "Christianity," a term that emerged much later. Coincidentally, the earliest term for what it meant to follow Jesus was called "the Way" (e.g., Acts 9:2, Acts 19:9, among others). This term, "the Way," in

Greek—*hodos*—ordinarily means "road," which ties into our song and our sense of confusion about life and planning our futures. On the one hand, to say that we don't know the way (*hodos*) could refer to the fact that we don't know the literal road to walk or on which to drive to get where we are going. Yet, on the other hand, the Hebrew Scriptures had already begun to develop a more metaphorical sense of "the Way," from simply meaning the road on which one journeys to a "manner of life" or way of living in the world. Such is the case with the very first verse of the very first Psalm: "Happy are those who do not follow the advice of the wicked, or take *the way* that sinners tread" (Ps 1:1). At the core of the early Christian movement was the realization that where one was and where one was going in life wasn't all that important, but *how one lived* and the manner according to which one went about living really made all the difference.

The spirit of Fastball's song "The Way" conveys the risk of leaving behind all the expectations, plans, personal interests, selfish desires, and values of the world to walk on the path toward the unknown, toward the high-*way* where those en route would be happy. Jesus calls us to do something likewise. To follow his way (*hodos*) is to surrender those things that create barriers in our lives, that compel us to look down at our detailed maps and personal plans, that focus on the wrong values and fleeting interests of our time and place. To follow Jesus is to live in a new manner, a new *way*, such that even if we don't know where we're going tomorrow or the day after, we do know how to live in relationship with others as God has called each of us to do.

Returning to the story that inspired the song, it can be easy to dwell on the tragedy of an elderly couple losing their way on the road, which leads to their deaths. It is important to recall that today's Gospel from John's fourteenth chapter is often proclaimed at funeral Masses, and the reason it is can help us to see an otherwise overlooked dimension of the story about Lela and Raymond Howard's last days. Jesus's comforting words to his disciples is twofold. First, we should not become distracted about the fleeting worries of the moment. To do so is to focus too much on an unknown future at the expense of the present. This preoccupation will lead us astray and likely cause us to draw into ourselves selfishly out of fear and anxiety. Second, in the present and in the future, Jesus is there both with us and ahead of us, drawing us back to God. "And if I go and prepare a place for you, I will come again and will take you to myself, so that where I am, there you may be also." How do we get to where Jesus is? How do we return to the Father? By following *the way*, not along a road on a map and not according to some spiritual GPS planner, but by living as Jesus did, in loving relationship with all people.

Jesus was, as he promised, with Lela and Raymond Howard that morning of June 28, 1997. Jesus is, as he promised, with us today. We might not know where the road on which we step or the journey that we begin today will take us in this life, but we have faith and hope that the God who raised Jesus on Easter will likewise raise us to new life.

We might not know where we're going, but we certainly know *the way*.

6ᵀᴴ SUNDAY OF EASTER

FRAN ROSSI SZPYLCZYN

Acts 8:5-8, 14-17
1 Peter 3:15-18
John 14:15-21

"I will not leave you orphans."

In the mid-1990's, Continental Airlines was the laughingstock of the industry. It had come through a terrible acquisition with Eastern Airlines that left both carriers decimated. Eastern went out of business and whatever was left was subsumed into Continental. The planes were a mess, the words "on time" did not exist, and finding your luggage when you got off the plane was chancy. Financially, a third bankruptcy was in the offing. Added to that, the employees were as depressed and beleaguered as could be; their attitudes contributed to making a bad situation worse. No one cared. Why should they? As for me, I don't need to refer to the history books for this one—I was a Continental frequent flier at the time. It was awful.

Later, something happened, and things began to turn around. In a reversal unheard of in the industry, everything changed very quickly, and all for the better. What was different? The big difference was that they had a new CEO, Gordon Bethune. He focused on ways to make employees the priority, and this was the source of a remarkable business transformation.

There had been so many problems, a great deal of which were symbolized in an odious employee manual. This manual was a life-sapping book that did not help anyone to do his or her jobs. In fact, it hampered them. It was hard for Bethune to motivate the staff and get them to believe in his vision. Seizing an opportunity for real change, the CEO decided to take a bunch of manuals, along with a group of employees, to an empty parking lot. He set the manuals on fire and replaced them with a new and clearer manual that inspired courage, vision, and employee participation. A new chapter was born for the airline, which went from "worst to first" in record time. The employees came to believe, leaving "beleaguered" behind.

Many of the people of Samaria in the time immediately following the Resurrection were beleaguered themselves. They were that way prior to the Resurrection, too! After the Babylonian captivity, the Samaritans returned home, but with their religious practices fractured. The people of Samaria were completely disenfranchised from the Jewish people; they were outcasts, decamped in their own territory.

You might remember the story of the Samaritan woman that we heard on the third Sunday of Lent; she had to remind Jesus that he should not be talking to her, a woman and a Samaritan! These were a people left out, excluded, isolated, and to be avoided. This is not exactly fulfillment of the dignity of the human person as God wills it.

In today's first reading, we heard about Philip, who went to speak to the people of Samaria to proclaim Christ to them. The Scriptures tell us that "unclean spirits, crying out in a loud voice, came out of many possessed people, and many paralyzed or crippled people were cured. There was great joy in that city."

In this Easter season, we are taught, reminded, and encouraged to come to know the resurrected Jesus, and the great power of what God has done for God's people. Of course we would all like to think that we know enough about that—that's why we're here—but do we know enough? Or do we need to be reminded? Do we believe it? Or are we beleaguered, too?

Our Gospel from John is one that we have heard time and again, but do we believe it? Jesus knows that he is going to be leaving the physical world, and he is promising the disciples that an "Advocate" or "Spirit" will be sent by God, to always be with and in them. Jesus adds that all who have his commandments and who observe them are the ones who love him. This is the key to unlock God's promise of eternal life through the revelation of Jesus in eternity. That all sounds good, but sometimes the instructions can appear like the old Continental employee manual— something that is too hard to read and understand, let alone follow! Do we believe it, or are we beleaguered? And if we do believe it, how do we bring others to the table to join us in the community of belief?

The new way given to us by Christ may not be so different from the old one; yet through the very being of Jesus it is expressed completely differently. Philip is expressing this to the people of Samaria, and they are able to hear and understand him, thus connecting them to God and to God's people. That all may be one is not some random thought, but the desire of God who has loved each and every person into being.

Now the second reading can help us to understand things a little more deeply. How do we proclaim Christ to others? Can we do this in a manner that will help their hearts to be transformed? Can we be like contemporary Philips who offer understanding and joy to people who may need both?

"Always be ready to give an explanation to anyone who asks you for a reason for your hope, but do it with gentleness and reverence," is what we hear from 2 Peter.

Do we believe? Do we hear, like the Samaritans, with one accord? And if we do, how do we communicate this to others? Do we look like people of joy, explaining with gentleness or reverence? Or do we present people with the dry and difficult-to-follow manual, leaving them to flounder while we feast?

This is where the Spirit comes in. If we are living with one accord in the promise of Christ, we make room for the Spirit that Jesus has promised to us. For the Samaritans, this meant Peter and John joining Philip so that the people would be given the Holy Spirit. We are sealed with the Holy Spirit at our Confirmation, and we must continue to seek the Spirit as we live. It is important to remember that the Spirit promised to us all is what brings the fullness of life. The Spirit animates and enlivens us, the Spirit frees us from our beleaguered past, putting us in the present moment of life.

Once we are given that Spirit, we know that we believe, but our belief must be tended to, over and over. Our belief must also be shared in ways that draw people to life in Christ. This should be done with joy, inspiring hope, and creating a life of common good, not simply by teaching people a one-dimensional set of rules from an outdated way of living.

Christ brings us new life, and here we are in the Easter season rising up in that life with the promise of the Spirit. Like those airline employees burning manuals in the parking lot, the Samaritans were freed from their past when they came to know Jesus. We are in the same need of being freed and freeing others. That is how we can all come move from being the beleaguered to the believers.

7ᵀᴴ SUNDAY OF EASTER

MICHELLE FRANCL-DONNAY

ACTS 1:12-14

1 PETER 4: 13-16

JOHN 17:1-11

"I am in the world no more..."

"*I am in the world* no more..." Placed as it is between the Feasts of Ascension and Pentecost, liberally laced with references to glory—you can almost hear the sparkling trumpets—it's tempting to read this passage from John's Gospel as if it were Jesus's final words before his Ascension (and scholars suggest that it might have been). But John deliberately places this dialogue just before Christ's passion, on the evening he was arrested and dragged before Caiaphas.

Perhaps John wants us to hear Jesus's words not as the words of the Christ who has conquered death, spoken to disciples exultant with the joy of the resurrection. Instead, he implies, listen to the words of a man who knows the cup he is about to drink, who grasps the inglorious, ignominious death he is going to die, offered to his Father on behalf of his closest companions. Perhaps John places this conversation between Father and Son here to remind us that the glory in which Jesus is wrapped is not the glory of the resurrection, but the glory of the cross.

Still, glory seems like such an Easter word, perhaps all the more so because we scrub it from our Lenten liturgies. We return to it at the Easter Vigil with exuberant voices; organ thundering, trumpets resounding and lights blazing in a church often filled to overflowing with flowers and worshipers, all brightly clad in the colors of spring. The joyous glory of Easter sparkles and spills out, its gold and white vestments perhaps even for a moment obscuring the image of a forsaken man dragging his own death through the dusty streets of Jerusalem while the crowd jeers.

This passage from John and the selection we read in Peter's first letter remind us that the glory of Easter is deeply entwined in Christ's passion and death. Rejoice, says Peter, when Christ's glory is revealed in you through suffering. What bursts forth from us in our Easter Gloria is not just our joy in the salvation of the world, though it is surely that, but also our willingness to be glorified ourselves—on a cross, should it come to that. As poet Daniel Berrigan, SJ wryly put it, "If you want to follow Jesus, you better look good on wood."

Cross or crown, mockery or honor, glory is our destiny. We hear over and over again in the scriptures the promise that we shall be clothed in glory. In his essay *The Weight of Glory*, C.S. Lewis tries to help us imagine what glory might look like on us, as if it were a cloak we are trying on now to see how it might fit on us in eternity. What might it be like, Lewis asks, to stand before God and have God appreciate us for who we are, what we have accomplished—to see in God's face how we are cherished, to know in our depths that God rejoices in what He has made?

It's an overwhelming thought. Even so, Lewis proposes flipping the contemplation around to ponder what is, at least to me, an even more oversetting reality: none of us are ordinary, that "[n]ext to the Blessed Sacrament itself, your neighbor is the holiest object presented to your senses." Imagine the driver that just cut you off, the neighbor whose political stance you find untenable, or the homeless woman foraging just after dawn in the dumpster behind the grocery store standing before God wrapped—as are you—in a garment of glory and light. Would you still blast your horn, tell them off, or walk past? Or would you be drawn to see them as they are, images of the glorified Christ, cherished creations of the God of glory?

In the Greek, *doxa*—glory—holds a tinge of expectation. Glory is for those who are thought well of, and consequently from whom good is expected to flow. Glory carries a certain weight of expectation. Glory gleams, but not with the tawdry glitter of worldly grandeur—it flashes its obligations, shimmers with possibility.

Origen, reflecting on the Gospel of Matthew in the third century, asks, "What cloak am I weaving in both word and deed to wrap around Christ, our King, who is cold and shivering on the street?" We might equally well ask what cloak of glory we are weaving for ourselves in word and deed. Jesus points us in this direction at the very end of this Gospel passage: "It is in them that I have been glorified." The cross Christ bore was ours— the weight of it, our sins.

So, too, our way to glory lies not in ourselves, but in those we come to serve. We are glorified not just in our own sufferings, through our own crosses, but we are glorified when we share in our neighbors' suffering, when we pick up the crosses that are not our own. This is the garment of glory we weave for ourselves — the cloak we wrap around the shivering man in the street, the tablecloth we spread on the table at the soup kitchen, the blanket we tuck around our dying spouse.

As we walk out of Easter's trumpeting joy, into the ordinary days, let us carry with us the promise and the reality of the glory made manifest in us. May we have ears to hear the poor. May we have eyes to see the root of injustice. May we have the courage bear the crosses placed upon us. May we have the will and the strength to take up the crosses that are not ours. And may we ever bear with joy and hope the weight of glory.

ASCENSION OF THE LORD

FR. PAUL HOLMES

Acts 1:1-11
Eph. 1:17-23
Matt 28:16-20

"I am with you always, until the end of the age."

S omeone once said that intimacy is a work in progress. Intimacy is that feeling of being "at one" with another person—and once it's started, it's never finished.

Husbands and wives certainly know this to be true, for how else could marriage work, were it not for the fact that intimacy is never a "done deal"?

Young lovers often mistake what they're feeling as a "done deal". They think, "I now know everything I can possibly know about you." (And this only minutes after they learn each other's names!)

But long-time friends know that intimacy is a work in progress because with each passing year, with each passing decade—and even though they can finish each other's sentences and have heard each other's stories a hundred times—there's always something new, something wonderful about being in each other's presence.

This is why Jesus *had* to leave us. There *had* to be an Ascension Thursday, when the disciples would be left staring up into the clouds, watching Jesus disappear forever. As he himself said, "I *have* to go, for how else can I send you my Spirit?"

When he said this, he meant that there had to be a way for all of us to feel "at one" with God and with each other. And sending us his Spirit was the only way for this to happen.

Of the three persons of the Blessed Trinity, the Holy Spirit is probably the least understood. Every Sunday, though, we proclaim that he is the "Lord, the giver of Life," and that he's "spoken through the prophets". And then there's all that "proceeding" stuff that ends with his being "adored and glorified."

We say it. But, if you're like me, the Spirit is a little hard to get to know.

Here, in these nine days between Ascension Thursday and Pentecost Sunday, we await the Spirit's arrival. When he came on that first Pentecost, he turned eleven uneducated and foolish fishermen into hearts-on-fire missionaries whose legacy is now over two billion Christians throughout the world!

But what is the Spirit doing in *your* life, and in mine?

Well, even though we don't say it in the Creed, the Spirit is the intimacy between God the Father and God the Son. And that same Spirit is drawing you and me close—close to God, and close to one another.

If we are ever to feel "at one" with God, the way we feel "at one" with a spouse or a best friend, it is the Spirit who will make it happen.

During these nine days, as we look forward to Pentecost, let us pray to the Holy Spirit. And pray that he will draw us close to the Father and Son and make us one. It's a work in progress. It started at our Baptism, but it's never a "done deal".

PENTECOST

FR. BILL BAUSCH

Acts 2:1-11
1 Cor. 12:3-7, 12-13
John 20:19-23

"The doors were locked, where the disciples were."

*A*rchbishop *Thomas Kelly of Louisville,* Kentucky, tells a story about the day he was appointed bishop. He made it a point, on the morning the news was made public, to have breakfast with his mother so that he could be with her when she heard the story on the radio.

So there they were having breakfast when her son's appointment was announced during the morning news. Mrs. Kelly was thrilled. She leaned across the table and asked,

"What is it like for you to be made bishop?"

Kelly explained to his mother how he felt, and as he spoke, his mother sat with her chin on her hand, seemingly in reverie.

When he had finished, there was a pregnant pause. Mrs. Kelly sighed and said, "You know, Tommy, if I had known that one day you would become a bishop and have your picture in the newspapers and on television, I would have had your teeth straightened."

Well, it wasn't quite what he expected. A bit of a surprise I would say.

For a real surprise, let's return to the gospel we just heard. It's a story of shut and open doors. The disciples of Jesus were hiding in fear behind closed and locked doors, shutting out the rest of the hostile world, a world for them full of suspicion and accusation. They felt better, safer, huddled together in isolation.

And then, a surprise! Into their isolation Jesus bursts. Through closed doors he walks. Past locks he breaks in. Oblivious of barriers he comes. Surprised and fearful, the disciples are stunned. *They* thought it was all over between Jesus and themselves. After all, their conduct these past few days had been anything but sterling: denials, betrayals, flight, leaving Jesus to go it alone, die alone. The only thing they had left was their embarrassment and guilty consciences. Truly, this bunch of failures deserved to be behind locked doors. Who wanted them? Who would speak to them? Let it cool off and they would slink away and go into hiding somewhere and be forgotten.

And yet. And yet there he was. He sought them out in their weakness, ignored the doors they thought would keep him out. Yes, he was there, and there to speak of forgiveness and, above all, to give them the gift of the Spirit: the Spirit of the Second Chance, the Spirit of a love greater than their shame, a Spirit that would break down doors and send them out, now as a community of wounded, forgiven healers, to preach the Good News of God's love. Oh, what a beginning, what a Pentecost that was!

Yet, I confess, I never realized fully what that all meant, how profound a story it was, until a priest friend told me the story of Tom. And on Pentecost, I want to share it with you. Here's my friend's story:

Tom was a forty-one-year-old man, dying of AIDS. His family was in total denial. His parents literally had him locked in an upstairs bedroom, although they did care for his basic necessities, like food and water. The first time I visited Tom at his parents' home, I was brought up to his bedroom. This huge, rather handsome man was now terribly thin and looked lost in his king-sized bed. I bent over to kiss him on the forehead and then sat beside his bed. I took his hand and said, "Now tell me what you want me to know." He said with tears in his eyes, "No one touches me any more." I continued holding his hand and let him unravel his story.

Eventually, Tom became so ill that it was necessary to hospitalize him. Each day I would drive over to visit him in the hospital. I would try to engage his mother and father in conversation. Nothing seemed to work. Knowing it was therapeutic for all of them to be able to talk about Tom's condition, I tried many different techniques. I was successful with his brother and sister-in-law, but the parents had built high walls around the subject.

Meanwhile, Tom's condition worsened daily. After about five weeks, the family seemed to look forward to my arrival at the hospital each day. There were times I spent alone with Tom. He wanted and needed to tell me other pieces of his story. He was a wonderful man who had made one decision that left its mark on him. Apparently he felt safe with me. I did not judge him. We even found things to laugh at, at times.

But what came across was that Tom feared that that he had been a failure. Though everyone who knew him described Tom as generous, kind, thoughtful, and attentive to others, Tom focused on the "mistake" he had made. He shared how embarrassed he was. What would others think of him? Tom never gave many details. I never really found out how Tom developed AIDS. Tom also worried about his friends from whom he had pulled away. So many unanswered telephone calls and notes! He admitted that he had gone behind closed doors, as it were, to protect himself. He went through waves of despair. He shared the loneliness that all of this created for him.

One day, Tom asked me to contact his friend Anna and ask if she would like to visit him. Tom and Anna had been very good friends but had not seen each other in over two years. Too ashamed, he never told her about his condition. When I contacted Anna, she felt betrayed. "Why didn't he tell me what was going on?" she cried. I wasn't sure if Anna would even go to visit Tom.

The next morning, however, Anna called me and asked what time visiting hours were at the hospital. I agreed to take her over when I went for my visit. When we walked into the room, at first both old friends seemed very frightened of each other. But when they embraced, the conversation immediately came more easily.

"What did I ever do that you cut me off?" Anna asked.

"You didn't do a thing," Tom replied. "I was so ashamed to tell you about myself."

Anna said, "It doesn't matter to me. I've missed you and have worried about you so."

All Tom could say was, "Anna, I'm glad you came. I'm so sorry. Please forgive me." Tears flowed. Two friends were reunited.

One of Tom's last conversations was with his brother. Tom told him, "I *do* have AIDS. But I know I am a good person, and I hope you love me."

Tom's brother went over to his brother's bedside and embraced him. "Yes," he said, "I love you. I love you so much. I don't care what you have. I love you."

Tom's father was a holdout. He still remained distant, but it seemed to me that even he and Tom had somewhat repaired their rift by the time of Tom's death. I recall the night of Tom's wake when his father embraced me and said, "You know, I wanted a perfect son. For a while I thought he was a failure. But these weeks in the hospital I started to learn who my son was again. I loved him so much. He was a good boy. I am proud of my son." Tom had died knowing that his father accepted and loved him and that even when we make mistakes we can be perfect.

When I heard this story, friends, I could not get it out of my head how much it was like the Upper Room that first Pentecost. Failure and shame and all kinds of doors. But, one by one, those doors opened as the Spirit exhaled its love, like the wolf in the fairy tale that huffed and puffed his way in. Once more, in the person of my friend and eventually Anna and his brother and his father, doors were gone through and with them Jesus walked in and breathed on Tom and said, "Tom, receive the Holy Spirit. Your sins are forgiven."

It's a Pentecost story. One by one my priest-friend, the brother, the sister, Anna, the father went through the closed doors. They had been sent by the Spirit. Pentecost is precisely that. It is about the birth of a sent community—you and me—whom the breath of God has touched, a community called church, a gathering of people inducted through baptism, sent to open shut doors and let out sin and despair and let in the Good News.

It's a formidable job we have been given, but we are not alone. As church, we have the Spirit, for as the Mexican poet Amado Nervo puts it: "Alone we are only an anthill / but in the Spirit we are a mountain." And he goes on to move us from drop to fountain, from feather to wing, from beggar to king. All because we have the Spirit.

Yes, and more. In the words of St. Peter, we are a royal priesthood, a holy nation, a people set apart. We are church.

ORDINARY TIME

2ND SUNDAY IN ORDINARY TIME

DEACON JIM KNIPPER

Isa. 49:3-6
1 Cor. 1:1-3
John 1:29-34

"Behold, the Lamb of God who takes away the sin of the world!"

The Cherokee Indians tell the story that when the plants and trees were first made, the great Creator gave a gift to each species. But first he set up a contest to determine which gift would be most useful to whom.

"I want you to stay awake and keep watch over the earth for seven nights," he told them. The young trees and plants were so excited to be entrusted with such an important job that on the first night they found no difficulty in staying awake. However, by the second night, it was not so easy, and just before dawn, a few fell asleep. On the third night, the trees and plants whispered among themselves in the wind, trying to keep from nodding off, but it was too much work for some of them. By the fourth night, even more fell asleep.

By the time that seventh night came, the only trees and plants still awake were the cedar, the pine, the spruce, the fir, the holly, and the laurel. "What wonderful endurance you have," exclaimed the Creator. "You will be given the gift of remaining green forever. You will be the guardians of the forest. Even in the seemingly dead of winter, your brother and sister creatures will find life protected in your branches." Ever since then, all the other trees and plants lose their leaves and sleep all winter while the evergreens stay awake.

This creation tale talks about the greenness in the midst of barrenness...
it speaks to light in times of winter darkness. And that is what this Sunday
is all about.

As you walked into the church this morning, my guess is that you could
not help but be struck by the relative barrenness of the sanctuary. Gone
are white and gold vestments, all the bright lights, the red poinsettias,
the green trees. But note: As we enter the period of ordinary time, and
relative spatial barrenness, the church reminds us with the use of green
altar cloths and vestments that Christ brings nourishing life into our spiritual journey and personal growth.

Today is indeed a Sunday of transition. Transition in nature, as we continue to move from the darkness of winter towards increasing amounts
of daylight—and transition in the church, as we move from the close of
the Christmas Season last week with the Feast of the Baptism of our
Lord to the beginning of Ordinary Time. It is a time when we move from
celebrating the manifestation of God to celebrating the beginning of
Christ's ministry on earth.

Manifestation comes from the Greek word *phaerosis*, which means to
make something visible, to reveal something. The root of this word means
"light", for in order to make something visible, there must be a light
source. When we celebrated the Epiphany, which means manifestation,
we celebrated the magi finding the Christ child through the light of the
star and revealing the Son of God.

But on this Sunday we hear in Isaiah that it is in the eyes of the Lord that
we will be made a light to the nations so that God's salvation will reach
the ends of the earth. This will be echoed in a few weeks, when we will
hear the Gospel where Christ tells us, his followers, that we are the light
of the world.

So as we now transition to Ordinary Time, it is interesting to note that every year we begin with a gospel from John. For where the Synoptic Gospels of Matthew, Mark and Luke provide focus on the Kingdom or Reign of God, it is the Gospel of John that focuses on relationships— Christ's relationship with God the Father and our relationship with Christ.

While each of the Gospel writers recounts the baptism of our Lord (last week we heard Matthew's), only in John's account do we hear John the Baptist's cry, which we repeat at each Eucharistic liturgy to this day: "Behold, the Lamb of God who takes away the sin of the world!" Unlike the other gospel accounts, which are a bit more passive, John the Baptist makes no bones about who is coming to him. Why? Well, can you imagine his excitement? He has been baptizing at the river Jordan day in and day out, with the faith that the Holy Spirit will enlighten him with the knowledge of who is Christ. For, up to that point, what does John the Baptist repeat in this passage? He says, "I didn't know him," or in other words...I don't see him.

How often have we said that to ourselves and others? Times in our lives that we do not feel connected...times of great difficulties...times of great conflict...times where we feel we are just not good enough...times of great loss.

A few days ago, we commemorated the anniversary of the earthquake in Haiti taking the lives of over 300,000 people, including a loved one here from St. Paul's—Christine Gianacaci. In those days, darkness fell on Christine's family and this parish. But as the healing began, within a very short time her parents decided to respond to their darkness with light. They quickly formed a foundation in her name (Christine's Hope for Kids) and within just their first year distributed over $75,000 to children in need.

Tomorrow we celebrate the life of Martin Luther King Jr., who spent a lifetime bringing light into the darkness of racial segregation and discrimination. While sitting in a jail cell in 1963, he wrote, "Darkness cannot drive out darkness; only light can do that. Hate cannot drive out hate; only love can do that."

And most recently, the coverage of the tragedy in Tucson has been exhaustive. A country tries to make sense of how one person could take the lives of seven innocent people, including nine-year-old Christina Taylor Green. Of course, there are no answers to the obvious question, "Why?" And so many ask, "How do we begin to find light in this carnage of darkness?" Actually, the best public response I have read is by our President, who said that we can only respond to such a tragedy by looking inward at how we live our lives and how we love others.

Indeed, it is with this type of inward reflection and prayer that opens our eyes to this indwelling of the Holy Spirit. Where in the face of darkness *we* may be able to cry out, "Behold—this is the Lamb of God, the Christ, who takes away the sin of the world." This is the Christ who called to sinners and prostitutes and tax collectors...this is the Christ who made the lame walk, the blind see and the deaf hear...this is the Christ who hung on the cross so that all may be saved. This is the Christ who calls to us to be light to others.

So our journey through Ordinary Time begins...and like the journey of John the Baptist, it is a developmental faith journey...a journey where we may be faced with times when we cry out, "I don't see him," and other times where we can feel the light of Christ shining upon us. But we take comfort knowing, as we heard in today's Gospel, that it is Christ who comes towards us, no matter where we are in our lives. It is the indwelling of the Holy Spirit who gives us the gift of sight. And it is our good and gracious God who calls upon us to be a beacon of light in times of darkness...an evergreen in barren land, a light to shine on others, as well as a reflection of Christ to ourselves.

3ᴿᴰ SUNDAY IN ORDINARY TIME

PATRICK WENRICK

Isaiah 8:23 – 9:3
1 Cor. 1:10 – 13, 17
Matt 4: 12 – 23

"They left their nets and followed him"

*S*ometimes, in order to hear the voice of Jesus, we need to be called out of the ordinariness of life to experience the extraordinary. That's what is happening in today's Gospel. Jesus approaches two brothers, Peter and Andrew, who are routinely doing what they do every day (which is casting their nets). Jesus asks them to come and follow him. The response is powerful: They left their nets. They left what they were routinely doing…they left what was familiar….they left what was secure. A little while later, Jesus approaches two other brothers, James and John, and says the same thing to these fishermen, who were doing something very routine, too, i.e. mending their nets so that they could continue with their job, which would put food on their table and clothing on the backs of their families. Yet, the leaving behind of nets by James and John entailed something more than the tools and source of income. It entailed letting go of their father with whom they worked, and at whose feet they probably learned the art of fishing.

Was the response of these brothers to Jesus so radical in nature? Would they never return to their father or to their occupations as fishermen? Perhaps it was, but more likely the call of Jesus entailed a gradual shift to what is really important in life. It's almost like they had to separate from ties that bound them in order to hear the message of Jesus.

What keeps us from hearing the voice or call of Jesus? Are we obsessed with our work, our relationships, and our routines? Are we sucked into our social networking, the gadgetry of iPads and cell phones, that we cannot hear the voice of Jesus calling us through our spouses, children, prayer, or others beyond our familiar circle? Perhaps we are in darkness and yearn to experience what the community referred to in today's first reading longs to see and hear: "The people who walked in darkness have seen a great light…those who dwelt in the land of deep darkness, on them has light shined."

Perhaps the darkness of our lives has roots that are much deeper than being caught up in the fast-moving world of technology? Maybe the roots of the darkness that we have become so used to is grounded in the trauma that we have experienced through physical, emotional, or sexual abuse? Darkness, fear, unhealthy guilt, lack of trust, and violence often swirl in our psyches if we have been exposed to conflict and hurt in our families of origin, or perhaps in the wars we have fought in. Perhaps our deafness, our blindness, to the call of Jesus is the result of disease or illness. In these situations we are not blinded by routine that we cannot see the light, but we are deaf to the call of Jesus who wants us to come into the light, to experience healing, and to help others to do the same.

Perhaps we need to pray for the ability to experience the voice of Jesus in the midst of darkness, to experience the presence of the Resurrected One even though we are stuck mending or casting our nets. Our prayer needs to be like that of Viktor Frankl who survived the atrocities of Auschwitz by giving meaning to focusing on a light in a farm house he could see in the distance from the concentration camp. Or perhaps we need to model our lives after Ben Underwood, who as a toddler lost his sight to cancer but stunned people near and far with his ability to "see" with sound. He played basketball, went rollerblading and walked to school without the aid of person or cane. He participated in karate, rode a bicycle, and did what sighted people do, only he was totally blind. Scientists and the medical professions were baffled. How did Ben "see" without "eyes"? Ben taught himself echolocation, similar to that used by dolphins and bats—by making a clicking sound with his tongue, there wasn't anything Ben could not do. He could even play video games by memorizing scenarios where characters had particular sounds. Ben was called to make a difference in the lives of others. He swam with dolphins, and danced on the Ellen DeGeneres Show. He befriended famous people like Stevie Wonder but through it all, his mother said, "he remained humbled and focused." Jesus called Ben in his blindness and he responded by teaching others the guiding system he developed. He taught others another way of seeing; he was, like Jesus, light in the darkness.

Ben Underwood's life on this earth ended in January of 2009 after a recurrence of cancer in his sinus cavity could not be arrested or eradicated. Yet, his responding to the call to leave his mending and casting of nets to follow the Lord lives on to this day. He followed the Light in spite of his darkness to where he now is immersed in the Light of God's eternal Presence. He was not focused on acquiring things in this life, but was tuned into love, which was more important than things.

May we answer the call of Jesus as did the brothers Peter and Andrew, James and John; and as Ben Underwood did in his ordinary life made extraordinary by his openness to the spirit of Jesus.

4ᵀᴴ SUNDAY IN ORDINARY TIME

ROB BELL

ZEPH. 2:3; 3:12-13
1 COR. 1:26-31
MATT. 5:1-12

"Blessed are the poor in spirit."

We often see in the Gospels Jesus interacting in some way with the "crowds." And in the case of today's popular story of the Sermon on the Mount, it is the "crowds" that are key to breaking open what Jesus was really teaching. For the "crowds" came from Galilee (A very Jewish area), the Decapolis (a very Greek non-Jewish area), Jerusalem, Judea and the region across the Jordan. And they were all following him. The "crowds" were Jewish, not Jewish, religious, not religious—covering the broad spectrum of humanity.

And, no doubt, there would have been people in that crowd who would have been taught from birth that in order to follow God they were to have absolutely no contact with the same people that they were now mixing among.

Jesus is surrounded by all of them. He goes up on a mountainside, sits down, and the crowd and his disciples gather around him. With this mass of humanity encircling him, he begins to teach by saying, "Blessed are the poor in spirit, for theirs is the kingdom of heaven."

How do you begin to unpack this? Remember there's a massive crowd of sinners, and tax collectors, and prostitutes, and really, really religious people, and really, really Gentile people who aren't really, really considered religious by the really, really religious people. There's this massive spectrum of humanity, and it's in the midst of this crowd that Jesus begins, "Blessed are the poor in spirit because theirs is the kingdom!" The kingdom of God is *theirs*.

What Jesus is doing here is so upside down. It is so brilliant and ultimately so shocking—and at the same time it's deeply comforting. So it takes a bit to absorb just what's happening.

First, the phrase "poor in spirit" is a negative term. The "poor in spirit" are losers, those at the end of the rope, those spiritual zeros, the bankrupt, the pathetic, the lame, the out of it—those without a trace of good—the morally empty, the pathetic. "Poor in spirit" is not a condition which we to try to attain. There's nothing praiseworthy, noble, good, honorable, or positive about being poor in spirit. Christ is not giving people a wonderful praiseworthy condition that one would aspire to.

Secondly, when Jesus says, "Blessed," it comes from the Greek word *makarios*. Which some have translated as "happy," as in "Happy are those who mourn." The scholar Fredrick Dale Bruner says, "To understand 'blessed' is to understand 'a divine.' It's a divine 'I am with you.'" It's God's way of saying "I am on your side." If you look at how the term is used throughout the Scripture and how the term is used by Jesus, it's the larger holistic sense of being fortunate because God is with you. Fortunate are the losers, the pathetic, the depraved, the lame, the spiritual zeros because God is on your side.

What Jesus is doing here is making an announcement. And an announcement is a fundamentally different way of framing something. He's not giving instruction—like the seven steps to get God's blessing. This is not a command—since he doesn't begin with here's what you need to do in order to be blessed. This is not advice—such as: "Well, I'm quite intelligent. Here's how I'd think you ought to approach the question." He begins the Sermon on the Mount with an announcement. He announces that God is on the side of everybody for whom there's no reason why God should be on their side.

When Jesus makes this announcement, it is fundamentally counterintuitive. Because if you are like me, your first impulse is to say: "What good is this condition of being poor in spirit that it deserves the blessing of God? What good thing makes me deserving of God's blessing?" Instead the announcement is, "Blessed are those who there's no reason why they should be blessed. Blessed are all the people who aren't humble. Blessed are all the pathetic, wretched sinners and tax collectors, and prostitutes, and alcoholics, and thieves. Blessed is everybody who doesn't believe in God. Blessed are all of the morally empty people who couldn't tell the truth straight if they had to. Blessed are all the people. The favor of God is now pouring down on everybody who doesn't deserve the favor of God."

This announcement of Jesus to this massive crowd of people from across the spectrum is, "Blessed are all the people who there's no reason why they should be blessed." That, my brothers and sisters, is the Gospel. That is the very Good News, but it can be terribly disturbing for religious people because it is very, very easy to become convinced that God's blessing is for particular people because of this particular thing they've done, or who they are, or what they've said. Jesus, on the other hand, says "Blessed are the totally pathetic losers without a wisp of religion, for the Kingdom of Heaven is theirs!"

Look back at what Jesus does during his ministry and trace through the things that Jesus says. He doesn't give much in the way of explanation about God other than *because God is like this*. He tells story after story after story, where there isn't really an explanation given and there really doesn't seem to be a point other than something intrinsic to who God is.

To all of those who feel that they don't deserve the blessing of God, the blessing of God is here and it's yours. You can see why the first people who heard this said, "Well that's good news." But some will immediately say, "Wait, wait, wait, wait. No, no, no, no. God only blesses the hard-working. God only blesses the morally upright-right? God only blesses all the people who make the right decisions. God only blesses the people who do the right things at the right time. God only blesses people who make the right confession of faith. God only blesses the people who go to the right schools. God only blesses the people who work hard and keep their nose clean." Which, in essence, says that God's love is only for the people who can earn it...

The moment we look down upon somebody because they aren't as disciplined, hardworking, upright, smart, responsible, moral, God-fearing, bible-believing, or Jesus-trusting as we are—because they've made idiotic stupid, immoral choices again, and again, and again—it is at that moment we are in fact rich in spirit and Jesus isn't announcing anything to us. Instead, it is in your pathetic, bedraggled, confused, morally ambiguous state in which there's nothing good within you that God announces, "I'm on your side."

Perhaps we could say it this way: If you are a church and you are in a gathering of people who take seriously the Gospel pronouncement of Jesus, then you have to embrace the simple truth that before it's a theology, or a system, or a doctrine, or a church, or a movement, or an institution, or a worldview, or a way, or a perspective—it's an announcement. God has sent His son into the world, His one and only Son because God so loved the world, His Son that did not come to judge or condemn. God came to save and God begins the epic Sermon on the Mount by starting not high-but low-with an announcement—a shocking, jarring, and strangely counterintuitive, exuberant, healing, comforting message.

Anyone think they are on the outs? God's blessing is now pouring out on you. The Creator of the Universe is not for only those who do right, but also for all those who do wrong. This God loves. The Kingdom of Heaven has now become available in a fresh new way for all the people who have absolutely no claim to it and who don't deserve it.

Blessed are those who there's no reason in the world why they should be blessed.

Isa. 58:7-10	*"You are the light*
1 Cor. 2:1-5	*of the world"*
Matt 5:13-16	

*T*his time of NETWORK's "Nuns on the Bus" and its various off-shoots has been a time of dazzling surprise so far—beyond what any of us could have created. It got started because of the Vatican censure of the Leadership Conference of Women Religious (LCWR) that mentioned our organization, NETWORK, as a bad influence. It was this notoriety and pain that resulted in last year's initial bus trip as we tried to use the media focus for mission.

Quite like St. Paul in the second reading, I feel that we "came among you in weakness, in fear and great trembling." We did not have a philosophical argument to persuade; rather, we had a heartrending passion to live in the Spirit. It was the Spirit that gave life to the whole adventure.

In this journey we have met all kinds of people along the road—people who agree and disagree with us, but each one with a unique story. And with each we try to encourage in the Spirit to be all that we are called to be.

The call that our nation seems hungry for is to be communal. It is not possible to live in individual isolation, though many would want us to pull up the drawbridge and hide out. The call of Jesus is to know that we are integrated into each other. The journey of the twenty-first century in the first world is to move away from individualism and self-satisfaction and live in relationship without fear of the other or the unknown.

It is almost impossible for me to think of myself not as just a single person. I think our English language is a part of the problem, because we use the same word "you" in the singular and the plural. If we read the Scripture in the plural, then we immediately see the communal call to live in relationship with those at the margins of our society. The collective is only alive to the extent that we embrace all. But if I read "you" as referring just to me as an individual, then I can readily think that "it is all about me" and I am the good news alone.

Into this hungry world we came with a message on our bus of joy and hope. Like Isaiah, our message of the call to share food, shelter the homeless, clothe the naked, and not turn our backs on our own resonated in a world starved for connection. Some tell us that this mandate is only for personal giving of food and shelter. But what we know is that the problems are so large that in a complex society individual charity is not enough. Rather, we must "do away with the yoke, clenched fists and malicious words." This needs to be done personally and as a society.

But we are not only connected as individuals; rather all of our actions are connected. I have been struck by the fact that Billy and his wife and two kids, whom we met in Milwaukee, use food stamps (SNAP) because their wages are so low that they are left in poverty. Some politicians want to believe that this is a "handout" to Billy. But what I realized is that it is also a benefit to the employer, since he can pay low wages and keep his costs down because of food stamps. But it is also a benefit to the consumer because food stamps help keep prices down. So the safety net is not just for those who use the benefits directly, it is a benefit for all of us. We need to "do away with the yoke and malicious words" that denigrate those who use these programs. We need to lift up the dignity of all, knowing that we are in this together.

When we know our interconnectedness and that we are all part of the problem and the solution, then the Spirit can shine in our lives and world. It is this Pentecost moment that lets our light shine out brightly on the lampstand. But we can tell if we are light, I think, not from ourselves, but only from the reactions of others.

As a "Nun on the Bus," I do not know if we are light or not. But what we have discovered in the thousands of people we meet is that they have seen our journeys as light. This light draws people into the warmth of community in challenging days. So I think that this may be the way for all of us. We are surprised when people find our lives as a witness to the Good News.

Light is understood from a distance, and we are called to be a vessel for light itself. What joy to embrace the vibrant mystery of God and live in loving relationship with all those who struggle! Then our God will say "I am here!" It is a surprise to all of us that this warmth of light is such a magnet. But we should know that it is God's practical love that is the flavor of our lives and the joy of our ministry. I pray that all those who respond to it "may give praise to our Father" knowing that if we "satisfy the needs of the afflicted, your light will rise in the darkness and your darkest hour will be like noon."

Sɪʀ 15:15-20
1 Cᴏʀ 2:6-10
Mᴀᴛᴛ 5:17-37

"You shall not commit adultery."

For thousands of years, people have been wrestling with the complexities, tensions, and heartaches of divorce. Divorce has never been simple, and we do a great disservice to others when we try to make it a nice, neat, clean transaction. It almost never is. People have a staggering variety of different thoughts, experiences. and reflections on divorce, creating a vast array of responses, hurts, wounds. and opinions. Which bring us to Matthew 5, because many who have been through divorce have had someone in a Christian community beat them over the head with this passage, telling them that they are out of line and are breaking the scriptures and being disobedient to Jesus. Context, of course, is crucial here, because in speaking about divorce Jesus was entering into a particular discussion of his day, and there's a chance that if we aren't familiar with that discussion this passage could be used to seriously wound others.

First, then, let's take a look at the word "divorce" that Jesus uses. It comes from the Greek word *apoluo* which means to loose or to unbind from, to send away. The root word does not mean a mutual parting, but rather one person unbinding, loosing, or sending another away.

Second, the discussion in Jesus's day surrounding divorce was based on a passage from the Torah—Deuteronomy, chapter 24—which involved a cultural context even earlier than Jesus's day. In that time, a wife was treated like property. The husband could get rid of her at any time for any reason he wanted to. If the husband sent her away, she would have no rights, no dignity, no protection and no provision. If you as a wife were dismissed or sent away by your husband, you were cast out of the tent, the clan, the tribe—you had nothing. You were a single woman in a barbaric, primitive world where you had no protection. You had no dignity. You had no rights. You had no way to provide for yourself.

In the Book of Deuteronomy, Moses doesn't condone or say that divorce is good, he simply acknowledges it's reality and says, "You must give a woman a certificate of divorce if you send her away." The Mosaic Law was such that if you were a man and you wanted to send her away, you had to go through the process of writing her an official, legal, recognized certificate of divorce. The thought being, first, if you have to go through that much trouble and take that much time, you may reconsider. Secondly, giving her a certificate of divorce was a way of restoring her honor and dignity and virtue in a culture in which a woman who had been sent away had none. This passage from Deuteronomy is a radical, empowering, pro-women legislation that actually was a giant, progressive, revolutionary step forward—not the last step, merely *a* step. The woman no longer is just cast out, but she has legal rights. She has dignity. She has honor.

So when Jesus uses the word "divorce", he is entering in to one of the most electric, controversial subjects of his day. Two great rabbis had, some time before Jesus, taken sides on this issue, one saying that to send a wife away all she had to do was burn the toast, the other saying that the only grounds for sending her away was adultery. Jesus sides with the latter, saying that if he does choose to divorce her, he must honor her and give her dignity and virtue in the process. He must not, at any point, treat her like a piece of property. This is where Jesus lands on the matter. He is entering into a specific discussion and debate, and he comes out and says, listen, you don't treat a woman like that. It is simply not right.

When we look at Paul, he actually expands Jesus's biblical grounds and says, "Oh, by the way, if somebody is married to somebody and this Christian is married to somebody who's not a Christian and they abandoned the marriage and walked away, then this brother or sister can let them go." So Paul actually expands what are called biblical grounds for divorce, but he doesn't just say they're free to walk away. He adds a sort of operative principle for the whole situation. They are not bound in such circumstances. He could've ended there. But Paul adds, "God has called us to live in peace", which is wholeness and health. Everything in its right place. Paul's message is clear: God has called us to live in peace. Paul doesn't just say, "I have a second reason it's okay to divorce: your partner deserted you." He adds a larger principle that drives these grounds: God has called us to live in peace. So the question to ask, then, is: Is there hope for peace in this relationship? Is staying together here in some way actually more disruptive and destructive because God calls us to live in peace? Are there some marriages where there are so many years of wounds that, while we believe in miracles, we believe in healing, we believe in divine intervention, and we believe that some things can be raised from the dead—that perhaps, at times, some things do die?

God has called us to live in peace. So how do we then approach divorce? Perhaps a way to say it would be simply this: "We are always for fidelity, reconciliation, endurance, and peace as far as this is possible." Be true to your spouse. Don't cheat. It's mean. It's nasty. It's horrible. It's destructive. It's sin. It's absolutely awful. It shreds marriages to pieces. Be true to your spouse. We are always for fidelity. We are always first and foremost for reconciliation.

When there has been infidelity, when there has been abuse, our intent first and foremost is always for reconciliation. Reconciliation takes two. It takes all sorts of things coming together, but we always want to see marriages healed. That's what we do. Our first instinct is always reconciliation. Endurance. We always want to see marriages last.

So our interest is always in endurance, but then, we add to that, peace as far as it is possible. Both witness profound respect for the sanctity of marriage, but at the same time, with the reality and honesty that sometimes some things die and you have to call it what it is.

The very practical truth is that Jesus invites you to go there. If you have been divorced, that is a wound, like a primal tearing. Marriage is the mingling of souls, and if there's been a divorce, souls have been torn apart. Divorce is a death. It's the death of a marriage. It needs to be grieved like you would grieve the death of a friend or a companion. Jesus's invitation, whether you have been through divorce or whether your parents were divorced, is to go into the heart of that wound and name that pain, understand it, pull it apart, see its components. As this begins to happen, it's no longer a dark mystery that has shaped you, and you can begin to have light and freedom.

Marriage is to be a place in the world that is supposed to be full of life and light. This is why divorce can be so traumatic: because it causes fractures leading to dark and deadness. It cuts to the very core of how we understand the universe. So if you're really serious about the sanctity of this bond, and you're really fearful of divorce becoming too easy, start in your own home with your own spouse. And do that well. Marriage is a precious, sacred gift, a union that spills out light and life to others. It is to be a unique bond that shimmers brightly and reminds people of what God is like.

Lᴇᴠ. 19:1-2, 17-18
1 Cᴏʀ. 3:16-23
Mᴀᴛᴛ. 5:38-48

"But I say to you, love your enemies."

Here's a joke: A priest is giving a homily based on the Gospel for today. "Now," he says, "I'll bet that many of us feel as if we have enemies in our lives," he says to the congregation. "So, raise your hands," he says, "if you have *many* enemies." And quite a few people raise their hands. "Now raise your hands if you have only a few enemies." And about *half* as many people raise their hands. "Now raise your hands if you have only one or two enemies." And even fewer people raised their hands.

"See," he says, "most of us feel like we have enemies. Now, raise your hands if you have no enemies at all." And the priest looks around, and looks around, and finally, way in the back of the church, a very, very old man raises his hand. He stands up and says to the priest, "I have no enemies whatsoever!" The priest is delighted and invites the man to the front of the church. "What a blessing!" the priest says. "How old are you?"

"I'm 98 years old, and I have no enemies."

The priest says, "What a wonderful Christian life you lead! And tell us all how it is that you have no enemies."

"All those bastards have died!"

Most of us still, sadly, go through life with, for better or worse, and no matter how hard we try, a few people we may feel are "enemies." Or, more broadly, people who seem to hate us. There are people whom we've offended, to whom we've apologized, but who refuse to accept our apologies. There are people at work whom we've angered, who are jealous of us, or who have set themselves against us. There may be people in our families who hold a grudge against us for some mysterious reason that we can never quite comprehend. And there are people who seem to dislike us or wish us ill for no good reason. It's a very sad part of human life.

And it's a hard part of life. And sometimes, when we read this Gospel reading today, Jesus's words may make it seem even harder.

In the Gospel of Matthew, Jesus contrasts what the disciples had heard in the past with what they must practice as his followers. "You have heard that it said, 'An eye for an eye.' But I say to you, offer no resistance to one who is evil... You have heard that it was said that you must love your neighbors and hate your enemies. But I say to you, love your enemies." And so on. Jesus is trying to move the disciples beyond what they knew into a realm of practice that will help them follow Jesus, to live according to a new law—the law of love—and to be "perfect."

But there's a problem: it seems impossible! How are we supposed to love our enemies sincerely? Are we really supposed to pray for....whom? For people who hate us? For people who work against us? For people who want us to fail? It seems almost masochistic. A recipe for psychological disaster.

A few things might help us understand what Jesus is saying here. Now, I'm not going to water down these passages, but as in all the Gospel narratives, it's important to understand the context of Jesus's comments and how they may have been understood in his time.

For example, when Jesus talks about someone turning the other cheek, many Scripture scholars feel that he's talking about a particular act. The

Gospel of Matthew specifies the "right cheek." This means the blow comes from the back of the assailant's left hand, and therefore constitutes an insult, not a violent assault. So, some scholars say that when Jesus says "the other cheek", the idea is that when you're insulted by a slap on the cheek you should turn away, and not retaliate. It's not so much an invitation for someone to keep hitting you as it is for you not to retaliate. So that may help us understand things.

Likewise, the word Jesus used when he talks about loving your enemy is not the same word that is used in other discussions of love. As you probably know, in Greek, the language of the Gospels, there are three words for love: first, *philios*, which was a kind of fraternal or friendly love (and from which we get the name Philadelphia). Second, *eros*, a romantic love,

But the word Jesus uses here is the third kind of love, *agape*, a sort of unconquerable benevolence, or invincible goodwill. We're supposed to *agape* our enemies. Jesus is asking us to *agape* people no matter what they do to us, no matter how they treat us, no matter how they insult us. No matter what their actions, we never allow bitterness against them to invade our hearts, but will treat them with goodwill. So it doesn't mean that we have to love our enemies the same way that we speak about "falling in love" with someone, or the way we love our family members. It simply means we must open our hearts to them.

And we must pray for them, too. I think it's easier to *agape* someone you dislike (or who dislikes you) when you pray for them. Because when you pray for them, God often opens your heart to seeing the person the way that God sees them, rather the way we see them. And you can often have pity for people who may be filled with a spirit of hatred towards you.

But even when you understand all these things, and even if you read Scripture commentaries, these remain difficult things to hear. Even harder to follow. Loving your enemies and praying for those who persecute you is *hard.* In my life I found it probably the most difficult thing to do as a Christian. For many years, for example, many years ago, I lived with a Jesuit in community who simply refused to talk to me. For several years. He despised me. And I couldn't figure out why, and efforts at reconciliation failed miserably. No matter what I did, nothing changed his attitude.

Over the course of many years, and in light of that experience, and in light of meditating on the Gospels, I realized several things about loving your enemies.

First of all, some people may simply dislike you. So it's useless to try to "get" them to like you, much less to love you. It's useless to try to change things. You can be open to reconciliation, but you have no control over whether someone will reconcile with you. Part of this process is embracing your own powerlessness. Letting go is paramount.

Second, turning away from insults, hatred, and contempt, and "offering the other cheek" is emotionally healthy. Now, some schools of pop psychology say that you should always give vent to anger (rather than let it fester), but always responding with vituperation or vengefulness is rather a childish thing to do. Only a baby gives vent to his or her anger all the time. You can acknowledge your anger, perhaps express any frustration you have in a calm way, but you don't have to respond in kind. Basically, and to put it less elegantly than Jesus, if your enemy behaves like a jerk toward you, there's no reason you have to act like a jerk towards him.

Third, loving your enemies and praying for those who pay you is liberating. Too often we can find ourselves in pitched battles with the people that hate us, always seeking the upper hand, always toting up who's up and who's down, always measuring every insult. You see this in families and even in office environments, where people are trapped into cycles of vengefulness. And it wears both parties down. I've seen couples, for example, whose marriages are utterly destroyed by the inability to forgive;

the two become like scorpions in a jar. Jesus is offering us a way out of all that.)

So what Jesus is telling us is hard, but it's not impossible, and it's necessary, too. Because ultimately he is inviting us not only to forgiveness and charity but something else: freedom and happiness. So you have heard that it was said, and you have heard that it was said to you by Jesus—who wants you to be happy.

8TH SUNDAY IN ORDINARY TIME

JOEL BLUNK

ISA. 49: 14-15
1 COR. 4:1-5
MATT 6:24-34

"Do not worry about your life"

The pink slip lay on my desk for days. It was a message from a social worker at Brookline, a local assisted living facility, indicating that they had a resident who "very much wanted a visit from a Presbyterian minister." Not recognizing the name from our congregation, and with plenty of other things to do, I set it aside.

Several weeks went by before I walked into Everett's room. I could see right away that he was frail and in failing health; he didn't have long to live. He was lying on his back, oxygen tube in his nose, on what turned out to be his deathbed. I should have come sooner.

"I've been expecting you," he said cordially, when I introduced myself. "How long?" I wondered to myself. "Days? Weeks? Years?" I was sure I was too late, but he immediately made it clear that I was, in fact, right on time. His graciousness caught me off guard, bringing relief.

We talked for a while, though it was hard for him to do so. Every breath was a struggle, and it took great energy and effort to speak; he did so deliberately and carefully. He shared that he'd become sick with pneumonia a year earlier and nearly died. He informed me that his 91st birthday was coming soon, the age his father lived to be.

I was surprised to learn that he'd worshipped at our church on numerous occasions, though he admitted it had been several years before. He'd grown up in a "Christian home" in Pittsburg, but as an adult his work schedule and the demands of caring for a family prevented him from attending church regularly. He and his wife Dorothy had five kids and he'd worked multiple jobs to provide for them. Sunday had long been just one more day to make ends meet.

He told me about each of his children in great detail and about his wife. In November of 1985, he and Dorothy were driving with their best friends and were struck head-on by another vehicle. He was so badly injured that twice his family was called to his bedside to say their goodbyes. He spent several days unconscious. When he finally came to, he was told that Dorothy didn't survive the accident and that he'd missed her funeral.

He told me all of this very matter-of-factly. It was clear that he had done his grieving long ago, and had accepted what was.

We finally got around to why he'd asked me to come. He seemed restless as he admitted to wanting to see a minister because he knew his own death was imminent and he was concerned about his relationship with God and his own salvation. Not wanting to presume anything, I asked him to tell me more.

He went on to say that he had several friends who were certain of their salvation. Some had talked about being "born again," but he wasn't sure if he was or not. He said he'd been baptized as an infant and that when he was nine or ten, out in the woods behind his house, he deliberately gave his life to Christ. But that was long ago, and he knew he hadn't honored his end of the bargain. He was concerned about that.

I tried to reassure him by sharing similar experiences from my own life, and stating my belief that God understands the human condition all too well, and our need to start over again and again. As much as we'd like to say that our personal decision for Christ set us on a new way once and for all, the reality is that most of us fall off the path regularly. Fortunately, I told him, God's love is steadfast, and God is there to pick us up each time we fall, giving us another chance.

I asked him if he wanted to pray with me for God's love and forgiveness, and to ask for God's saving help once again. I told him that I could stand to pray that prayer myself and that he was welcome to join me, if he liked. He said he very much wanted to. Not wanting to speak for him, I told him I'd begin the prayer and then give him a chance to add anything he wanted. I took hold of his hand, we closed our eyes, and we prayed. I don't recall what I said, but after a few moments I stopped and gently squeezed his hand. His words have stayed with me, spoken slowly and deliberately between gasps for air, "Forgive my sins...for they are many. Welcome me back...into your loving arms. I can ask no more than that. Amen."

I was touched by the simplicity and gravity of his words. He'd gotten right to the heart of it. Before I left he had one more request, to celebrate the Lord's Supper a final time.

It was a few days later when I returned. Again, he was expecting me. This time, though, I'd called ahead and made an appointment. He was visibly weaker, but also calmer, more at peace, resigned. After we shared the bread and cup, he labored to speak, "It's been a long time...since I had Communion. I was skeptical. But I feel differently. I strayed so far...but now I've come home. I feel like the prodigal son."

I shared with him my favorite part of that story: when the father, who had reason to be angry and scolding, hikes up his robe and runs down the road to meet his wayward son, embracing him with a kiss.

"That's comforting to me," Everett said.

There was silence, peace, a calm in the room. Finally I added, "Are you ready to die, Everett?"

"Yes!" he said emphatically. "I feel better having partaken of the body and blood of Christ." And he said it again, as if to make sure I'd heard him earlier: "I've come home." And he added, "Thank you to my brother in Christ for coming."

He closed his eyes and took a deep breath; I thought it might be his last.

It was a few weeks later when all five of his children showed up in my office. It was surreal to be face to face with his family, hearing stories that filled in the gaps of his 91 years. I couldn't help but think how my life, though full and vital, is so often spent far less alert and awake than Everett's last days. I told his children that I treasured the time I spent with their father, that in his dying he taught me about living. They just smiled in an understanding way. I mentioned that we'd spoken together about God's saving love and had celebrated the Lord's Supper. One of his sons asked when that was. When I told him, he reasoned it coincided exactly with a new found peacefulness he noticed in his father.

As we began to plan his funeral, one of his children mentioned that he often quoted Matthew 6, "Consider the lilies of the field, how they grow; they neither toil nor spin, yet even Solomon in all his glory was not arrayed as one of these..." It was read at Everett's service—a text about priorities and about the place of material things in our lives. Jesus reminds us that we often give far too much attention and worry to what we're going to wear, or eat, or to the things we have. When we do, "things" can get in the way of our intimacy with God. "Why do you worry about these things?" Jesus said. "Don't you know life is more than food or clothing? Instead, seek God and God's ways first and all these things shall be added."

Things—all things—are gifts from God, not ours to cling to, but meant to be appreciated, shared, and entrusted to God.

When I met Everett, he was without things; he was eventually even without the worry of what tomorrow would bring. All had been stripped away from him: his health, his home, his concern for appearances, his preoccupation with work, family and friends. Life had done this to him; he lived long enough that all that was left was himself and God. And in that moment he willingly turned again to the one who had given him everything, grateful, at peace.

It may not happen for us the same way it did for Everett, but we, too, are invited to come home to God, right now, and let go of all that preoccupies us and ties us down. Perhaps a simple prayer can help:

> *Forgive my sins, for they are many.*
> *Welcome me back into your loving arms.*
> *I can ask no more than that. Amen.*

DEUT 11:18, 26-28, 32 ROMANS 3:21-25, 28 MATT 7:21-27	*Talk is cheap. And it's getting cheaper every day.*

L iving in a world today shaped by technology that expands our speaking potential into capacities nearing the infinite—24-hour news networks, satellite radio, streaming Internet entertainment, blogs, twitter, Facebook posts, iPods, iPhones, iPads, and the like—has left us with an overdose of words and not too much to show for them. Furthermore, at a time when everybody is full of promises—whether politicians or infomercials, fast-food ads or cellphone plans—is it any wonder that so many of these oaths turn up empty?

Today's Gospel is a first-century play on the popular adage: "You can talk the talk, but can you walk the walk?" In the course of his teaching, Jesus confronts his followers with a difficult message that was hard to hear in his time, and might be even more challenging to hear in ours.

Jesus makes a clear distinction between "talking the talk" of Christian discipleship and "walking the walk" of true faith. "It is easy," we can imagine Jesus reiterating, "to claim to be my follower, to recognize me by name ("Lord, Lord"), and to talk to others like you understand what it is I've taught you all these years." However, he would continue: "But talk is cheap and, when it comes to authentic discipleship, one's actions always speak louder than words."

Sacred Scripture is saturated with this message that comes across today in Matthew's Gospel. If we return to the Hebrew Scriptures, to the Book of Deuteronomy, from which our First Reading is taken, we are told that we should put God's *words* in our "heart and soul" (Deuteronomy 11:18). At first glance, it might appear as though this contradicts the spirit of Jesus's insistence that words are not enough, that talk is cheap. However, the Hebrew word for "word" (*dabar*) has another meaning or sense. It is both the word that is spoken *and* it means the action one takes. To place the "words of God" in our hearts and souls means more than committing a bunch of ideas, thoughts, or affirmations to memory. There is no oral exam for ascertaining whether or not one is a just or righteous person, whether or not one is a good disciple. The true test is found in how the word expresses itself in action.

We hear this in another challenging passage from Scripture, this time in the Letter of James:

> What good is it, my brothers, if someone says he has faith but does not have works? Can that faith save him? If a brother or sister has nothing to wear and has no food for the day, and one of you says to them, "Go in peace, keep warm, and eat well," but you do not give them the necessities of the body, what good is it? So also faith of itself, if it does not have works, is dead. Indeed someone might say, "you have faith and I have works." Demonstrate your faith to me without works, and I will demonstrate my faith to you from my works (James 2:14-18).

The mark of true faith is what is communicated not just in verbal affirmation of belief or expressed in creedal tenets, but what is lived and done in one's works.

It is truly easy to speak the "right words" that, in fact, have no meaning. The question presented to us in the Letter of James is to pause and discern how we demonstrate what it is we claim to believe. If we really have faith that Jesus Christ is the Incarnate Word of God, *Emmanuel*, God-with-us, then shouldn't we always be ready and willing to proclaim the good news at all times? Jesus himself sets that stage for his earthly ministry when, in the Gospel according to Luke, he begins his public work with a reading from the Book of the Prophet Isaiah and announces that what has been heard about the coming servant of the Reign of God has been fulfilled by the one who has proclaimed the reading. Jesus says that "The Spirit of the Lord is upon me, because he has anointed me to bring good news to the poor. He has sent me to proclaim release to the captives and recovery of sight to the blind, to let the oppressed go free, to proclaim the year of the Lord's favor" (Luke 4:18-19). In other words, Jesus has been sent by the Father to *do something* and not simply to pass along some interesting ideas or teachings. Those who bear the name Christ as Christians are likewise called to do the same, to *do something*. How Jesus announces the Reign of God is not just with words, but by doing *something*: loving the unlovable, forgiving the unforgiveable, embracing the marginalized, healing the broken and broken-hearted.

St. Francis of Assisi is often credited with having said, "Preach the Gospel at all times, and, if necessary, use words." While we have no historical record of his actually speaking this adage, we can say that this expression bears the true spirit of the Saint from Assisi who, in his Earlier Rule or "way of life" for the friars, wrote: "Let all the brothers, however, preach by their deeds" (*Regula non bullata* 17:3). Francis of Assisi, the man most revered among all the church's canonized saints, understood what Jesus was telling his disciples in today's Gospel and he wished that all who might look to him for inspiration or a model of Christian living would do the same.

Can we, like St. Francis, follow in the footprints of Jesus Christ and preach the Gospel with our whole lives and not simply with our words?

May we, like the wise man in Jesus's parable who built his home on rock, build our faith on the solid ground of concrete action. Only then can we walk the walk we profess in our talk.

Hosea 6:3-6
Rom. 4:18-25
Matt. 9:9-13

"For I have not come to call the righteous, but sinners."

As a religious leader, I've heard a great deal about the "Nones." When opinion polls ask people what sort of religious affiliation they claim, a growing number of them will skip over the categories of Christian, Jew, Muslim, Buddhist, Hindu, and "Other." Then, they check the box marked "None". The "Nones" are more highly concentrated in adults in their twenties and thirties, which causes a great deal of hand-wringing for those of us who love the church.

The reasons for this rejection of religious categorization abound. Looking at it from a Christian perspective, we know that some people aren't part of a particular church because they are too busy working, moving, or being broke.

Often it's a spiritual issue, as people have been hurt by the church. Others don't go because they've become frustrated with the conservative politics or gender issues that certain Christians espouse.

Some people can't settle on checking one box because even though they are part of a church, their spouse is part of another faith tradition. Their family celebrates Christmas and Passover. They teach their children the ways of both paths. With their blended families, they don't feel like they can claim just one tradition. If they have to mark one box, they mark "none."

Others feel like they sense God more outside of the church or any religious institution. They experience the divine when they walk along the beach at sunrise more than they do in a sanctuary or at a potluck.

Sometimes people don't want to claim a particular religious affiliation because to put a label on a person means that they are excluding another person. This can create an "us versus them" mentality that they feel harms society. People look at the wars that have been fought for religious reasons and they believe that there might be more peace if people stopped trying to claim labels that divide.

Still others are a part of a growing group of non-theists, atheists, or agnostics.

Whatever the reason, it's uncomfortable for those who are part of institutional religion to read that the fastest-growing religious group in our country is the "Nones." Those tiny check marks indicate that our churches are losing influence. The changing popular tide threatens our way of doing things. And when we couple this survey data with our aging congregations, dwindling memberships, and ecclesial downsizing, we panic.

We know the way church ought to work. Babies ought to be baptized, teens should be confirmed, adults should join a congregation. Adults need to have babies so that the cycle can start over. That's what creates healthy, vibrant communities of faith. When this life-cycle breaks down, when a new generation feels more comfortable at Starbucks than at church on a Sunday morning, then the whole enterprise gets sick.

When something looks queasy, then we want to know the cause. So we start diagnosing. We berate parents for not doing a good enough job at keeping kids connected to worshiping communities. We blame the pastors and point to the lack of leadership or boring sermons. We point our finger at the liturgy and cry that the ancient words are outdated. We look at our buildings, which need endless maintenance. We hate ourselves for not being relevant or authentic enough. We can look at the world and wonder why it's so sick. We look askance at our academic institutions that are filled with atheists. We can look at younger generations, and say that it's their fault. They shouldn't be so self-centered and lazy. They are the cause of the sickness and so there is no way that we can help them.

We could do all of those things, or we can realize what a time of great opportunity this is. We can recognize that we are in the place that we are supposed to be. Jesus said that he didn't come to serve those who were well. He came for people who were sick.

Jesus ate with the sinners—women and men who drank wine to excess, traded sex for money, and finagled bribes with taxes. When people wondered why he hung out with all of the riff-raff, he explained that he did it because he didn't come to serve the healthy, but the sick.

Likewise, if we're going to step in the shoes of Jesus, we will also need to serve those who are sick. We are a hospital for sinners. We have had churches that have served the upstanding, healthy people of our society for a long time.

Now we know that the "Nones" are on the rise, we have a decision to make. Will we blame them for not being healthy? Will we shame them for not being a part of our shiny hospital? Or will we see this as an opportunity to walk alongside Jesus, reaching out to the sick? Will we understand that our calling and our ministries are not for those who are well, but for those who need healing?

May we continue to be people who continue to work for the health of all, to the glory of God our Creator, Liberator, and Sustainer. Amen.

Exod 19:2-6ᴀ
Rom 5:6-11
Matt 9:36—10:8

"The harvest is plentiful but the workers are few."

In today's Gospel from Matthew, we find Jesus at a critical part of his ministry. Upon seeing the crowds, he realizes that there is much work to do. There is an abundance of harvest, but he cannot do it alone. He needs help. He needs to choose disciples. While Matthew only lists the names of the twelve that were chosen, it is the Gospel of Mark that gives us the stories of how Jesus came up to them and invited them to follow him.

To help break open this morning's Gospel, I think it is important to understand the process of a first-century rabbi in Galilee choosing his disciples. The people of this area firmly believed that God had spoken to Moses and handed him the Torah—the first five books of the Bible—and thus it was a focus of their educational system.

Jewish children at the age of six would begin their schooling with a Torah teacher. This first level of education was called Beit Sefer and lasted till they were about 10 years old. By that point, the brightest children had the complete Torah memorized and the rest of the children had shifted the majority of their time away from school and were at home learning the family trade of their father.

But the few that were the cream of the crop continued their education and moved onto what was called Beit Talmud. Over the next few years they would memorize all of the Hebrew Scriptures. With the weight of all these requirements, by the age of about 15, the vast majority of the kids were relegated to working in the family business. But for a select few who were considered the very best , those students were the ones who moved on to Beit Midrash. At this point they would need to seek out a rabbi, looking to become of one of his disciples. Which meant more than just knowing what the rabbi knows: It was to actually be like the rabbi, to walk in the steps of the rabbi, to do what the rabbi did.

During those days the particular biblical interpretations of each rabbi were called the, "yoke of the rabbi. " Sodiscipleship of a rabbi required you to learn his yoke. Therefore a student would apply to the rabbi who in turn would grill them on his interpretations of Scripture and if he felt that the young man was not up to the task , he would encourage the student to prac- tice his family's trade. But if the rabbi thought that the student had what it was going to take, he would say, "Follow me," and the student would leave everything—family, home, loved ones, belongings—and devote his entire life to be like the rabbi, for this is what it meant to be a disciple.

So if chosen to be a disciple of a rabbi, it would mean that you physically followed that rabbi each day, all day, every day, through the towns, down the dusty roads….listening to his words, watching his interactions, mod- eling yourself to be just like him, to the point where at the end of the day you would be covered in everything the rabbi had stepped in, and the followers would often bless others by saying, "May you be covered in the dust of your rabbi."

So now let's circle back to our gospel and the Jewish rabbi, Jesus. What does his yoke look like? Cleary, he shows a preferential option for the poor—which were over 95% of the population. And Jesus has driven out demons, given sight to the blind, speech to the mute, cleansed the lepers, and calmed the waters. So as the time had come for Jesus to select his disciples, he walked along the shore and came across Simon and Andrew, brothers who were working their fishing boats. And Jesus said to them, "Follow me."

But we know that if they are fishing, they are not associated with any other rabbi, and therefore they are nowhere near the best in class. And we are told that they immediately dropped their nets—which now makes some sense, since rabbis only picked the very best—when Jesus told the brothers to "follow him". He was saying, "Hey, I think you can do what I do!"

Then he came across James and John, who are fishing with their dad. At the age of 17 or so, they are apprenticing and learning the family business. So they, too, missed the mark at school. But again, Jesus chooses them. But why? This is far from what the other rabbis have been doing when they are only selecting the best! There is no doubt that the very clear message Jesus sent to them, and to us, is that his way is for everybody—not just for the best of the best, but for you and me and everyone else who is not the best.

Jesus says, "You did not choose me—I choose you." The rabbi does not choose you unless he thinks that you can do what he does! And the good news is that we are all chosen, we are all disciples, just the way we are: with all of our imperfections and sin, we are simply called to stay on the journey with God whether we are doing right or not! He simply says "Follow me and I will show you how to do it." "Follow me" is different than giving people maps—it is going on a journey. And the Good News for us is that God doesn't care if we have the right map or the wrong map. God will use whatever map we have to get us closer to God. But we tend to get focused on the quality of our maps. Worse, yet, we judge the maps that other people are using.

A story recently ran in the wires, reporting that a pastor in a Catholic parish in Minnesota filed a restraining order against an autistic boy to keep him out of the church because he felt the boy was causing too much of a distraction. A distraction? Possibly.... A disciple called by Christ? Absolutely! That teen is as worthy as you and me because we are all called and chosen by Christ to be followers—even those people who annoy us!

And just as Jesus changed Simon's name to Peter and upon him he built his church, we too are reminded that God not only sees what we currently are—broken and sinful—but he sees and knows how we can change and what we can become if we just follow him.

God believes in all of us and he calls us forth to go out and make more disciples—to go and gather everyone, without exception, no matter what map they are using, to come to his table.

At the conclusion of every mass, the priest or deacon concludes the liturgy by saying, "This mass has ended—go in peace." If you go back to the literal translation of that closing phrase, the translation is closer to a sense of "Get going, get moving, get out of here. There is much work to do and he cannot do it alone—we are called to follow him!!"

So this week, spend a bit of quiet time and pray and meditate on a scene where Jesus is walking up to you, without judgment or prejudice, knowing that you are not the best of the best and asking you not to be concerned or worried, but simply saying. "Follow me." What does that sound like to you? What does it look like to you—how do you respond? Jesus knows that we can be like him, and he calls us to simply walk behind him on the dusty trails of our life.

12TH SUNDAY IN ORDINARY TIME

MICHAEL DOYLE

JEREMIAH 20:10-13
ROMANS 5:12-15
MATTHEW 10:26-33

"*Do not be afraid of anything.*"

O*n April 3, 1968, Dr.* Martin Luther King, Jr., in concluding his speech in Memphis, Tennessee, spoke these words:

"*I got into Memphis, and some began to say the threats, or talk about the threats that were out, or what would happen to me from some of our sick white brothers. Well, I don't know what will happen now. We've got some difficult days ahead. But, it really doesn't matter with me now, because I've been to the mountain top. And I don't mind.*

"*Like anybody else, I would like to live a long life. Longevity has its place, but I'm not concerned about that now. I just want to do God's will. And He's allowed me to go up to the mountain. And I've looked over, and I've seen the Promised Land. I may not get there with you. But, I want you to know tonight, that we, as a people, will get to the Promised Land!*

"*And so, I'm happy tonight. I'm not worried about anything. I'm not fearing any man!*

"*Mine eyes have seen the glory of the coming of the Lord.*"

Dr. King knew Chapter 10 of Matthew's Gospel, from which the passage for this Sunday is taken. In that chapter, Jesus called his 12 disciples by name and sent them out, "like lambs in the midst of wolves." He clearly gave his command: "Do not be afraid of anything" (Matt.10:31). This call to courage rolled off the tongue of the *Drum Major for Justice* with cadence and power unequalled in any Church. His congregation heard the splendid sound, like the ringing of a bell on a frosty morning. He spoke bravely with the perfect pitch of heartfelt truth.

He finished his memorable speech to the striking sanitation workers and their supporters in Mason Temple in Memphis, Tennessee. It was April 3, 1968. His last lines echoed Jesus in Matthew 10: "I'm not fearing any man. Mine eyes have seen the glory of the coming of the Lord." With that, the speech ended to thunder-loud applause rising to the roofs and silent tears falling on the faces of close friends listening with anxiety. He walked from the podium to a chair, where his body slumped in utter exhaustion. Less than twenty hours later, he was dead—murdered in Memphis.

Jeremiah, in the first reading today, alludes to "The whisperings of many: 'Terror on every side!' We can take our vengeance on him" (Jeremiah 20: 10). "Whisperings" in Memphis and "whisperings" in Washington, DC, and elsewhere. "Whisperings" is a good word for conspiracies. Classified documents from the case of the killing of King cannot be seen by society until 2027. Why? In today's gospel, Jesus promises that "nothing is concealed that will not be revealed." I hope that covers the "whisperings" that circled the plan and the killing of the great civil rights leader. On April 4, 1967, Martin Luther King condemned the war in Vietnam. One year to the day later, his blood flowed on the balcony of a Memphis motel. In this tragedy, amidst the whirl of written words and whispers, there is one shining truth in the darkness: Dr. Martin Luther King, Jr. was a star of admirable courage.

He knew that Jesus promised the gift of the Holy Spirit. He knew of the mighty wind that walloped the place where the disciples of Jesus cowered in corners. He knew that fear fled, that courage came, and not one of them ever flinched again in the face of terrible struggles, sufferings and death. A constant command on the lips of Jesus is: "Do not be afraid," and "Fear not." Jesus knew that fear is the most crippling of all emotions. So much good has not been done in the past, so much good is not being done in the present, and so much good will never be done in the future because of the lack of courage.

The great poet and exponent of truth in laser language, Maya Angelou, was admired by Dr. King, and vice versa. Invited to work for him, she shared his dream. She was devastated when he was shot and killed on her 40th birthday. She knew his courage, a virtue she always celebrated. "Courage is the most important of all virtues," she says, "because without courage, you cannot practice any other virtue consistently."

Speaking of courage! On May 7, 2013, I saw and I heard a sermon in Sacred Heart Church in Camden, NJ, that will forever change me. No better was ever experienced there since March 7, 1887, when the first one was preached. His name is Kyle Maynard, and he spoke to Sacred Heart's seventh and eighth grade students and eighth graders from four other schools in Camden. He entered the church in a wheelchair, climbed out of it, and made his way to the front, where he climbed up on a chair and spoke for forty-five minutes. Kyle Maynard. One could change that seven-letter name, Maynard, and make it into the seven-letter word Courage. He has made that word into his own flesh and spirit.

His visible presence on this earth began 27 years ago when his mother, Anita, brought her first born child into view for her husband, Scott Maynard, to meet and greet. They were shocked to see that their precious baby had arms cut off above where elbows would have been, and legs cut off above where the knees would be. Says Anita, "We concentrated on his face. He had a most beautiful face." The baby grew. There came a time when he wanted to move around and he moved without wobble on all four little limbs. Says his father: "We just placed things in front of him and let him figure them out." He was a most determined, energetic, and into-everything child. He would use his bits of arms to connect with things. Time brought him three sisters to love and enjoy. He was and is so very adept at using his limbs in marvelous ways that his parents set out, heroically, to create for him a path to normalcy. He learned at an early age to feed himself with the tools he had. Congenital amputation is the full name of his condition. Artificial limbs were tried when he was five, but had to be discarded, because they got in his way. He was blessed with an unrelenting determination to courageously keep trying, regardless of his failures and disappointments and the sufferings he had to bear to achieve his goals. He went to school, moving on the floor on all fours as he did on May 7, 2013 on the terrazzo of Sacred Heart Church.

He is a very intelligent person. In 6th grade, he went out for wrestling. The coach backed him and his parents supported him, but in that first year he lost every match he entered, thirty-five in all. He had to summon great fortitude to go on, and on he went. The next year, he began to win. Today, he has an honored place in the Wrestler's Hall of Fame, and he is the nation's top disabled athlete.

God blessed him with parents of unending courage, and encouragement. He set out to try football in school, and his father supported him, and he began blocking big kids with his unique "Kyle tackle" near the ground. It is said: "What makes him different is not his body, but his heart." In other words, his courageous perseverance against all odds and failures. Scott says of his son: "One of the things we tried to do with Kyle was to focus on what he can do, focus on his abilities as opposed to his disabilities." His mother added: "Not on what he cannot do." They succeeded.

Today, millions of people of all ages have seen what he can do and are inspired with courage to pursue worthy goals. They are motivated to stop complaining, stop making excuses. Kyle's best-selling book is titled, "No Excuses."

People watching him in our Church and listening to him were mesmerized, enchanted, inspired, and motivated. Especially the students. One could live three lifetimes and never experience anything like it. The courage that it took to do ordinary things that we all take for granted. He told of his struggles to swim with no hands and no feet, to type with no fingers, until he could do 50 words per minute. He learned to use weights, and reached the unbelievable level of lifting nearly 400 lbs with straps and chains attached to his precious bits of arms. Once, at home, when he was 14, he was invited to go to the movies while his parents were out. He called his mother, but she was not able to come home. He had a big problem. He could not put on all his clothes. He tried. Socks! How! Eventually, he thought of a paper clip. With it, he put on the first one. It took 30 minutes. The second one, 15 minutes. He had never zippered his pants, but with the paper clip, he pulled up the zipper and went to the movies. Then, in front of our eyes, he pulled off a sock and put it back on, in 3 seconds.

Yet, nothing prepared us for his final story. On January 5, 2012, Kyle Maynard set out, with nine others, to climb a mountain. He had to crawl every inch of the way to the top. He crawled over paths of deep dust with his mouth and nose so near the ground. Over sharp stones, over steep rocks and dangerous ice. His body ached with terrible pain. At times, he cried. He felt he could not do it. But, the promise he made to the mother of Corey Johnson helped him to go on. Her son was killed in Afghanistan. Her son was a young man who wanted to see the world. And he promised her that he would carry some of her son's ashes to the top of a mountain.

And so it was, on January 15, 2012, a Sunday (as Easter always is), Kyle Maynard "strove with his last ounce of courage, to reach the unreachable...." He reached above the clouds and cast the ashes of Corey Johnson towards the heavens from the white high altar that is the snows of Kilimanjaro. A high altar indeed, where the courage in the heart of Kyle Maynard ascended to a peak of transcendence...19,431 feet above the sea.

Do not be afraid of anything. The great and beloved poet Seamus Heaney, in the last minutes of his life, proclaimed in a text message to his dear wife, "Nolle Timere" (Don't be afraid).

13ᵀᴴ SUNDAY IN ORDINARY TIME

MARY ELIZABETH SPERRY

---

2 KINGS 4:8-11, 14-16
ROM. 6:3-4, 8-11
MATT. 10:37-42

"He who receives you receives me"

The *"butterfly effect" conjectures that* the flutter of a butterfly's wings can cause a hurricane on the other side of the world. Thus, even a small action can have an enormous impact. Most of us don't remember our baptisms, but this simple action, a washing with water, has a profound impact.

As Saint Paul tells us in today's second reading, baptism changes everything. Through baptism, we share in the death and resurrection of Jesus Christ. We become part of the Body of Christ, one with our brothers and sisters in him. We die to everything that is temporary and superficial and set our sights on the things of heaven that last forever.

In this light, Jesus's words in the Gospel are less shocking, but no less subversive. He calls those who would follow him to move past the values and vision of this world. No longer do we focus solely on caring only for those close to us, letting others fend for themselves. "Charity begins at home" is not part of the Gospel message! Concern for our families cannot be an excuse for ignoring the needs of others who are children of God just as we are.

Because concern for others, especially the most vulnerable, is fundamental to the Bible's message, hospitality plays a critical role throughout Scripture. The Bible portrays welcoming guests—be they friends or strangers, rich or poor—as an act of righteousness. In today's first reading, a woman of Shunem welcomes the prophet Elisha into her home, going out of her way to ensure his comfort. In gratitude for her kindness and welcome, Elisha asks the Lord to give her the gift of a son who will care for her in her old age. In the Gospel, Jesus assures his hearers that anyone who welcomes a disciple welcomes both Jesus and the Father who sent him. By opening our hearts and our homes to the children of God, we open our hearts more fully to God, who awaits our invitation to enter.

At the same time, we must be willing to accept the hospitality offered to us. With gratitude, Elisha accepted the invitation he received. Jesus counseled his disciples to accept the hospitality offered when they went out to preach. The Gospels often show Jesus accepting invitations to dinner—even when those invitations came from simmers and outcasts. Jesus does not recognize "others" or "outsiders." Conformed to Christ in baptism, we die to self and sin and live both for and in him. In the new life of baptism, we break out of the familiar routines of life. We are called to welcome, to befriend, and to care for all of God's children, especially the most vulnerable.

Hospitality was extremely important in the Bible, as many people were nomads and much of the land was desert and harsh wilderness. In such an environment, offering a cup of water was literally a matter of life and death. We tend to take water for granted. Fresh, clean water seems plentiful. We turn on a faucet, and there it is. The same is not true for everyone.

In the southwestern U.S., people risk their lives crossing the desert in search of opportunity, the basic essentials of life, and hope. Each year, hundreds of these people die. Groups of volunteers travel through the desert, leaving water in places where the sojourners can find it. In untold instances, these gifts of water are the difference between life and death.

Much of the world's population—about one of every eight people on the planet—lacks access to clean water. Giving these people access to clean water has a profound impact on their lives. Digging a well can change an entire community. Reliable irrigation can improve crops, giving the people access to better nutrition. Clean water can help to prevent the diseases that cause the deaths of thousands of children. Easy access to clean water changes the lives of the girls and women, who in many countries are charged with getting water from distant water sources and carrying it home. This task may require carrying jugs weighing forty pounds over several miles of rough and often dangerous terrain. When getting water becomes as simple as turning a faucet at a village well, significant amounts of time become available for other productive work or for additional schooling, changing the lives and futures of girls and women.

Opportunities to offer the welcome of Christ abound if we choose to see them. People sitting in this church today feel unwelcome, unwanted, unrecognized. Perhaps they are newcomers to the area or they have been away from the Church for a while. Perhaps they are unfamiliar with the culture or the language or they feel overwhelmed by the circumstances of their lives or the weight of their sins. Does the welcome we offer extend beyond passing them the collection basket or handing them a bulletin? Do our actions on the other six days of the week reinforce the welcome offered at Sunday worship? Do we expect newcomers to become more like us before we accept them?

Living in the new life in Christ that God gives us in baptism, we look at the world with new eyes. We do not see strangers and outcasts, but brothers and sisters in Christ. We seek out opportunities to offer welcome, to lend a helping hand, to extend loving concern.

What ripples will our baptism make?

ZECH. 9:9-10 ROM. 8:9, 11-13 MATT. 11:25-30	*"For my yoke is easy, and my burden light."*

If you leave St. Patrick's Cathedral by the front door, on Fifth Avenue, you can't help but be jolted by the figure greeting you as you leave.

It's Atlas: a mammoth, four-story-high statue of the Greek titan, cast in bronze, his arms spread wide has he carries the universe on his back. He was created by artist Lew Lawrie in 1937. It's the largest sculpture in Rockefeller Center—bigger, even, than Prometheus, down by the skating rink. The Atlas statue aroused controversy when it was unveiled, with some people complaining that the face of the statue looked too much like Mussolini. But someone noted, to the contrary: "It looks the way Mussolini *thinks* he looks."

Whoever he resembles, the Atlas we meet as we leave the cathedral makes a powerful statement. As we pass through those massive doors, we leave the house of God...and return to the world of gods. The gods of deadlines and headaches in midtown Manhattan. And Atlas welcomes us back.

Welcome back, he says, to everything you've been praying about.

Welcome back to the invoices that are overdue and the line to get on the elevator. Welcome back to the boiler that doesn't work and that unemployment that's running out and the accident causing problems on the subway that is going to delay getting home.

Welcome back to things you want but can't afford. Welcome back to Tiffany's and Saks and Harry Winston and Cartier.

Welcome back to the world—and all the burdens, the weight of the world, that every one carries on their back.

But in today's gospel, Jesus offers us help.

"Take my yoke upon you and learn from me," he says. "For I am meek and humble of heart; and you will find rest. For my yoke is easy, and my burden light."

What a relief!

Jesus wasn't talking, of course, about the misery of midtown Manhattan, or the headaches of modern life. He was talking, specifically, about all the regulations that the Pharisees had laid out for the Jewish people— more than 600 in all. Rules that, to a lot of the Jews of the time, must have felt like the weight of the world. But Jesus offered another way. Later in Matthew's gospel, he would make it clear that you don't need hundreds of regulations, but only two commandments—love God, love your neighbor.

That sounds so simple, and that does lighten the load. But it doesn't completely remove the "yoke". For when you think about what it means to love God and love your neighbor—*especially* to love your neighbor!—well, you can feel your shoulders start to sag.

Yet, what Jesus offers is not meant as an imposition. Love is never an imposition. It is a choice and a gift. There, from the depths of our hearts, is where we find the strength to carry that yoke—trusting that the God who makes all things possible will also make it possible to bear any burden, to carry any load. And if we do, Jesus—"meek and humble of heart" Jesus—assures us that he will give us that most blessed of gifts, rest.

As St. Augustine put it so beautifully in his famous prayer: "Our hearts are restless until they rest in you." In Jesus, our restless hearts find comfort. Reassurance. Peace.

Rest.

Today's scripture reminds us that it's not found by attaching ourselves to this world, with all the things that weigh us down.

As we heard from St. Paul, writing to the people of Rome:

"If you live according to the flesh, you will die, but if by the Spirit you put to death the deeds of the body, you will live."

In other words: don't fall prey to all the problems that plagued ancient Rome—or modern New York. The kinds of things that the great statue of Atlas sees happening around his feet every day—and that people file in and out of St. Pat's to pray about, or seek forgiveness for. These are heavy "yokes" of the world that can weigh us down. Instead, take on the yoke of Christ—the bearable burden of love.

He is our rest. And he is our strength. He's the one who helps us when we feel like we are carrying the weight of the world.

If you look closely at that great statue of Atlas, you'll see that he has one sphere on his shoulders that represents the north-south axis of the universe. It is marked to point us toward the North Star. For centuries, that is the star that sailors have used to navigate, to determine where they are, and to find their way home. It is the determining point on every compass.

As Catholic Christians, our North Star is Jesus Christ. He gives us direction, guidance, surety. He leads us home.

Remember that, the next time the worries and weight of the world seem to be too much.

He is ready, meek and humble of heart, to lead us where we belong.

And it won't be as hard as we may fear.

For his yoke his easy. And his burden is light.

15TH SUNDAY IN ORDINARY TIME

FR. PAUL HOLMES

ISA. 55:10-11
ROM. 8:18-23
MATT: 13:1-23

> *"Whoever has ears, ought to hear."*

*T*he *"Parable of the Sower"* is perhaps not Jesus's most famous parable, or even his most colorful. But it *is* the first of many parables he told about the Kingdom.

And I think we've missed the point of this parable for a long time! What congregations are probably hearing all across the Christian world today is that Jesus is the Sower, and that he sows the Gospel everywhere, and that it's up to us to be the "good soil" and make that seed bear fruit.

That sounds good, doesn't it? It's just that I don't think that's what the parable is saying at all. First of all, Jesus is *not* the sower. *God* is. And *God* is sowing His seed, namely *Jesus.* In fact, He isn't exactly *sowing* Jesus (in the present tense)—He's *already* sown His Son. And He's sown Jesus *everywhere.*

This was shocking to those listening to Jesus from the seashore. They were Jews, and believed that God would only "sow his seed" among *them*—and no one else. They were special. They were God's chosen ones. So why would God want His seed *anywhere* but in Israel?

It's still a shocking story today, at least to all those who feel that God has given His Son to only one group of people—to Christians, or even better, to Catholics. And everyone else is just plain "out of luck." But the parable we just heard tells us that God is as generous with his Son as a God could be. He's given His Son to everyone! He's "scattered" the "seed" of His Son not only for Catholics, but for Baptists and Presbyterians, too. And not just for Christians, but for Muslims and Jews and Buddhists and Hindus. And for atheists and agnostics, too.

What we hear in most parables is true about this one. God just ain't like us, at all!

You see, *we'd* be careful about where we sowed our seed. But God sows it indiscriminately, almost as though it didn't matter *where* it goes. It goes everywhere! *We'd* be stingy with our seed, worried we might run out of it. But God seems to have no end of it, an inexhaustible supply, so He can be much more generous than we'd be. *We'd* be worried about making sure the seed bore fruit. But God seems to feel that His seed, his Son, has already been fruitful—that he's fruitful no matter where he's sown! And *we'd* be sure not to waste any seed on those who don't deserve it. But God seems just as happy to "waste" His son Jesus on everyone!

Our job as Christians is, of course, to become "good soil" for Jesus the Word. But our job is *also* to imitate Jesus—in what he said, and in what he did. What he said was "Follow me." And what he did was die.

Let's do that. And stop worrying about who gets the seed, and who doesn't. That's the Sower's job. And *He* doesn't seem to care!

16TH SUNDAY IN ORDINARY TIME

DEACON JIM KNIPPER

WIS. 12:13, 16-19 ROM. 8:26-27 MATT 13:24-43	*"Let the wheat and weeds grow together."*

This Sunday's Gospel, taken from the 13th chapter of Matthew, picks up where we left off last Sunday and is probably one of the most hopeful and consoling gospels written. If you remember, Jesus has pushed off in a boat, enabling the large crowd gathered to hear him teach using a series of parables—parables, in particular, that describe what the Kingdom of Heaven is like.

But before I dig into the three parables given to us today, I think it is important to break open this term, "Kingdom of Heaven", because many people hear that phrase and think, "Oh, Jesus is describing what heaven must be like—isn't that nice." Remember that Matthew is a Jew and is writing predominantly to a Jewish community, and thus instead of using the term coined by the other gospel writers, "Kingdom of God", he alone uses the term "Kingdom of Heaven." But when modern linguists and theologians look at the early text, they say the best translation is really "Reign of God" or "God's Domain", or perhaps the best translation is simply "God's Love", which is, indeed, the core message found throughout the Bible.

So, in today's Gospel, Christ tells us that God's love is like:

- A sower of good seed whose field yields both wheat and weeds,
- It is like…a mustard seed
- And it is like…yeast

As a consummate teacher, Christ most likely chose these three metaphors because the crowd gathered along the shore knew what sowing seeds and baking with yeast was like—it was part of their everyday lives.

In the first parable, the sower of good seed finds his field has yielded weeds along with his wheat. So what is Christ communicating to the crowds, and to us here today, when he tells us that this sower of the good seed stops his workers from pulling up the weeds, for fear of pulling up some of the good wheat? He tells them not to focus on separating the two—rather, to allow them to grow together. So why leave the weeds? Why not identify and clear all the bad weeds out so the focus can just be on the good wheat?

But, being a parable, we know Christ was not describing how to tend our fields, but rather how we should live our lives. For, don't we often find ourselves spending much of our time trying to identify the good wheat and the bad weeds? Everyday our egos feed on identifying who is right and who is wrong, who is in and who is out, who is worthy and who is not…and in actuality, who are *we* to be judging anyone? We are *all* wheat and weeds. You can't have one without the other, and Christ knows that and instructs us to let them grow together. Christ calls for us to stop judging who or what is wheat and weed and understand that we are all children of God and that God's love is unconditional—God takes our weeds, our faults, our imperfections, and fills them with God's grace and holiness. If you look through the Gospels you will never find Jesus admonishing a sinner—rather, only offering forgiveness. And so, all we are called to do is recognize who we truly are and to give it back to God as a gift…blemishes and all!

The best metaphor I can give you is this: think of the times when your very young child came to you with the picture they just drew with their crayons. With a proud smile all over the face they presented a picture that was by no means perfect from an artistic viewpoint, but was treasured by you and hung on the fridge because it was given as a gift. That is how God loves us—imperfections and all—just waiting for us to give ourselves over as a gift back to God!

Next, we hear that God's love is like a mustard seed, the smallest of all seeds, yet a seed that rapidly grows into a bush 10 to 12 feet tall. At first glance, one may hear this parable and read a number of metaphors into it, such as how love or faith can begin small and with nourishment can grow and grow—and all of that is good. But I think we need to take a second and deeper look into this parable. You see, the crowd listening to this story knows all too well that the mustard seed is an invasive weed! It is the last thing anyone wants in their field. A farmer would not only want to get rid of such a plant, but also rid themselves of the birds that are hiding in the bushes and eating all the good seed!

No one in their right mind would ever sow mustard seeds. Well…no one, unless you are God. Remember, in these parables Christ is describing God's love—and like the sower who casts the mustard seeds that are re-jected by most, this parable reminds us that God's love encompasses all and reaches even those that are rejected…those who are on the fringes… those who are broken. God's love reaches the divorced, the gay, the de-pressed, the homeless, the jobless, and the addicted. Our personal weeds grow together with our wheat. But no matter how many mustard seeds we have, God's love reaches each of us and fills us with forgiveness. And the best news yet? It is freely given by God to all of us and can't be earned—there is nothing we can do more of or less of in order to gain more favor or more love from God. All we are called to do is to be open to this incredible gift of God and, in turn, to reach out to others with this same love. But all too often, as we are reminded in the first parable, we allow our egos to take over focusing on what we want, what we think, based on our own reference points, and thus judging who are the worthy and unworthy, rejecting others. And, worse yet, rejecting ourselves, and thus rejecting God.

Which brings us to the third parable of today's gospel, which tells us that God's love is like yeast. But to get insight into this metaphor, we need to understand what they are referring to as "yeast" in this story. It certainly wasn't that yellow and red packet of yeast granules that you get in the food store and add to warm water to make your bread rise. What Christ was referring to is better translated as "leaven". How many here have used sourdough flour starters you got from a friend or perhaps started yourself? That is leaven…and they can be kind of scary looking as they sit on your counter, doubling in size each day.

What is most interesting is that to begin a starter you simply add water to flour, and it is through the baker's daily care and nurturing that the natural yeast found in the flour and the bacteria coming off the baker's hands interact with each other and the mixture becomes leaven. All that you need is right there—flour and water and encouragement—and you have life and growth. It is then the addition of a small portion of this leaven kneaded into the bread/flour mixture that allows the dough to rise and to come to life and, when baked, becomes the bread that nourishes our bodies.

That is the yeast that Christ talks about in his parable…and now can you see why Christ described this unconditional love God has for all of us as leaven?

We all already carry that indwelling spark of the divine. We carry the yeast, the good seed, and we also carry the bacteria, the weeds, and through the nurturing of God's love we are transformed, like leaven. God's love is a source of growth and life. It is transformative. It changes us. It enlivens us. It hides in the weeds and the raw flour of our lives. It is to be shared and passed on to all we touch. And, nourished by our desire, it grows rapidly, like a mustard seed.

As I said in the beginning, this is indeed a gospel filled with good news—a gospel that reminds us of a love that consoles us when we are lost in the weeds, nurtures us when we are empty, comforts us when we are lost, and accepts us as we are, both wheat and weed. God does not love us for what we do or don't do, God loves us because God created us to be in relationship with God.

And so may you be open and present to experience this great love God has for all of us…

May you discover God's desire to be in relationship with you, with an abundant love that accepts you as you are, both weed and wheat…

And may you never forget, no matter what, that you are a cherished child of our God—a God who is, indeed, pure Love!

1 KINGS 3:5, 7-12
ROM. 8:28-30
MATT 13:44-52

"Ask something of me and I will give it to you."

If you've been a parishioner here at St. Ignatius Loyola for more than a few weeks, you'll know that this is a Jesuit church. That is, it's a church that the local bishop asked the members of the Society of Jesus to staff, way back in 1851. And if you've been a parishioner here for a few years, you'll probably know something about St. Ignatius, about Ignatian spirituality and maybe even a little Jesuit lingo.

So when I say that I'm about to tell you a story about my "provincial," you'll know that that's the regional superior of the Jesuits. Now, even though I work in New York, I'm actually a member of the New England Province. So I'm going to tell you a story about the Provincial of New England, whose name is Myles. Some of you might remember him from a few years ago, if you were at my Final Vow ceremony. He was the presider with the Boston accent.

Myles is a good friend and a Jesuit physician. Now, that does not mean that he is a physician that takes care of Jesuits only, which is a job I wouldn't wish on anyone! No, he was a physician—specifically, a gerontologist—before he entered the Jesuits. And for the last 15 years he worked at Loyola Medical Center in Chicago, a large teaching hospital, where he not only cared for patients but headed the gerontology department, where he was a beloved faculty member. Myles was known as a great doctor—smart, caring, sensitive. He even won some local fame by caring for Francis Cardinal George, the archbishop of Chicago, during the cardinal's bout with cancer a few years back. Consequently, Myles became a familiar presence on television in Chicago, updating the press with news of Cardinal George's surgery and eventual recovery.

Myles also has a splendid sense of humor. When Cardinal George asked why it was taking so long to recover from his surgery, Myles said, "It's the devil!" which made the cardinal laugh.

Anyway, a few years ago the Jesuits of New England were looking for a new provincial. Well, that's not entirely accurate. We don't really "look". Rather, the provincial's term ends after six years—a good idea from St. Ignatius, by the way, who wanted Jesuit leaders to return to the ranks after they finished their terms. And a new one is appointed. So the superior general of the Jesuits in Rome started to look for a new provincial. Of course, as in any group, there was a rumor mill about who were the top candidates. In this case, the top three candidates, which is the traditional number of candidates for positions in the church and the Society. Myles's name was mentioned by many New England Jesuits when they talked among themselves, but usually set aside.

Why? Well, we thought, Father General would never ask someone in Myles's position to give up his medical work, since it takes so many years of study to get there, or to give up such a high-profile job, to become provincial. He would be great, we thought, but it'll never happen.

Well, guess what? One day we all got an official email from Rome announcing that Father General had chosen Myles to be the next provincial. Well, I was delighted, of course—it's not such a bad thing to have a friend as provincial!—but also surprised. Would this mean he'd be giving up his medical career?

That day I called him up in Chicago. I said, "Oh, congratulations, Father Provincial." And he laughed and said, "Oh, Jim, we're old friends. Don't call me Father Provincial. Call me *Very Reverend* Father Provincial!" And we both laughed.

Now, I know a little about physicians, and how they regularly have to take certification exams and the like in order to stay "board certified." And I knew that Myles probably wouldn't have much time to study for those exams, and I wondered how he would keep up his certification. So I asked him, "What does that mean for your medical career?" "Oh," he said, "that's over."

Now, let me tell you how edifying that was for me to hear. How inspiring. It represented the very best of what we Jesuits call "indifference". Which is another way of talking about freedom. As much as Myles loved being a physician, he wasn't so attached to it that it prevented him from hearing God's call in his life to do something else, something new, something unexpected.

His example was edifying and, as a friend said to me, terrifying, too. Because if Myles asked you to give up a ministry you loved to do something else, it would be hard to say, "Well, I can't give *that* up!"

Why am I telling you that story? Because it's a kind of parable. The same kind that Jesus told. It's a story that helps us understand a rich topic. And the parable of Myles the Jesuit physician is very much like the parable of the pearl of great price.

The fellow in today's Gospel finds something so valuable—that famous pearl, something that he desires above all other things—that he's willing to let go of all he has to purchase it. Likewise with the fellow who finds the treasure in the field, and who sells all he has to buy the field. They know what's important in life and, moreover, they don't let anything get in the way. Myles knew that the pearl of *greatest* price was not his being a physician for the rest of his life—as wonderful as that is for people, and maybe for some physicians here today in this church—but following God's voice in the Society of Jesus.

Obviously, most of your lives are different. There aren't many Jesuits in the congregation today, so you're probably not going to be asked to drop everything and become a religious superior. But you *will* be asked to make choices in life that reveal your priorities. To choose between one set of goods and another.

So here's a question to ponder: What's *your* pearl? Sometimes, when our lives are not ordered correctly, that pearl could be money, or status or power. Other times, when they're ordered a little better, the pearl is family, or friends, or love. The greatest pearl though, the biggest treasure, is God. It's Jesus. It's following his Word in our lives, in big ways and in small.

Of course, all this requires freedom—detachment, or "indifference," as St. Ignatius would say, making sure that nothing gets in the way. Once again, you could be a physician who cares for his patients and his family and friends and serves God in that way. It's not about what you do as much as it is for whom you do it.

So the question is not "What's your pearl?" but "*Who* is your pearl?"

Jesus told parables like this, about pearls and fields, and fishes and buckets, and wheat and weeds, to help people understand the Kingdom of God. I'm telling you about my friend Myles to help you understand Jesus's parable, and about what's important.

But let me close with a story about *another* gemstone, from a Jesuit named Anthony De Mello. De Mello was a great spiritual master, an Indian Jesuit who told stories from the Eastern traditions to illuminate Gospel truths.

It's called "The Diamond." And it, too, is about freedom.

The wise man had reached the outskirts of the village and settled down under a tree for the night when a villager came running up to him and said, "The stone! The stone! Give me the precious stone!"

"What stone?" asked the wise man.

"Last night God appeared to me in a dream," said the villager, "And told me that if I went to the outskirts of the village at dusk I should find a wise man who would give me a precious stone that would make me rich forever."

The wise man rummaged in his bag and pulled out a stone. "He probably meant this one," he said, as he handed the stone over to the villager. "I found it on a forest path some days ago. You can certainly have it."

The man gazed at the stone in wonder. It was a diamond, probably the largest diamond in the whole world, for it was as large as a person's head.

He took the diamond and walked away. All night he tossed about in bed, unable to sleep. The next day at the crack of dawn he woke the wise man and said, "Give me the wealth that makes it possible for you to give this diamond away so easily."

18ᵀᴴ SUNDAY IN ORDINARY TIME

JOEL BLUNK

Isa. 55:1-3
Romans 8:35-39
Matt 14:13-21

"They all ate and were satisfied"

*I*t can easily be argued that we Protestants don't celebrate the Lord's Supper enough. It often comes down to what's convenient and practical rather than our real need to be fed. I recently spoke with a fellow Presbyterian ministry who told me his congregation is now celebrating Communion once a month during Ordinary Time and every week during Advent and Lent. He said they considered the possibility of celebrating every Sunday, but he kept hearing comments like, "Celebrating Communion less frequently makes those rare times we do more meaningful!" He told me he finally smiled and said, "Then would it be okay if I only preached every once in a while?!"

Meal celebrations are a common biblical practice, and are certainly meant to be a part of our communal life today. Even when it's not Communion, congregations often hold activities centered on a common meal. It's a natural and meaningful way to gather. God knows that—God, who rained down food from heaven for the wandering Israelites; God, who established the Passover Meal, which remains significant for our Jewish brothers and sisters; and Jesus, a faithful Jew himself, who said, "Remember me in the breaking of bread."

Our text for today, the story of the feeding of the five thousand, contains the heart of the gospel—it's evidence of the love of God, it indicates what true discipleship entails, and it's an example of how God takes a little and turns it into a lot.

This is the only miracle story told in every gospel. It's not a story Jesus told, but it's a story told about Jesus; it's a story about something Jesus did, and, as we're reminded today, he did it with the help of a few others. Not insignificant in the least.

In the late 80's, my wife Kristen and I visited Central America with about ten others as part of a Presbyterian Health Seminar. We toured Guatemala, El Salvador, and Nicaragua. It was a time of upheaval in those countries, marked by political corruption, civil unrest, and war.

While in El Salvador we were taken to a small farming village on the outskirts of the city. As we toured the tiny neighborhood we saw men and women hard at work carrying water, pounding wheat, baking tortillas. After a while it became obvious that they were preparing a meal, and we were to be the guests of honor. They didn't have much, but out of their scarcity, they offered a feast to us.

They served up beans and rice, and stories from their lives, sharing what it was like to live in a war-torn land while trusting in Jesus. Helicopters could be seen and heard in the distance carrying war wounded to the hospital in San Salvador nearby. We knew their lives were hard, that they had very little, but they opened their hearts to us and abundance sprang forth. It was a kingdom moment, a real-life loaves and fishes experience for all of us.

God, in Christ, cares about our basic needs. What happened on that hillside so long ago is intended for every person, and for all of creation. As poet and author John Phillip Newell says in his paraphrase of the Lord's Prayer, our prayer is that "there may be food for the human family today, and for the whole earth community." God intends for our hunger to be met, and while Jesus recognizes that we may not live on bread alone, he also knows that "without bread we cannot live."

The disciples, though, were a bit slow to catch on. They recognized that the need there that day was great and that the resources at their disposal were scarce. Still, it would be better, they reasoned, if people were just left to fend for themselves, that they be sent home or back to their towns to raid their own refrigerators. But Jesus wouldn't have it. He knew that he had the power to provide, albeit with the disciples' help, exactly what the people needed. And so Jesus took action.

Just listen to the verbs in the story: He saw, he had compassion; he ordered, he took, he looked, blessed, broke, and gave... He moved toward the need of those around him and he invited the disciples to do the same. He asked them to give the people something to eat. He modeled for them and with them what life in the kingdom of God is like.

A student wondered about the difference between heaven and hell, and so approached his teacher. "In heaven," the teacher said, "there is a large banquet table with every imaginable delicacy you can imagine, every plate is full, every chair is occupied—it's a bountiful feast. And hell looks exactly the same, a great banquet, but there, everyone is starving." "Why is that?" the student asked. "The forks are too long," the teacher said, "and they can't feed themselves." "How about in heaven?" the student asked. "Ah," said the teacher, "in heaven, they feed each other."

Though we think of Jesus feeding the five thousand that day, it's really the disciples who do it—with God's help, of course. Jesus tells them to give the crowd something to eat. Blessing and breaking the bread, he gives it not to the crowd, but to the disciples first, and they in turn pass it around...and are amazed to find there is plenty for everyone, with lots to spare.

Discipleship requires participation on our part and a willingness for us, like Jesus, to take action. When we do—acting with and for Christ— miraculous things are possible. It's up to us to feed each other.

That may seem like a daunting task, given the magnitude of need we see in the world today, but the story of the feeding of the five thousand serves as evidence that God multiplies our efforts and provides what we alone cannot. All we can do is be faithful with what we've been given and do what we're asked, like the disciples on that mountainside that day.

When Jesus asked them to feed the crowd, their first response was, "We have nothing!" But Jesus knew better. And to the disciples' credit, they did what he asked. What they found as a result were basketfuls left over— full stomachs, satisfied people, meager resources turned into abundance.

This story is a kingdom story, an example of more being fed than ever expected. In this story it's five thousand, a huge number compared to the five loaves and two fish; yet, no one went away hungry. What about the over 7 billion people in the world today, what about the vast creation in need of healing, care, reconciliation? This story says that no staggering number is insurmountable with God. God's abundant love can meet the needs of the world, *if* we're willing to do our part.

There is an expectation that disciples, like you and me, will pass out the food, that we'll act as Christ in the world, doing for others what he's done for us. For us to be Christ-like today, we must express our faith in tangible ways, working for justice, loving our neighbors, and showing compassion to others. When we do that, even modestly, God is able to multiply our efforts.

Some years ago, my family and I spent Holy Week in a West African village. We were celebrating the Last Supper in a packed sanctuary. As people came forward to receive the meal, music played on brass instruments and drums. The congregation made their way up front to receive the elements, but what should have taken 10 to 15 minutes for all to be served stretched on and on. I actually began to wonder if people were coming back for seconds! Then I noticed the front door of the church was open—the windows, too—and there were crowds of people streaming in to be served. How would there be enough to go around? The service went on and on. Communion alone took well over an hour. It seemed as if the whole village showed up to be fed! Imagine that, imagine the whole town eager to receive the love of God in a piece of bread, imagine people lined up outside to get in, waiting for a turn at the table.

Jesus demonstrates God's miraculous ability to provide in this little story; passing bread to the disciples, who in turn hand it to the multitudes. Imagine us doing the same. The promise set before us in the gospel—in this simple story—is that God intends love, peace, and justice for the sake of all.

What God in Christ is really offering is life in its fullness. That promise was kept on that hillside in Galilee. And it's a promise kept with us today.

We are called now as partners in Christ's service. We are the ones who must pass the loaves around. If we don't do it, who will? Like the stories Jesus told of the mustard seed and yeast, from meager beginnings, amazing things will rise!

The invitation here is to see greater possibilities, to dream a bigger dream, for ourselves and for the rest of creation. The disciples discovered that firsthand. They thought they didn't have enough, but their meagerness in the hands of Jesus became a bounty.

Imagine that now. What would it mean for us to dream bigger, to see more than meets the eye at every turn? What would it mean for us to trust that with God there are no limitations? What would it mean to believe that our little basketfuls, when placed in the loving hands of Jesus, become a bounty? Or that when we dare to live as people fully alive out there in the world, a multiplying effect happens because God is living through us in ways we can scarcely see in the moment?

When we step back, like we can from this story, we begin to see it—how lives are changed, how the world is healed, how love expands, because we dare to take Jesus's request seriously, giving others something to eat.

Give them something to eat, Jesus said. It's time we went into the world fully alive ourselves, offering the best of who we are to anyone we meet, meeting them where they are, trusting God to give everything that's needed and more. Our God is an abundant God, full of love enough to go around. All we're asked to do is trust in that and serve. God will take care of the rest.

19ᵗʰ SUNDAY IN ORDINARY TIME

FR. BILL BAUSCH

---

1 Kings 19:4-13
Rom. 9:1-5
Matt. 14:22-33

"The Lord was not in the wind."

The first reading will occupy our time. The prophet Elijah is at his lowest ebb, contemplating suicide. As the story tells us, he's discouraged. The wicked Queen Jezebel is after him. All his work seems down the drain. Nothing is going right. He's at a very bad part in his life. So he treks across this desert, physically and mentally exhausted, sits beneath the broom tree, and as you heard, asks God to take his life. He's had it: "Enough already; I'm ready to die!" He's given up. He's in despair. He is one tired and desperate prophet.

His mood is not unknown to us. It is found everywhere today, communally and individually. The press reported this week that the ugly and horrible war in the Mideast has already killed more than one hundred Israelis, most of them military, and over fifteen hundred Lebanese, most of them civilians. Or as the Jesuit magazine America says, "Lebanese casualties have outnumbered Israeli deaths more than ten to one. A third of them have been children." Factions in Iraq are routinely killing thirty-five to fifty people a day. Iran is making nuclear weapons. Terrorists are emboldened and airports are fortresses. Gas prices keep climbing. Daily revelations of corruption in the corporate, sports, political, and professional worlds are numbingly commonplace. The vulgarity and sleaziness of the media disgust us. Thus subconsciously burdened, we all feel an unspoken unease as we go about our lives.

Then there are our personal lives which force us brooding beneath the broom tree. There are those who have suffered loss, the loss of a child or spouse through death. The loss from divorce. The loss of physical or mental health. The loss of a job or an opportunity. The loss of virtue. Loneliness. Betrayals and disappointments, addictions, and simply spiritual flatness plague many. Some people are sick and tired of being sick and tired. We all have Elijah moments. So let's go back to the Elijah story and see what we can learn. Two things, in fact.

The first thing we learn is the value of Elijah's solitude, the time when one is forced by circumstances "to be still." Elijah sat exhausted beneath the broom tree, but in that stillness he had a chance to regroup and recover, to listen to the Lord. One of Grace Noel Crowell's poems speaks of his condition—indeed of life itself—as a reservoir that needs filling up just like a slow rain fills an empty cup. She proposes:

Hold up your cup, dear child, for God to fill.
He only asks today that you be still.

That's a lovely metaphor. It's starting to rain after a long dry period, one or two drops and then more, and you turn your cup upside down; and gradually, drop by drop, the cup begins to fill again. Those of you who are hurting, grieving, in sorrow, or just struggling with something, the poem says that maybe you need just to sit awhile and rest, and turn your cup upside down to God; and little by little, let your dry reservoir fill up again. *Be still.* Stop trying to control. Be still.

The second thing we notice is that as the exhausted prophet wakes up from his stupor of despair he unexpectedly spots a little hearth cake and water. Where did that come from? Maybe it was there all along but he never noticed. Being so "down," that was the last thing he expected, but there it was and it picked him up a little. In discouragement, the Elijah story says, be alert to the little signs.

Here's another example: a pagan philosopher of some note, a man with a reputation of some fame, yet he's unhappy. His life is a shambles, his religious doubts are plaguing him, his personal life is a disaster. His relationships— with the woman he is living with and his illegitimate child—are strained to the breaking point. He's depressed. To throw him into further despair, he's just received news that two common Roman soldiers had converted to the Christian faith. Here these ignorant soldiers have found something and they're happy, and he, Augustine, the great intellect, is in a terribly depressed state. Dejected, he goes into his garden and just sits under *his* broom tree, and great man that he is, he puts his head in his hands and he simply weeps. As he's weeping, he tells us, he hears a small voice say- ing, "Take and read, take and read," on the other side of the garden fence.

So in a half daze he goes into the house and picks up the Christian Bible, and in his own words in his autobiography he says,

I seized, opened, and in silence read that section on which my eyes first fell: "Not in rioting and drunkenness, not in chambering and wantonness, not in strife and envying, but put on the Lord Jesus Christ." No further would I read, nor needed I, for instantly at the end of the sentence, by a light, as it were, of serenity infused into my heart, all the darkness of doubt vanished away.

Under his broom tree of despair, prompted by a child's voice, he found a new direction in life.

So for this woman. It was one of the worst days of her life. Newly sepa- rated, she was tired, sick, lonely, hot, and discouraged. It was all she could do to lift her little boy into his highchair for dinner. She put his food on the tray and began to read the mail. Another bill she could not pay; it was the last straw. She leaned her head against the tray and began to cry. The little boy looked at this sobbing mother, then took the pacifier out of his mouth and offered it to his distraught mother. She began to laugh through her tears and hugged the source of such total unconditional love. Again, the lesson to learn in times of being at the end of one's rope is to be alert to the small signs.

So in bad times, be still. Maybe bad times are a sign that you're running on empty and simply need the time to hold your empty heart up to God to be refilled. Second, notice the little signs: summer, spring, flower, a kindness.

There are all kinds of people sitting under the broom tree. I suggest when shortly I lift up the paten and the chalice, you might think of someone under the broom tree and say in your heart: "I am placing Mary or John on this paten and in this chalice. May they too be lifted up to God." Or when you approach for Communion, bring someone in your heart with you. Let them share the "hearth bread" of life, this sign that they are not alone.

Thus strengthened by that food, may they begin to walk forty days and forty nights to the mountain of God.

Reprinted from Once Upon a Gospel: Inspiring Homilies and Insightful Reflections *by William J. Bausch, ©2008. Twenty-Third Publications. Used with permission. All rights reserved.*

20ᵀᴴ SUNDAY IN ORDINARY TIME
REV. CAROL HOWARD MERRITT

Isa. 56:1, 6-7
Rom. 11:13-15, 29-32
Matt. 15:21-28

"*Woman, you have great faith!*"

I can't help but notice that I am raising my daughter much differently than the way that I grew up.

The main distinction is that my mother always thought that the number one thing that a parent needed was consistency. Once my mother made up her mind about something, she would not change it. She would not be moved. No amount of tantrums, or crying, or pleading would make the answer different. Mom got her intended result—I was not a whiny child, and I figured that what she said might as well be written in stone, because she was not going to change her mind.

There are many things that I learned while growing up, and many things that I am thankful that my parents gave me. I learned how to be compliant and respectful, but my mom and dad's style of parenting did not allow me to develop the art of negotiating. That was something I had to learn as an adult.

As a parent, I'm more flexible. People might even call me a softie. That's okay, because I've made a conscious decision to allow my daughter to negotiate. Respectfully, without whimpering, I let her change my mind. I will say, "What is your best argument? Give me a good reason to alter my position." If she succeeds with well-articulated reasoning, then I will let her win. I made this decision because I'm hoping that she will have the confidence to argue and acquire the skills to challenge people who have authority over her.

I also think negotiating is a Biblical concept. Through Jesus's stories about women and his conversations with women, he has respect for the woman who overcomes great adversity and persists in getting what she needs.

The same sort of woman often shows up in the Gospel stories. Throughout the parables, there is often a persistent woman, a woman who will not quit looking for her coin until she finds it, another women will not quit knocking on the judge's door until she gets the answer that she wants.

Jesus interacted with determined women as well. One woman who had been bleeding for twelve years reached out and touched the hem of his garment, even though she was "unclean" and not supposed to be touching any man. Another woman's back was bent for eighteen years. She received healing, even though it was the Sabbath. It was not lawful for either one of them to be healed, but they still made sure that it happened.

Our passage is no exception. We have a woman who is not Jewish, asking Jesus to cast a demon out of her daughter. Jesus says no. And he's rude about it. He says he's not going to heal her because that would be like taking the children's food off of the table and giving it to the dogs.

The woman swallows the insult, but she doesn't walk off offended by his words. Her daughter is suffering, and she knows that Jesus can heal her. She is not deterred by his refusal. Instead, she negotiates with Jesus and reminds him that even the dogs under the table get the children's crumbs.

I imagine Jesus laughing at this point. Jesus changes his mind. Jesus heals the daughter.

We can learn a lot from these persistent women—women who reach out, women who persevere, women who are not afraid to state what they need, women who negotiate.

We can learn a lot from these ancient women whom Jesus championed. In our modern day, women make 75 cents for every dollar that a man makes. The wage gap has stayed the same for the last 13 years.

The more prestigious the position, the more disparity there is between men and women. As women acquire more education or move up the corporate ladder, they are more likely to make much less than their male counterparts.

I've heard women say that they don't like negotiating. I certainly don't. One businesswoman, Pat Heim, has a theory about this. She wrote that women are socialized to play games that are fair and equal—games like dolls or house—while men are encouraged to play competitive sports. She says that men like to negotiate because they are used to playing football and soccer, and because of that, they are socialized to win, while women are socialized to build relationships.

(That's why Title IX, the Equal Opportunity in Education Act, which encouraged so many women's sports programs, was so important. It allowed a whole generation of girls to compete.)

Even in such a different time and culture, Jesus upheld these women who broke the rules, who were persistent, who reached out when they were supposed to keep their arms to their sides, who gave their last dime, who knocked until the door was finally open. I think there's a message for us here, in this woman who taught Jesus.

She gave in a bit, but she refused to take no for an answer. She was clever in her answer. And it seemed that she taught Jesus something. He changed his mind.

May we go out with a longing to do justice. As bosses, as employees, as men, and as women, let us remember the persistence of these women that Jesus upholds, and let us live in their example. To the glory of God our Creator, God our Liberator, and God our Sustainer. Amen.

Isa. 22:19-23 Rom. 11:33-36 Matt. 16:13-20	*"Who do you say I am?"*

*O*ver *the past few weeks,* we have listened to stories of Jesus on the road with his disciples, healing, preaching and teaching. We heard the parable of the weed and the wheat, of the mustard seed and of the yeast. We heard of the Jesus who calls those who labor and are burdened to come to him to find rest. We read of a Jesus who feeds the multitude, and just last week of the Jesus who finally responds to the unrelenting faith of the Canaanite woman.

But today's Gospel opens up telling us that Jesus has taken his disciples on a 25-mile hike north from the Sea of Galilee to the foothills of Mt. Hermon, near the city of Caesarea Philippi. Since words were not wasted as these stories were told and retold over the centuries, why is this piece of information recorded in the gospel? Why did he take them on a long hike to this place? And why did he simply enter the region, but not the town? Why did he travel so far to simply ask them the one question: "Who do you say I am?"

And what we see is that the question was more than just Jesus doing a popularity poll with his disciples. As a matter of fact, that question was so important to his mission that Jesus sets the stage by bringing them to this region due to its physical geography as well as its political significance.

For one of the most prominent pieces of landscape in all of Israel is the massive wall of rock at Caesarea Philippi. It is upon this sheer cliff, well over 100 feet high and 500 feet wide, that this city was built. In 14 A.D., Caesar Augustus died, and around the time of Christ's ministry, the marble temple was enlarged and rededicated by King Philip to honor Caesar, who had considered himself a god. And it was during those times and throughout the years that hundreds of people would carve niches into the side of the cliff and, in homage, place statues of their pagan gods so that they could be worshiped.

But the opening line of today's gospel clearly states that Christ took them to the *region* of Caesarea Philippi, but not into the city, and the reason has to do with one's viewpoint. You see, Christ was looking for the perfect backdrop to make his point—to ask his question. And the only way this enormous rock formation can be seen is for the viewer to be outside and below the city. For if you were in the actual city, all you would be able to see is the view from the top of the rock. Your viewpoint would be one of power and control, and you would miss seeing the rock itself!

Now, can you better envision the picture that has been painted for us in today's Gospel? It seems clear that Jesus took his disciples on a 25-mile journey in order to make a point. With this massive rock in the background, with a marble temple that honors an earthly emperor sitting atop it and niches to pagan gods carved in the side, Christ begins to query the disciples by asking: "So who do people say I am?"

Did they see him as just another one of those gods being honored by another temple? Was he simply just another god to fill in another niche in the wall? You can almost see the disciples shrugging their shoulders as they begin to answer him that some say he is Elijah and others John the Baptist. But then Christ cuts to the chase as he pins the disciples down and asks: Who do you say I am?

Can you imagine the look on their faces? Christ standing before a backdrop of a temple to Caesar, with a massive rock wall honoring false gods, looking them in the face and asking them, "Who am I….just another one of those gods? You have walked with me, listened to me, watched me heal the sick and feed the hungry—have you figured it out? Reach inside yourself and tell me, who am I?"

And it is Simon who steps forward with the answer—"You are the Christ, the Son of the living God!" And with that 10-story-high rock in the background, Jesus looks at Simon and calls him Kephas, Aramaic for "rock", translated in Greek as Petros or Peter. And it is Christ who proclaims that it is upon that kephas, that human rock (not that rock wall behind him) that he will build his church.

And look at who Christ chose: Peter! A rock? A shaky rock, perhaps at best. In the prior weeks we heard the stories of how the disciples were looking to send the multitudes away hungry rather than feed them. They wanted to shoo off the pagan Canaanite woman who was seeking help. It was Peter who lost his faith and began to sink in the waters as he answered the call of Christ to walk on the water. And next week we will hear Christ call Peter a "Satan" and an obstacle and to get out of his way. Peter, wheat and weed, is called "rock" and is called to *be* a rock—to be a foundation that Christ will use to build this church.

So where are we within this Gospel? How does this all relate to our lives today?

Easy! The same scene that we heard described today in the Gospel is played out each and every day with all of us. We all have our Caesarea Philippis…and it begins with the walls that hold up what we worship. Maybe it is our work, our drink, our food, our toys, our image, our egos… it is all the things that we hold near and dear but are simply empty falsehoods. And Christ comes to each of us, with our weeds growing from within our wheat, carrying the same faults and indiscretions found in Peter and his disciples, and asks you and me the same question—Who do you say I am? But before we answer that question, we need to know who we are!

The answer is right there in the gospel. "Upon this kephas Christ will build his church." But notice: it is "church" with a small "c" and not a capital "C". Remember, Christ was not a Catholic, Christ was a Jew. He did not come to necessarily start a new religion or build large cathedrals fed by a hierarchy—but rather Christ came to teach a new way for an ekklesia, an assembly of the people (you and me), a church (with a small "c") to live and to love as God loves.

But for over 2,000 years we have taken the church with the small "c" and made it a Church with a capital "C", with a pyramidal structure and hierarchy, and we missed the point that we are all foundational, we all have a role, we are all various forms of rock, with various talents and gifts. We are like the seed scattered on fertile soil which yields wheat as well as weeds, we are like the yeast hidden and growing in the dough, we are all called to be part of the church. We who are the body of Christ, we whom Christ dwells within, we who are being called to open ourselves to God's love, versus living our lives focused on what we love.

So Jesus continues to ask us, "Who do you say I am?" And where does the answer come from? Look at Peter: His answer did not come from years of Catholic education, it was not derived from Church doctrine, dogma, or encyclicals. We are told that it was revealed to him by God—in short, it came from within. It is Paul, in his letter to the Romans, who tells us that it is God who touches our spirit, our being, and confirms who we really are so that we may know him and know ourselves. And it is this internal revelation that clicked within Peter. Even with all his imperfections—and one could even say it was because of his imperfections—that

Peter opened himself up to the flow of God's love, the revelation of this indwelling. God simply waits for each of us to be open to this gift...waits for us to walk away from the pagan gods in our lives...waits for us to walk away from our Caesarea Philippis, our false rocks, and to simply be a true *kephas*, like Peter.

You see, by virtue of our baptisms, we are all called to be the rocks of foundation for Christ.

Through our discipleship we are called, not to be perfect, but to be part of a growing and nurturing foundation that Christ can use to build a church, an ekklesia, a community that loves as God loves and that forgives as God forgives.

Through the way we serve others, we make Christ more visible to those around us...and so by seeing who we are in Christ, and who Christ is in us, we become like Peter—whereby our eyes are opened to the gift of the one who is truly the Son of the Living God.

JER. 20:7-9

ROM. 12:1-2

MATT. 16:21-27

"Whoever loses his life for my sake will find it."

---

*W*e're led into this challenging Gospel by the first reading from the prophet Jeremiah, "You have seduced me, Lord, and I've let myself be seduced." Sometimes it's translated, "You have duped me, Lord, and I let myself be duped." I'm told by scholars that these are both softenings of the original text. What Jeremiah is really saying is closer to, "You have raped me, God, and I have let myself be raped."

Jeremiah seems to be saying, "I set out on this journey with You that I thought would be wonderful and consoling and gratifying and self-promoting; instead it's turned out to be a life with an awful lot of suffering. I don't know why I ever followed you."

This lament prepares us for the Gospel. Today's Gospel reading is quite a reversal from last week's, an earlier part of Matthew 16 where Jesus is praising Peter, "You are a rock, Peter. You're the leader. You've got the keys of the Kingdom of Heaven. You did it right." You can just see Peter strutting around with immense self-confidence, thinking, "I'm the best."

And now, just a few verses later, the infallible Pope shows himself, in fact, to be very fallible when Jesus goes so far as to call Peter a devil. How can one who got it so right now get it so wrong?

Well, I hope that is comforting, because it's true of all of us—both sides can coexist in the same person. I remember the first time I visited Rome and looked in the great church of St. Peter; there, written in Latin around the top of the cupola, it says, "Thou art Peter, and upon this rock I will build my church." This is as it should be, but I've wondered why there wasn't a second ring of Latin words saying, "Get behind me, Satan, for you think like men and not like God," as it says in Matthew 16:23 today. We acknowledge the positive, but we conveniently forget the negative—it's human nature, I guess.

When we start on our journey toward God, we don't realize it, but the motivation is almost all about ourselves. It's a career move. We're looking for personal advancements. We're buying our eternal fire insurance policy. This isn't love of God yet. It's very well-disguised self-interest. We're not in it for God; we're in it for ourselves, but it takes a while to recognize that.

That's why Jesus says it so strongly: "If you don't lose your life, if you're in this to gain your life, you haven't yet understood what I'm talking about. You're missing the point."

Jesus isn't just saying this to Peter; He's speaking to all who seek to follow Him. We start the journey largely out of self-interest, taking care of ourselves while thinking we're worshipping God. But we're doing the "work of the Devil," as it were, precisely because it is passing for love of God, but it isn't. Whoever wishes to save his own life must lose it, because it's still all about "you" and your private gateway to heaven. It's not about God, truth, love, others, or the bigger world.

How could such smallness be God's great salvation? Why would that show any transformation, which is what the second reading talks about? "Be transformed in the very nature of your mind" (Rom. 12:2). This is Peter's moment of initiation, when he turns from earlier, selfish motivations to being drawn by actual desire for God and God's Big Picture. It's probably the ultimate challenge, a complete reversal of engines for each of us when somewhere in the middle of life we have to ask the question, "Why am I doing what I'm doing? Why am I coming here on Sunday morning? Does God need me to come to church?" I don't think so. God is doing quite well without you and without me, and yet God invites us into the great dance.

We're really not coming here for God. We're here, I hope, for ourselves, to find out what it's all about. What does it all mean? It's we who have to change. It's we who have to reverse engines and recognize that it's in letting go of what we think is our identity that we actually find our true self. That's the great paradox.

Let me say it plainly: Your life is not about you. You are one little instance of this Mystery of life that's been going on for billions of years, and all you can do is surrender to that Mystery that is larger than you, bigger than you, more wonderful than you, and which will draw you forward, almost in spite of yourself.

All you can do is trust it and allow it and suffer it and surely enjoy it too. It's not a matter of doing it right, it's a matter of "doing it"! It is a matter of letting go and losing who we think we are, to fall into who we really are, and always will be.

EZEK. 33:7-9
ROM. 13:8-10
MATT. 18:15-20

"For where two or three gather in my name, there am I with them."

*M*ost *of us don't actually* know very much about living in community. Ours is a society in which individualism reigns supreme. We think about what is best for ourselves and perhaps for our spouse or our children, but the idea of thinking first of the community around us is somewhat foreign. After all, the foundational stories of the United States feature the rugged individualist, and so it is no wonder that we are not as attuned to the larger community as we are to our own selves and families.

Therefore, this passage from Matthew is hard for us to put into the context of community, where it belongs. The concern in the story is about the overall health of the community, which in Matthew is small and young and fragile and new, and the sins that are to be corrected are worrisome because of the effect those sins have on the community itself. It's not so much about "you sinned against me," but about the health of the whole.

Sadly, these verses are more often used, now, in a way that I don't believe Jesus was advocating to his disciples. I don't think Jesus had the idea that we should go on television or on our blogs or otherwise stand in our various bully pulpits and call people out in public because we believe they are sinful and wrong. For one thing, Jesus advocates addressing one another privately. And for another, standing in judgment of one in the community is the very antithesis of what Jesus in Matthew is about.

For in Matthew's view, it is accepted that there are both "wheat and weeds" in the community and that it is God's job, not ours, to sort that out in God's good time. Constant weed pulling, Jesus told his disciples in the (unique to Matthew) parable of the wheat and the weeds (Matthew 13:24-30), was an unhelpful disruption to the community. Tender shoots of green wheat were liable to be damaged by all that digging around to pull up the weeds, he said. Leave them alone and let God sort it out.

And yet we sometimes feel it our duty to call out others in public and even to shun those who we deem to be weeds, citing Scripture as the basis of and justification for our behavior. We like to keep things stirred up and look to align ourselves with those of whom we approve and castigate those of whom we disapprove. Which, of course, is about puffing ourselves up and not about building up the community of God.

The Gospel stories show Jesus again and again standing with those whom others shun, whom others disapprove and ignore. He stands with the outcast and the broken. He dares the "righteous" to throw the first stone, provided they are without sin themselves, which of course they know they are not. He touches lepers and allows women to touch him. He says that the poor and grieving and imprisoned are blessed.

Will we ignore all of these actions and words of Jesus so that we might feel justified in separating ourselves from others because of this passage?

Yes, we offend one another. We hurt one another. We are sinful creatures one and all. We all stand in need of correction. None of us is pure. None.

And so, let us read on to see that the next thing Jesus says is to remind us that where two or three are gathered in his name, he will be in the midst of us. These words bring us back to the true sense of sacred community, where we gather around Jesus and ask him again how we are to follow him now.

And he will remind us, when we ask and listen for an answer, that we are made to live in community, and yet that community is a mixed bag. It will never be pure. That's just how it is. Our constant attempts to uproot weeds will do nothing to increase the harvest that belongs to God alone.

Keeping our eyes on Jesus, rather than casting about for sinners to exclude or call out, is how we will keep in The Way, that glorious way that is founded on love. When we are together on the way, Jesus is among us. Thanks be to God.

SIR. 27:30-28:7
ROM. 14:7-9
MATT. 18:21-35

"Forgive your neighbor's injustice."

*Y*ou've *no doubt heard the* statement, "To err is human; to forgive, divine." What we hear in the Gospel reading today is that to forgive is to be fully human—and therefore divine. God passes on the mystery of this impossible, unconditional love from God's self to all of us.

It seems that to the degree we know we need forgiveness and to the degree we actively receive it, to that very degree we can pass forgiveness on to others. If you've never felt in need of forgiveness, you likely don't know how terrible it feels to be unforgiven. You're not motivated or inspired to free others unless you know how wonderful it is to be liberated in love.

Brothers and sisters, without forgiveness all of history and human relationships devolve into a cold, deep freeze. Everything stops. Everything grinds to a halt. The very fact that Jesus tells us to forgive "seventy times seven" indicates that Jesus assumes that even good people are going to disappoint one another. He assumes failure. It is part of the deal. He assumes we won't live up to our highest ideals. The best of people hurt one another. There's really no point in saying, "He's evil," or "She's terrible," or "She's going to Hell." To refuse to forgive a serious offense is to be in hell ourselves—now.

What we hear in this passage is that God loves all of us in an unearned way, and that's what forgiveness means. Every time God forgives, God is breaking God's own rules and saying, "I would rather be in relationship with you than be right!" Forgiveness breaks down the logic that frames our very lives, a logic that says, "I deserve, and you owe me." It's the human logic of death. It keeps everyone isolated and insulated from one another and from life. Inevitably, people with bad intentions and even good people with the best of intentions will hurt one another, so our thinking goes that we have to protect ourselves.

But if we don't learn the mystery of forgiveness, we stay stuck in this cold, hard logic and we stay that way until we die. We close up our hearts and our minds; even our bodies constrict. Perhaps you've seen people with tight, rigid bodies who can't reach out, who can't open their arms. The body pulls into itself. It can't smile, hug, experience delight, or love.

Now, after saying all of these wonderful things, there's a bit of a conflict in this Gospel, too. Jesus has clearly said to Peter, "You must forgive seventy times seven." Now, we know that God could not ask something of us that God, Himself, Herself, does not also do. Yet what follows is a strange little tacked-on parable where God appears to not follow God's own advice. In fact, it seems God tortures people and throws them into the darkness if they do not do it right. It really does not fit the context at all, but contradicts the major point. (Probably some later scribe got upset at God's generosity!)

You have to put all Jesus's teachings on forgiveness together and see where He is going—He clearly says that the condition for your sins being forgiven is to forgive one another. That's the prerequisite. I wonder why we ignored that to make the condition for forgiveness of sin going to a priest and telling him the "kind, number, and circumstances" of our failures. That might indeed be very healing at times, but it is not what Jesus ever says. Your sins will be forgiven to the degree that you are forgiving of other people. That's the teaching. It's very clear. And that's the point Jesus is making in this story of the servants: "You received mercy, so why don't you forgive your brothers and sisters?" He inserts forgiveness into the entire community to keep it from freezing up, and does not limit it to one official forgiver (as good as that might be on occasion).

I don't know where the Gospel writer, Matthew, got this, but he puts in a Gospel impossibility at the end, and shows God torturing those who don't forgive. That can't really be the case from what we know of Trinitarian love, which only flows in one direction. But I think Jesus is talking about self-torture. It's not God who tortures you; humans most assuredly torture themselves and one another—and then project that onto God.

I'm sure you know how it goes. You remember and replay an offense done against you, perhaps for the rest of your life, and each time it gets tighter and more hateful. In your mind the offender becomes even more evil and you become more the victim. Many people live in a kind of obsessive-compulsive trap, replaying the video in their mind over and over and over again, trying to decide who is right and who is wrong, who deserves torture and who deserves exoneration. What a waste of energy.

I believe this is what the parable is teaching. You will be handed over to the torturer, and the torturer is your own mind, heart, and spirit. Brothers and sisters, you have to forgive or you'll never be free. You have to let go or there is no future to anything. If you keep holding on to the wrong-doing, evil and injustice you've experienced, blaming someone else, then you do yourselves and everyone else no good.

Forgiveness, in my experience, is the only action that reveals three *goodnesses* at the same time: First, you have to grant the offending party some degree of dignity and goodness themselves. You must not demonize them.

You have to honor the divine presence in them, even with the mistakes that they've made. That's high-level consciousness, of course.

Second, you also have to recognize a capacity for goodness inside yourself. You have to draw from a deeper place, bigger than you, that is not so easily offended. In fact, it is unoffendable. It's the soul, the place where God dwells, a holy temple within you. When you draw from that place, you don't need to count the cost or measure the offense because it's an Abundant Source and all counting is meaningless. You're living inside such a bigger love that little hurts really don't matter. They're not worth carrying around.

And the third goodness, of course, is that you have to recognize the total and unconditional goodness of God, who has always shown you kindness and mercy. As the mystics and saints all realize, the center of this universe is kindness and mercy, not hardness and coldness. This abundant love unlocks everything. It frees reality so we no longer need to count the cost, hate, or blame, or attack anyone! Yes, I said anyone. If God is kind and merciful, then we who are God's children can only, somehow, become the same. We become the God we worship, and God is forgiveness itself.

ISA. 55:6-9 PHIL. 1:20-24, 27 MATT. 20:1-16	*"So the last will be first, and the first will be last."*

If I've read one, I've read fifty homilies on the Internet this week, and almost every one of them interpreted Jesus's parable as a treatise on labor relations or employers providing a just wage for their workers.

I'm sorry, but Jesus was not a labor attorney. And even though he would absolutely stand up for those who are treated unfairly in the workplace, this parable was *not* his way of doing so.

To understand this parable, all we have to do is remember that the word "wage" has nothing to do with money. The "daily wage" Jesus is talking about is really "heaven". The whole story is about God giving "heaven" to anyone he pleases.

What seems unfair is that God seems to be offering the same "heaven" to latecomers as he offers to those who have been at it from the beginning. That's why this is probably the most disconcerting and distressing parable Jesus ever told. What's distressing is that he seems to be saying that God can give heaven even to those who haven't worked very long to earn it.

And, let's face it, if you can be rewarded with heaven after only an hour's work, it doesn't seem fair to those who have been working all day.

When the laborers who were hired early in the day get angry, it's because they *catch on*—they realize immediately that the "work" they've done doesn't matter. In other words, they've learned the most important lesson there is to learn: If the work we do to get into heaven doesn't matter, it must be because *you can't earn heaven!*

As Americans, especially, this sounds like heresy. Our whole culture is based on the "American Dream": that with hard work, and the sweat of your brow, you can pull yourself up by your bootstraps and become a millionaire! What Jesus seems to be suggesting is a kind of "divine welfare"—that you can work hardly at all and get the same reward as those who work their tails off.

Jesus seems to be saying that you and I can come to Mass every Sunday, say our daily prayers, and go to novenas; that we can be kind and gener- ous to our neighbor; that we can love our enemies, even—and that we'll get the same reward as someone who has a deathbed conversion! This flies in the face of our sense of justice!

Well, that's why we heard from the Prophet Isaiah this morning. He tells us that "God's ways are not our ways. His thoughts are not our thoughts." And God's generosity will therefore stick in our craw for the rest of our days until we *give in*. Until we surrender. Until we admit that *we are not in control.* I can't *work* my way to heaven. I can't *pray* my way to heaven. I can't control who *gets* to heaven, and especially who *doesn't get* there.

There's too many things wrong with the world that I *can* control. Let's leave who gets to heaven to God. I guarantee you: It'll free up a lot of our spare time!

Isa. 5: 1-7
Phil. 4: 6-9
Matt. 21: 33-43

"The stone that the builders rejected has become the cornerstone"

Martin Luther said that sometimes you have to squeeze a Biblical passage until it leaks the gospel. I find myself doing just that trying to figure out exactly what is going on in Matthew's version of the parable of the evil tenants in the vineyard. But that's what parables are supposed to do, right? Biblical scholars tell us that Matthew is actually preaching his own homily on Jesus's words concerning "the stone rejected by the builders becoming the cornerstone" (Mt 21: 42) in reference to the despicable behavior of the tenants in the vineyard leased to them.

In his homily, Matthew points his finger at the religious authorities of his day saying:

> *Therefore, I say to you, the kingdom of God will be taken away from you and given to a people that will produce its fruit ... When the chief priests and the Pharisees heard his parables, they knew that he was speaking about them.*
>
> Mt 21: 43,45

Using the image of the vineyard not producing the proper yield because of the wicked tenants, Matthew gives us pause to wonder who the tenants are and who the landowner is. Most likely, the Temple leaders thought they were the landowner who was wronged, and more likely than not, as we hear the parable today we think it is God who is the landowner and the tenants are the Jewish authorities. As Jesus nears his approaching death, the tension between him and the Jewish religious leaders is at its most intense. Even though this is the case, how unfortunate that much anti-Semitism has ensued from a simplistic understanding of this parable.

So, as we squeeze the Biblical texts today for the good news to leak out, what is it we discover? Three things come into focus for our consideration: The vineyard may actually be the zip code we live in, the stones rejected by the builder may be the unwanted dimensions of our own personalities, and the landowner, like God, does not give up too easily!

First, the parable challenges us to ponder whether we are producing fruit in the vineyard that bears the address where we live, which is necessary for building the Kingdom of God. St. Francis de Sales addresses this precisely:

Don't sow your desires in someone else's garden; just cultivate your own as best as you can; don't long to be other than what you are, but desire to be thoroughly what you are. Direct your thoughts to being very good at that and to bearing the crosses, little or great, that you will find there. Believe me, this is the most important and least understood point in the spiritual life. We all love what is according to our taste; few people like what is according to their duty or to God's liking. What is the use of building castles in Spain when we have to live in France? This is my old lesson.

We hear about a new evangelization and that the Gospel has lost its taste, its freshness, and its luster in much of our culture today. The reigning gods of secularism, consumerism, and materialism erode our confidence in the truths of our faith. We are confronted with untold acts of terrorism at home and abroad. Yet, in the midst of all of these givens, we are called to repropose the Gospel in our own neighborhood, and to do it in the ordinary, everyday moments of our day.

Second, think about those wild and sour parts of ourselves we don't like, those parts of ourselves we want to hide, those things we keep secret. And now, recall the words of Jesus: "Did you never read in the Scriptures: *The stone that the builders rejected has become the cornerstone; by the Lord has this been done, and it is wonderful in our eyes?*" (Mt. 21:42). What are the rejected stones comprising the edifice of our own personality? And, often when we look at what we reject about ourselves, there's the clue to something wonderful, something new, and something exciting. Richard Rohr makes this point in so many varied ways in his writings, but most especially in what I believe to be his mantra: "Everything belongs."

There is a saying in the Salesian tradition, attributed to St. Francis de Sales: "Love your abjections." This is another way of saying that everything belongs. Certainly, we do not welcome our sin or unhealthy behaviors, but by coming face-to-face with our own faults and flaws, we can learn to love even the negative as we turn it to the positive.

Third, God does not give up on us too easily, even as we need to do more tending to the vines in our own gardens. Often we are like the wild grapes spoken of in both the reading from the prophet Isaiah and the gospel from Matthew. We scapegoat and cast the blame on the other, forgetting the mercy God grants in our regard. Jesus asks his audience, the chief priests and elders, "Now when the owner of the vineyard comes, what will he do to those tenants?" The tenants offer the obvious answer: "He will put those wretches to a miserable death, and lease the vineyard to other tenants who will give him the produce at the harvest time" (v. 41). Imagine that God is pointing his finger at us as we tend the vineyard right now—what have we got to show for it?

Thomas Merton wrote: "A witness of a crime, who just stands by and makes a mental note of the fact that he is an innocent bystander, tends by that very fact to become an accomplice." In the vineyard of the world today, we witness gruesome and unimaginable horrors, we see widespread and unnecessary waste, we hear silent or eerily audible screams of the vulnerable—do we make mental notes of these crimes, or are we stirred to action in some concrete way?

The warning in the parable reminds us that we are accountable for what we do with our faith, and the God of love and compassion desires a response from us. And, just like in the parable, God does not give up too easily!

At this Eucharist, we ask God for the passion we need to live in the garden where he has planted us, for the clarity we desire to accept our complex personalities, and for the determination to accept responsibility to produce a good yield in the vineyard of the world.

ISA. 25:6-10
PHIL. 4:12-14, 19-20
MATT. 22:1-14

"Come to the wedding banquet."

*M*y children are among that generation of youth who received trophies for participation at the end of every sports team season. I used to joke that we needed to add a room on to our house in which to display them all. Trophies for each soccer season, medals for each basketball team, math competition, music group, you name it. I have boxes full of them in the attic.

Fortunately, as they grew older, the broad "participation" accolades lessened and trophies only were given for particular achievements. They were much happier feeling that their award actually meant something. "I got this because I did something special," my younger son explained, "and so it means something to me. I don't think I deserve a trophy for just showing up."

That's kind of what we have here in this story from Matthew. Jesus tells of the king who plans to throw a wedding banquet for his son. It's an allegorical story, to be sure, and the way Matthew treats this story (somewhat differently from Luke) suggests that it is a miniature version of the story of the people of Israel who ignored the prophets and were destroyed, set alongside the story of the inclusion of everyone through the work of Christian missionaries.

The parable outlines the initial invitation, based on the wonderful news of a royal marriage, which is then rejected by those who received the invitation—because they are too busy, or because they don't think this banquet is important enough for their notice. Some of the invitees even commit violence against the king's messengers. So the king instructs his messengers to forget the original list and instead invite everyone they see right out there in the streets to this wonderful feast.

And so, in the end, everyone is invited (both good and bad, according to the lens through which Matthew always writes) to the wedding banquet.

One guest, however, turns out not to be wearing the wedding robe, which, apparently, everyone else is. Now, in Matthew's time, the robe was the symbol of conversion. The Christian, on becoming a Christian through baptism, received a new identity, putting away the old life and embracing the new. This was symbolized by the putting on of a white robe, a new set of clothes appropriate for the new way of life. And that new way of life is characterized by bearing fruit, a prominent theme in Matthew. This guest has accepted the invitation but has not done anything else in response. He seems to signify that the invitation didn't actually mean that much to him.

In other words, it's not enough to simply show up. One has to recognize the value of the banquet and is called to do something in response to God's invitation. That is what "being Christian" is!

Now, I want to go back to my initial illustration of my children and their trophies to add the caveat that Jesus is not talking about earning one's way into heaven here. Heaven is not a prize to be won by work—it is a gift that has already been given. But we still have to do our part in response to that gift. First, we have to actually accept the gift. And second, we have to appreciate the value of it. Third, we respond by living a life that bears good fruit.

This is a hard teaching, especially for those of us who want to focus simply on the "everybody is invited" part, because Jesus wants us to remember that accepting the invitation is only part of the story. There is more to it. Jesus expects something from us in response.

To whom much has been given, much is required or expected. So says Jesus in St. Luke, and so has said many a teacher, preacher, parent, coach, and politician. Big things are expected of those with prodigious talent or great wealth. And how much has been given! Heaven has been given! Salvation has been given! Life abundant has been given! *Everything* has been given to us.

And so, yes, something is expected. We have been given no less than heaven. Oh, what a gift! It is not ours to simply hold and be glad of, but to share with a broken and weary world that desperately needs healing and hope. We may not be rich or athletically or musically or mathematically gifted, but we nonetheless have been given everything we need in order to bear fruit worthy of the gift of heaven.

So let us not simply show up and pose for the picture while holding our trophy. The gift of salvation has to mean something! Let us in love and gratitude share the riches of God's grace far and wide, through acts of love toward those who are broken and hurting, because we have been given no less than everything.

ISA. 45:1, 4-6	
1 THESS. 1:1-5	*"Is it right to pay taxes to*
MATT. 22:15-21	*Caesar or not?"*

*Y*ou'd think Jesus was running for office. The Pharisees throw another Gotcha question at him. They think they have him this time.

First they butter him up: "We know you're honest. You're impartial and don't play favorites. You teach the way of God." Then they let him have it: "Does God want people to pay taxes to the emperor? Whose side are you on, God's or the government?"

Of course, the issue wasn't taxes. It was about making Jesus look the fool. Jesus was direct: "Show me a coin you use to pay the tax."

One of the Pharisees held out a coin in his palm, with Caesar's face staring up at him.

"So then, give the government what you owe the government," Jesus said, "and give to God what is God's."

Jesus refused to debate. In a debate, the issue is never the issue. That's why he asked the questioner to display the coin he held dear. It was two-faced, just like the Pharisee himself.

Jesus verified that the Pharisee's flattery—"You teach the way of God"—was the truth. The only kingdom Jesus was interested in was a spiritual one. "Be more interested in the kingdom of God than anything else,"

Jesus taught, "and all these other things will be added to you" (Matthew 6:33). A denarius bore the image of Caesar, who demanded more of the same in return. The Pharisee, and everyone else everywhere, wore the image of God, who asked for nothing and gave peace and joy. That's what Jesus was talking about.

He was neither a politician nor a pundit. He voiced no opinions and taught in parables. Can you imagine Jesus on one of today's talk shows?

"Mr. Jesus, you're not on Facebook, but you have more than 2 billion followers. That said, do you really think a camel can get through the eye of a needle? Really!"

Jesus smiles, stands up, and walks away. "Come follow me," he says, "and I will give you rest."

"Huh?"

Jesus also said, "In this world you shall have tribulation. But be of good cheer, for I have overcome the world!" – John 16: 33

A sure way to experience tribulation is to debate, dispute, and disagree. Nobody wins. Everybody gets mad, and some get sick. Jesus showed us another way—the way of understanding. He clarified forever the difference between kingdoms made on earth and the one created by God. "The Kingdom of Heaven is *within* you" (Luke 17: 21). In the gospel of the former tax collector Matthew, Jesus shows us more than 50 times the way to this Kingdom that is not in a palace or above the sky or beneath the sea but "at hand" (Mt. 4: 17).

- "The Kingdom of Heaven is like a mustard seed which a man sows in his field. It is the least of all seeds, but when it is grown, it is the greatest and becomes a tree so that the birds of the air come and lodge in its branches."—Mt. 13: 31-33

- "The Kingdom of Heaven is also like a merchant who seeks valuable pearls, and when he finds one pearl of great price, he goes and sells all that he has and buys it."—Mt. 13: 45-46
- "Truly I tell you, unless you change and become like little children, you will never enter the Kingdom of Heaven. Therefore, whoever takes the lowly position of this child is the greatest in the Kingdom of Heaven. And whoever welcomes one such child in my name welcomes me."—Mt. 18: 3-5
- "Blessed are the poor in spirit, for theirs is the Kingdom of Heaven."—Mt. 5:3
- "So not lay up for yourselves treasures on earth where moth and rust destroy and where thieves break in and steal, but lay up for yourselves treasures in heaven where neither moth nor rust destroys and where thieves do not break in and steal. For where your treasure is, there your heart will be also!"—Mt. 6: 19-34

And of course:

- "It is easier for a camel to get through the eye of a needle than for someone with too much baggage to enter the Kingdom of Heaven."—Mt. 10:25

Isn't it interesting how today's gospel sheds light on one of the raging debates of our or any time?

Paying taxes? Petty change.

Following Jesus? Priceless!

Exo. 22:20-26 1 Thess. 1:5-10 Matt. 22:34-40	*"You shall love your neighbor as yourself"*

A crew team made up of Jesuits couldn't get their boat moving in the right direction, let alone moving fast. Every day they'd struggle to get into the boat. If they didn't capsize it, they'd still only get it going in circles. So they finally sent one of their Jesuit crew members over to spy on what the Franciscans were doing on a nearby lake for their practices. He comes back and tells his fellow Jesuits, "We're doing it all wrong. The Franciscans have the secret." The Jesuits ask him, "What is it?" "They have eight guys rowing and only one guy yelling!"

Today's readings call us to ponder the relationship between love of God and love of neighbor. Jesuit theologian Karl Rahner called these loves two sides of the same coin. To love one's neighbor is to love God, and no one can claim to love God if such love doesn't usher forth in love of those persons in our world who need our love. Linking love of God and love for neighbor makes our love effective and transformative. St. Ignatius teaches that love has to be expressed in deeds, not mere words. Love has to get us rowing the boat together, in the right way, and in the right direction.

Our first reading today calls attention to one social issue that impels us to practice transformative and effective love. Love of our God today must be expressed in love of those who are our new neighbors, those who have often risked life and limb to travel to our lands. Many of them take the worst-paying and most dangerous jobs in our society. I am talking about our new neighbors, our immigrants.

The Catholic Bishops of the USA have a great website, www.justice-forimmigrants.org. There we learn that immigrants do learn English. Immigrants, even the undocumented, pay taxes. Immigrants don't increase crime or take jobs from "Americans". Undocumented immigrants are not a drain on the economy of the USA, nor a burden on the health-care system.

According to the Pew Research Center, in the USA today, nearly fifty percent of Roman Catholics under the age of 40 are Latinos. Many are turning to Evangelical churches, often because our parishes can be cold and unwelcoming. The April 15th cover story of *Time* magazine chronicled how Hispanics' religious choices will radically affect the future of the Catholic Church in the USA.

In May of 2013, Michael Sean Winters of the *National Catholic Reporter* wrote that Cardinal Dolan of New York City noted that 77% of U.S. Catholics support immigration reform that includes a pathway to citizenship (Winters, NCR May 6 2013). In *Strangers No Longer: Together on the Journey of Hope*, the Catholic Bishops of the USA and Mexico teach that the earth belongs to all peoples. Countries have the right to "control their territories," but when people must migrate to find employment or flee war and persecution, their human rights must be respected. "Regardless of their legal status, migrants, like all persons, possess inherent human dignity which should be respected. Government policies that respect the basic human rights of the undocumented are necessary." How many of us know a "Jose" or a "Maria"? They are our brothers and sisters in Christ. We cannot claim to love God if we close our hearts and our society's benefits to those among us who are in a precarious legal situation. Most especially, we must find a way to accommodate the dreamers, those who do not have the status of citizenship but who have lived their whole lives in our communities. A kid brought to the USA at the age of two or three, who has lived his or her whole life here, who cannot even speak Spanish fluently—such people need to be given the opportunity to study and work and become productive members of our society. We certainly welcome them into our armed forces and allow them to risk their very lives to protect our freedoms.

"Thus says the Lord: You shall not molest or oppress an alien, for you were once aliens yourselves in the land of Egypt. You shall not wrong any widow or orphan. If ever you wrong them and they cry out to me, I will surely hear their cry."

Our God hears the cry of the poor. Do those yelling about immigration on talk radio and cable channels hear the cries of the poor?

There's been a lot of yelling about immigration these past few years. Too little conversation has begun with the idea that we are called by our God to love our neighbor.

Let's put ourselves in an undocumented immigrant's shoes. Imagine you have to emigrate today to Korea or Iraq or Russia. Imagine having to pay a coyote thousands of dollars to float you over on a rickety boat or sneak you in on an unsafe train or plane. When you get to those foreign shores, you must walk several days in horrible weather. If you survive the passage, you need to find food and shelter. You have to begin to learn the language. You need to make a life in a land that differs radically in so many ways, culturally, religiously, sociologically. You miss the USA and Memorial Day, the Fourth of July, and Labor Day. In Korea or Iraq or Russia, those are just days on the calendar. Attending a Catholic church may be a dangerous choice. Imagine having to go and live in a foreign land. There's no work for you where you were born. You have to live the rest of your days in a place where you are never fully accepted or afforded the status of "being one of us."

That's the situation for millions of our brothers and sisters in Christ with surnames like Garcia, Vasquez, or Jimenez.

God wants us to love by loving our neighbor. We all need to grab an oar and start getting the boat of immigration reform moving in the direction God wants it to go. We need to steer the boat of immigration reform toward truth and justice, peace and love.

As we come to this table of the Lord, the same table to which millions of our undocumented brothers and sisters come this day, let us pray.

31ST SUNDAY IN ORDINARY TIME

FRAN ROSSI SZPYLCZYN

MAL. 1:14 – 2:2, 8-10
THESS. 2:7-9, 13
MATT. 23:1-12

"The greatest among you must be your servant."

In the early '80s, I worked in the sales department of an upstate New York TV station. I coordinated the national commercial orders that came in from New York and other cities. My boss was a great man, and a real role model for me.

One day someone told me that there was a state law that mandated two daily breaks. My co-worker and I began to talk about what was due to us. Determined to stake our claim, we made an appointment with our manager.

Sitting in his office, we talked about what we wanted. Smugly, I presented facts and figures about employment law, including those breaks. He sat back in his chair, shaking his head in a way that seemed to express affirmation. As soon as I completed my pitch, he leaned forward, smiled broadly, and said that he would give us our breaks. Victory!

We thanked him profusely, surprised that it was so simple. As we got up he said, "Oh, by the way…" We turned around, as he continued, in a voice rich with concern, "I realize that sometimes you have to come in late, or leave early. You both often need a longer lunch. I'm really sorry we won't be able to accommodate that any longer."

We were stunned! What? He went on, telling us that what he thought was important as a manager was to offer us flexibility, but that if we wanted mandated times, he was happy to go along with it. Needless to say, after hearing about the non-mandated benefits we enjoyed through his wisdom, we left minus our breaks. It was one of the most powerful lessons in both management and in ownership of one's own power that I've ever known.

Today we hear the prophet Malachi railing against the priests of his time. It is late in our liturgical year, and it is late in the time of the Israelites, who long for a messiah. They are weary, living under the burden of oppressive leadership. The people turn to God, but they find no support from the priests, only burdens. The priests have broken the covenant of Levi, are profaning God and harming God's people.

Our Gospel reveals other tired people, first century Jews of Palestine living under Roman occupiers. They find little relief from the men of God of their age; their frustration with the hypocrisy of their religious leaders is high. Again, weariness has set in, along with a profound desire for the messiah who will redeem them. Little do they know, he is in their midst.

It must have been frustrating when Jesus told them to "do and observe all things whatsoever they tell you." We are to do what we are told, but we must also observe; learning what *not* to do is as important as learning what to do. As satisfying as it might appear to use God's law against others, and for our own self-justification, it is very wrong and morally corrupt. Isn't that exactly what Malachi and Jesus are saying about the temple leaders of their times? Those who used the law to burden or harm, and not to serve God and others?

The Catechism of the Church teaches us that we are all baptized to be "priest, prophet, and king." This calls us to a particular responsibility to live intentionally, giving witness to our faith, making an offering of our lives. Taking potshots at the big shots might assuage our anger, but what does it do for God? Perhaps we need to look within and ask ourselves about what we are doing with our own priesthood? Are we living up to our baptismal promises?

How do we accept the responsibility conferred upon us at baptism? Both Jesus and Malachi speak to the burdens put upon God's people that cause them to falter, or be further from God. Do our priesthoods bring others closer to God or drive them away? Do our priesthoods illuminate lives or darken them? How do we do the right thing?

In the second reading from Thessalonians, Paul speaks of the loving care given to those in his charge. He gives us the powerful, intimate image, "As a nursing mother cares for her children." God nurtures us; can we live within the law in the same way? Do we treat with compassion or with contempt? Following Jesus mandates a loving model of taking responsibility for the power given to us and compassionately living it with both strength and tenderness.

That all sounds good, but just how do we live into the law with love?

This is difficult if we are very weary and worn down. Perhaps we are exhausted from economic insecurity, employment challenges, discord at home, or more. Maybe it is the weight of the seeming hypocrisy of our faith leaders on our mind. Do we feel like failures, making it hard to live with kindness for others? And what about compassion for ourselves?

Sometimes it may seem easier to focus on the rules alone, leaving our overtired hearts out of it. That might have us reject others under the guise of the "law" even if it is hurtful. Some of us may abdicate our responsibility by declaring the law absurd, and rejecting God.

If we listen to Jesus, if we "do and observe all things" with his model of priesthood, we might grow closer to what God seeks. God asks us to do this; we always have the right to say no, come what may. But saying "yes" offers us the chance to be part of the dynamic deliverance in our own time.

We come here to be "one body", consuming "one bread". Do we do so in love, which is the foundational law? Do we leave here feeling the overflowing generosity of God? Or do we depart feeling smug and superior because we have done "the right thing"? I am painfully aware that my own loving compliance is extremely flawed at these moments.

The dynamism of the covenant is about both giving and receiving in love. The Eucharist empowers us to live into the gifts of the covenant of our nurturing God. This is God generously giving us the opportunity to love one another into our collective priesthood, and fulfillment of God's dream.

We are asked to find ways to remain engaged in the tender care of one another. The priesthood of Jesus Christ is a gift bestowed upon each of us at baptism, a heavy but beautiful gift to carry. No matter how frustrated or weary we might feel, that responsibility calls us to live in a particular way, giving and receiving, obeying, neither blindly following nor fully rejecting.

This is why I am reminded of my old boss. He listened with care, he responded by offering us the chance to define our own rules, and then he reminded us of what we shared, and what we risked if we made our own way. That long-ago lesson lives on in my heart today, a small reminder of what Jesus gives us today, and always.

WIS. 6:12-16
1 THESS. 4:13-18
MATTHEW 25:1-13

"The wise brought flasks of oil with their lamps."

"*T*he *Kingdom of Heaven will* be like this," Jesus said, and he told the parable of the Ten Bridesmaids. I have to tell you, I hope the Kingdom of Heaven isn't going to be one big wedding reception. That feeling of mine might be something of an occupational hazard. But with all due respect to the weddings I've done, the weddings I will do, the weddings in preparation now, the Kingdom of Heaven yet to come, and the glimpses of the Kingdom of Heaven now—it better be more than beautiful attire, an open bar, and forever dancing to the song "Shout!"

If you treat this parable as an allegory, you can drain all the meaning out of it. You can squeeze it so tight that every detail means something; squeeze it until there's not much life left to it. That Jesus is the bridegroom, that the maidens represent the church, that the banquet is the Kingdom, that the closed door is Final Judgment, that the delay of the bridegroom is the Second Coming. Well, if the Kingdom is all really about a wedding, if the Kingdom will be exactly like a wedding, then the delay of the bridegroom isn't about the Second Coming of Jesus, it's just all about the photographer. Who are we kidding? When Jesus begins with "the Kingdom of Heaven will be like this," it's not the wedding that draws me in.

The core of the parable, the focus of the story, the creative center, the plot turn, it all has to do with the oil. It really is all about the oil. All ten maidens were ready for the ball. All ten had to wait. All of them became drowsy. All of them slept. All of them heard the shout. All of them got up and lit their lamps. These ancient lamps didn't hold a lot of oil to begin with. The burning life of a lamp, the length of the burn, would not have been a secret to anyone. The wise ones took a flask of oil along in order to keep the fire burning. It wasn't gallons, but it was enough; enough for the wait, enough for the party, enough for the day, enough for the night. As one preacher put it, "it's not about how much oil you have, it's about how much you carry with you." But it is all about the oil.

When it comes to the history of interpretation of the Parable of the Wise and Foolish Maidens, in the history of an allegorical approach, the oil has been understood as good works, faith, spiritual practices, deeds of discipleship, acts of love and mercy. Hearers of the Word shouldn't be asked to pick one. You drill down too far on the oil, you get too specific about what it means, and the parable loses some of its luster. What sets the wise apart from the foolish is not simply that they act on the teaching of Jesus. The parable goes deeper than the Epistle of James. It's not all about the works. It's about the oil. The wise draw upon the resource necessary to live the faith-filled life today, and tonight, and tomorrow. The oil? Is it faith? Is it spiritual practices? Is it deeds of discipleship? Is it acts of love and mercy? The answer is yes. All mixed with a bit of grace and the Holy Spirit, a bit of fellowship and praise and a lot of prayer. A Kingdom life. Yes, they all had to wait for the bridegroom to come, but when the lamps were trimmed, their light had to shine right then and there, right now.

I stood in line at the grocery store the other day behind a woman who was reading a magazine she picked up there at the checkout. The older man working the register greeted her, and she said nothing, just kept reading. She held out her card to be scanned without looking up. After all her purchases had gone through, the clerk reached for the magazine to ring it up. "Oh no, I'm not buying this, I'm just reading it," she said, without looking up. He bagged all her groceries while she read. She waited for her receipt with her hand in the air, still reading. He said, "Thank you," she said nothing. Never even looked at him. Just walked away, back around the register, still reading, to put the magazine back. Someone should have tapped her on the shoulder and asked, "Have you not had your grace today?" A little dose of kindness. An act of generosity. A warm greeting. It all starts with being claimed by grace; God's grace for each and every day. Good works, faith, spiritual practices, deeds of discipleship, acts of love and mercy. A life of faith-filled generosity…it can only start with you being claimed by God's grace. The oil you carry. A spark of grace. A light that shines. Just a dose of grace, every day. *will do you*

In the novel *Gilead*, the father and preacher and narrator of the text that is in the form of a letter to his son is Rev. Ames. At one point Rev. Ames tells of standing in the sanctuary one Sunday morning after everyone had left the building. "The elements were still on the table and the candles were still burning," he writes. "Your mother brought you up to me [in her arms] and said, 'You ought to give him some of that.'" (this referring to the bread and wine there on the table.) "You're too young, of course, but she was completely right. Body of Christ, broken for you. Blood of Christ, shed for you. Your solemn and beautiful child face lifted up to receive these mysteries at my hand. They are the most wonderful mystery…" Just a dose of grace.

Your faith filled life today, tonight, and tomorrow. Good works, faith, spiritual practices, deeds of discipleship, acts of love and mercy. Now. Right now Not their light, or his light, or her light, not your grandmother's light, or your child's light, or your neighbor's light. Your light today, tonight, and tomorrow. A spark of grace and your Kingdom life that shines.

"Keep awake, therefore, for you know neither the day nor the hour," Matthew's Jesus said after the parable was finished. That's kind of odd, since the wise, along with the foolish, fell asleep. If it's all about the oil, make sure you carry enough with you for today, and tonight, and tomorrow. Live the life that Jesus teaches right now.

Prov. 31:10-13, 19-20, 30-31

1 Thess. 5:1-6

Matt. 25:14-30

"Well done, my good and faithful servant."

ere's one of my favorite definitions from theology studies. It's a definition of a parable, from the great Scripture scholar C.H. Dodd, who wrote an entire book on the topic. A parable is "a metaphor or simile drawn from nature or common life, arresting the hearer by its vividness or strangeness, and leaving the mind in sufficient doubt about its precise application to tease it into active thought." So rather than giving people precise definitions of, say, the Kingdom of God, or who your neighbor is, Jesus of Nazareth tells somewhat mysterious and poetic stories.

So a parable leaves the mind in sufficient doubt about its precise application. Which is the opposite of the way we often think about the parables. We tend to have them boxed in. We already *know* the point. The parable about the Good Shepherd and the Lost Sheep? It's about God going to great lengths to bring the sinner back into the flock. The one about the Prodigal Son? It's about forgiveness. The parable about the guy who sows seeds, with some falling on rocky ground, some on fertile ground, and some getting choked by thorns? That's about the various kinds of reception that the Gospel gets. In one Gospel, Jesus even *explains* it for his disciples like that.

But some Scripture scholars say that *that* explanation by Jesus may have been added by the Gospel writers later on, because the early Christians didn't like things too vague.

Well, neither do we. We like the parables to be clear. As a result, our minds may not be teased into active thought the way that Jesus wanted them to be. Because we already *know* the parables. Right?

Not so fast. Recently, I read an article that completely changed the way that I understood today's parable of the talents. Turned it on its head.

Now, the normal way of understanding the story is this: The man going on the journey gives his servants three measures of money. And, by the way, there is a little intentional humor in this story, which we usually overlook. A talent is a *huge* amount of money—maybe 15 or 20 years' worth of wages. And one servant gets five talents—75 years of wages. That's like Jesus saying, "A man gave one servant a million dollars!" You can imagine the crowd perking up or even laughing, "A million dollars!" And you can see why Jesus uses some over-the-top examples: to help people remember things, and encourage them to pass them along. "Hey, did you hear that story that Jesus told about a guy who gives his servant a million dollars!"

But back to the parable. As you heard, the servants take care of their talents in various ways. And the one who invests wisely, and gives his master a good return on his investment, is rewarded. Now, the English word "talent" is used for *talanton*, the Greek word for that unit of money. As a result, this parable is usually understood as encouragement to use our talents. Not to squander what God has given us—whether it's our talent for administration, or music, or friendship, or singing, or parenting, or counseling, or listening, or writing, or working with the poor, or being a good doctor or businessperson or lawyer—use the gifts that God has given you. So it makes sense that for the one who uses them, more will be given. Using generously the blessings God has given you, following your vocation, brings you happiness and joy to you and those around you. And that's *true*.

But that *may* not be the way that the first hearers of the parable heard it, or the way Jesus meant it. And now I'm going to shake you up a bit, like I was shaken up.

Recently in *America* magazine, Barbara Reid, a New Testament scholar who writes a weekly column on the Sunday readings, said that the common understanding is wrong. People in Jesus's time did not live in a capitalist system, where the one who invests was celebrated. There was only so much wealth to go around, she says, and the one who amassed great wealth was seen as taking it from others. You can tell this from Jesus's story about the man who stores up his treasure in barns; he's greedy, and he gets punished.

Barbara Reid suggests that the man going on a journey is *not* to be seen as a stand-in for God, and the parable is *not* meant to be an exhortation for people to use their God-given talents to the full. While that's an important thing for Christians to do, it was probably not the way that Jesus's first hearers understood the parable, since *talanton* does not have that connotation in Greek.

And in Matthew's Gospel, she points out, this is the third of three parables that stress the need for disciples to be faithful in the time between Jesus's departure and his Second Coming. So it's part of a larger point he's making. In contrast to slaves, who live in fear of a greedy master who punishes those who will not go along with his program for wealth, Jesus's disciples live with trust in God, whose love helps them to work for justice here and now, while awaiting ultimate fulfillment. The last servant who does *not* invest is the model, not the one who does invest.

Barbara Reid also believes that the parable shows what happens when someone exposes a corrupt system, and stands outside the normal ways of doing things: he's punished. That makes the very strange verse about the ones with more getting more and the one with little getting less make sense. And for people in first-century Palestine, that would have been Bad News: the rich get richer, and the poor get poorer. Many Christians have found that unjust. Well, it is unjust, says Reid. That's what she thinks Jesus is saying.

Now, that's pretty confusing, isn't it? I may have just upended the way that you've thought about that parable. But many of Jesus parables are *supposed* to be confusing, to "tease the mind into active thought."

So what *did* he mean, exactly? What are we supposed to take from it? Well, all of this points out the need for some serious Scripture study, but also some serious soul-searching. What does the parable say to you? Are you called to use your talents more, or are you called to work against unjust systems? Or are you called to do both? Because both points are valid: use your talents, and work against injustice.

The Risen Christ continues to speak to us through parables, and just like the disciples we may find them quite mysterious. But trust that the Holy Spirit is at work in you as you read them and trust that Gods want to move you in unexpected ways through this Living Word.

Which is the "right" interpretation? The one that moves you closer to the Kingdom of God, that challenges you, that moves you to conversion, that increases your love, that builds us a just world. The Spirit is always at work in the Scriptures, even when you're confused. And while it's important to read good scholarly works on the Gospels, to read commentaries and listen to those who teach, it's also important to trust the Spirit is at work in your heart. Use your head, but trust your heart.

You know, at one point when I was a young Jesuit working in East Africa, I made my annual retreat. And I was in the midst of something of a vocational crisis. Anyway, my spiritual director listened to what was going on in my life, and he gave me an assignment to pray over: The Book of Samuel, Chapters 9-12.

But when I got back to my room I realized that there are *two* books of Samuel! And my spiritual director was away for the evening and I couldn't ask him which he meant. In the First Book of Samuel those chapters are about Saul being chosen as King. In the Second Book those chapters are the story of David and his adultery with Bathsheba, the wife of his friend Uriah. Those are two very different stories. So I read both of them.

The next day I went to my director, somewhat confused, and said, "I couldn't remember which one you assigned. Which one did you mean for me to pray?" Rather than answer directly he said, "Well, which one helped you the most?"

And I said, "Oh, definitely the second one, the story of David's betrayal of his friend, because it spoke to me about fidelity and the need to do the right thing."

He smiled, and said, "Then that's the one you were meant to pray."

FEAST DAYS

Exo. 34:4-6, 8-9
2 Cor. 13:11-13
John 3:16-18

"God merciful and gracious, abounding in steadfast love"

Math has never been my favorite subject of study. As far back as I can remember, the thought of math class, math homework, and math tests have elicited a sense of anxiety in me that is not particularly rational, but is nevertheless real. Not everybody dislikes math as much as I do. For example, my younger brother is actually a math teacher who has taught at both the high school and college levels. He entered college with math as his declared major, reflecting a deliberate choice he made to pursue the field in deep and technical ways. Regardless of how much he and those like him love math, I have a feeling that there are a great many others who are more inclined to react to the proposition of solving complicated mathematical word problems in the same way that I am: we just would prefer not to deal with them.

This is one reason why I think so many people do not think deeply about the Christian doctrine of the Trinity. At first glance, the dogmatic claim that God is triune—three *persons*, one *God*—seems like an impossible math problem. "How is it," we might ask, "that one plus one plus one equals *one*?" Is this something out of a high school calculus textbook? The reaction that some people have to the idea of the Trinity is not unlike the answer one gets from finding the square root of a negative number: they claim it's imaginary! (OK, I promise that's the first and only math joke I'll mention). But in all seriousness, the apparent incomprehensibility of the concept leaves many scratching their heads and resigned to simply saying, "it's just a mystery."

In truth, it is a mystery, but mystery is not a word that means "completely unknowable," according to Christian faith. We might never fully understand the meaning of the Trinity, but that is also true about all things that relate so directly to God. Nevertheless, we can affirm the truth of God-as-triune not just in some vague way, but in real ways that come to us from God's Revelation and are passed on to each new generation through Scripture and Tradition. This is what we celebrate today on the day specifically set aside to recall this dimension of our faith, but if we're really honest, every day is a celebration of the Most Holy Trinity.

Instead of thinking about the Trinity in terms of a complicated and confusing math equation to be solved, I believe that we might benefit more from considering an ancient approach to envisioning what the Trinity is all about. The Trinity is about God's ability to hug us!

While it might sound weird at first, the idea that the Trinity is about God's ability to hug us goes all the way back to the second-century theologian Irenaeus of Lyon. At a time when Christianity was still a novel religious movement, Irenaeus found himself frequently responding to critics of the faith, and among his many contributions to Christian theology, he said that the Son and the Spirit are like the two "hands" of God. Although Irenaeus never actually used the term "hug," the point of his illustration was to highlight how God acts "outside" of God's self, how God creates, sustains, and saves all of creation.

What's particularly interesting to me about the idea of the hands of God imagery is the way in which it does lend itself to imagining God as the Divine Hugger. One of my former theology professors used to love "performing" what he thought Irenaues might have had in mind. He'd lean forward and reach his two hands outward. They would meet in front of him with his arms forming a circular shape as if closing a net. This would be the one hand, the Son, and the other hand, the Spirit, working in creation. Then he would draw his arms back as the hands passed one another, reaching around his forearms, elbows, and torso, giving himself something of a one-man bear hug. This latter movement was what he said Irenaeus meant about God's saving act. God's creating, sustaining, and saving all of creation was one cosmic act of the Trinity. At no point in the demonstration do the "hands of God" ever depart from that which is lovingly and personally brought into existence, held in the hands of the Creator, and brought back—in and through those hands—to God's self. God is not some distant clockmaker or disinterested deity, but a deeply relational and personal Creator.

Catherine Mowry LaCugna, a theologian who died far too young at the age of 44, wrote an impressive book on the theology of the Trinity. The title summarizes in three words what the whole theology of the Trinity and what the "hands of God" imagery of Irenaeus conveys: *God For Us*. What the doctrine of the Trinity conveys at its most basic core is that God's history is intertwined with ours and that what we understand through Divine Revelation is that God is consistently more and more a "God for us." God's love isn't some abstract ideal or concept (like a mathematical equation), but is real and concrete.

We hear proclaimed in our first reading from the Hebrew Scriptures about how God discloses to Moses *who* God is: "A God merciful and gracious, slow to anger, and abounding in steadfast love and faithfulness, keeping steadfast love for the thousandth generation, forgiving iniquity and transgression and sin" (Exodus 34:6-7). This is an expression of a God who is deeply concerned about humanity and all of creation, a God who is *for us* and a God who *will be there* for us. Moses's response to the LORD's self-revelation is to request forgiveness for his and his people's slowness to understand what it means to profess faith, hope, and trust in such a God. Far too often, we, like the Hebrew people in Moses's time, are quick to forget that the God who brought us into existence and continues to sustain us today also journeys through life and history with us, loving us faithfully and forgiving our sinfulness.

We hear proclaimed in today's Gospel yet another summary of the truth of the Trinitarian faith: "God so loved the world that he gave his only Son" (John 3:16). This is the culmination of Divine Revelation, the fullness of God revealing to creation who God is as *God for us*. To understand fully what this line—quoted on so many bumper stickers and tattooed on so many bodies—is about, we must return to the beginning of John's Gospel. Most people look at the first chapter of John and basically stop at 1:14, which reads: "And the Word became flesh and lived among us." Yes, this is absolutely important and essential to our faith. However, it is four verses later, in the very last line of the Prologue, that we get the key insight that illuminates today's Gospel passage on this day dedicated to the Trinity. "No one has ever seen God. It is God the only Son, who is close to the Father's heart, who has made him known" (John 1:18).

As the author of the Letter to the Hebrews says, God has revealed God's self in "many and various ways" from the beginning (Hebrews 1:1), but now in Christ Jesus we have the *fullest* and complete revelation of God. Jesus, the Incarnate Son, makes God known in creation. The promise that God makes at the beginning of creation, that God will always be *for us*, comes to the highest expression in this person Jesus of Nazareth. What John 1:18 is saying is that if you want to know what God is like, look at the Son, who is one hand of God active and present to all of humanity and creation. Because Christ is the fullness of Divine Revelation, we can look to his life and ministry as a concrete manifestation of what God is like, and what we see is the truth that God desires nothing more than to draw near to us and for us to accept that relationship in turn by reflecting God's love to others.

Yet, the Incarnation is not the only sign of God's continued and close presence to us. In John 16:12-15, Jesus tells his disciples about the coming of the Spirit, the advocate, the one who will be ever-present and guide us. If this were a play with stage instructions, then the script would read, "Enter the Second 'Hand of God.'" The Holy Spirit is the other assurance of God's immanence in and throughout creation, because the Spirit is God. The Spirit is the one that maintains communion, that is the continued creative presence of God in the world, that we worship as the LORD and the giver of life. The Spirit is the second hand of God that reaches out in the single Divine Act of creation and salvation. The Spirit is the one that will guide us back to the Creator.

Instead of trying to make sense of an apparent mathematical contradiction, perhaps we need to think more about what God is like and less about how God exists. The mystery of the Trinity will inevitably remain, but its meaning—that God is a *God for us*—continues to be lived and experienced at every time and in all places. But do we acknowledge that? Can we see it? Can we accept that to talk about the Trinity is to talk about a God whose very *being* is love and love *for us*?

Only if we come to understand that this is what the Trinity is about can we embrace the blessing the St. Paul gives us in the Second Reading: to encounter the grace and peace of our Lord Jesus Christ; to accept the love of God; and to be united to the Creator and all of creation in the communion of the Holy Spirit (2 Corinthians 13:13). Will you let God hug you?

MOST HOLY BODY AND BLOOD OF CHRIST

FR. JAMES J. GREENFIELD, OSFS

DEUT. 8: 2-3, 14-16
1 COR. 10: 16-17
JOHN 6: 51-58

"The bread that I will give is my flesh for the life of the world"

*I*n his column, *The Amen Corner*, Nathan Mitchell offers an important challenge for today's Solemnity of the Most Holy Body and Blood of Christ:

> The greatest threat to Christian Eucharist is precisely [a] moral numbness that prevents our seeing God's presence in the least and the littlest, that prevents our seeing the Risen One among the most vulnerable citizens of our chaotic world. The greatest threat to Eucharist is world hunger. (It is not for nothing that the great Indian teacher of non-violence, Mohandas K. Ghandi, once said that "if Christ ever comes to India, he'd better come as bread.")

And, for even more context on this feast day, of the 7 billion people alive on the planet, 1.1 billion subsist below the internationally accepted extreme-poverty line of $1.25 a day.

Jesus was born in Bethlehem, translated as "the house of bread." Jesus left this world telling us to be bread for others, wine poured out in loving service to all. We hear Jesus say that whoever eats his flesh and drinks his blood remains in him and he in us. Yet, do we understand what it truly means to *remain* in him?

To remain in Jesus is to accept his challenge: not just to receive him, but also to see the world through his eyes, to engage the world with his passion, and to feed the world with his generosity—and to do this literally! The word "remain" conjures up connections, family and societal ties, to be together in the house of God. This is what it means to be a member of the Body of Christ. Thus, how can we receive Christ in the Eucharist and not *give* Christ in the household of God to the world.

Later in John's Gospel, Jesus tells us that he has come to give us life and to give it abundantly—*not* wanting us just individually to survive, just solely to function well on any given day! He wants all of us to be fed and nourished on the good things that this life has to offer, *not* to subsist below a poverty level, as 1.1 billion people do today. As Paul describes it in his letter to the people at Corinth: "Because the loaf of bread is one, we, though many, are one body, for we all partake of the one loaf." But does everyone get a share in the loaf?

Moses reminded the people that the manna was not just food for their bellies but also food for their journey through the desert. The manna was a reminder of God's covenant to his people to care for them and to be with them always. In Jesus, we witness the amplification of God's covenant, as he himself becomes manna for God's people, fulfilling the law and the prophets. It is the bread that Jesus is that will now feed the whole world, and not just Israel. This is why Jesus warns the people that they should not go after the bread that perishes and spoils, like the manna of the Exodus. Rather, they should seek what he now gives them as food that will endure to eternal life.

And, just verses before, in our Gospel text for today, notice that little unnamed boy who comes forward with his five barley loaves and two fish, and Philip wonders what good these gifts will do for so many? But, we know that one of the greatest themes of Scripture is that God can do so much with so little! Like that little boy, whose name we do not know, but who plays a privileged part in the miracle of the feeding of the multitudes, need we wonder what good can come from the paucity of our own gifts, the ordinariness of our own talents, and the limitedness of our own time? In the words of St. Francis de Sales, "There is nothing small in the service of God."

Perhaps our names will never appear in a newspaper or other media outlet, but the Scriptures remind us that the world is transformed, one person at a time, by our efforts at "doing" Eucharist—being bread for others. As Jesus met the real and concrete needs of the hungry on the hilltop, we, too, can direct the energy of our lives to help others as their needs are made known to us in the *present tense* moments of our lives. St. Teresa of Avila's prayer rings true:

> *Christ has no body now but yours, no hands but yours, no feet but yours. You are the eyes through which Christ's compassion must look out on the world. Yours are the feet with which He is to go about doing good. Yours are the hands with which he is to bless us now.*

Furthermore, only when Jesus met the concrete needs of the people of his day in need of food and drink was he then able to meet the deep desires of their hearts. It is Jesus himself who does the feeding in John's Gospel, underscoring that it is God's desire that no one should ever be hungry or thirsty. This is the deep, rich, and abundant life that he promises to us as we struggle to remain in him.

The challenges of remaining together as the Body of Christ are manifold. It is always a temptation to simply spiritualize the miraculous feeding as a metaphor for Jesus doing all the work to make all things better. What happens gradually to the crowds in John's Gospel is that Jesus challenges them not just to look for the earthly bread he gives them. He wants them to feel a deeper hunger and to desire another feeding that has to do with buying into God's plan. Eucharist, a part of God's plan, does the same for us—it helps to unify us in our deep and real differences as the Body of Christ, knowing that as we eat and drink of the Lord we can look beyond our own differences and see the Body of Christ we already are and are fully becoming.

The chrism prayer at baptism asks God to keep us always as members of Christ's Body. Seeing all of our sisters and brothers as equally needy and hungry members, we are faithful to Jesus, and the promise of our baptism, and the call of the Eucharist.

Yes, the greatest threat to Eucharist is a moral numbness that prevents us from seeing Christ in the least and littlest ... and in the politically conservative and liberal, the happily married and divorced, the liturgically retro and grounded, the spirited straight and gay, the zealous activist and contemplative, and so on.

On this feast day, we hear the words of St. Paul to the people of Corinth, who were receiving the Body of Christ but not acting like the Body of Christ, who had great liturgical festivals but did not flow from worship into service. This puts us on notice!

As Fr. Pedro Arrupe, SJ, once remarked: "If there is hunger anywhere in the world, the celebration of the Eucharist is somehow incomplete everywhere in the world." What are the varied hungers right in front of us requiring our real sustenance, and what are the dreams we need before us beckoning for creative substance to meet them? Remaining in Jesus, let's feed and dream because so many are hungry. And we're among them.

FEAST OF ALL SAINTS

JAN L. RICHARDSON

Rev. 7:2-4, 9-14
1 John 3:1-3
Matt 5:1-12

"*Then he said to me, 'These are they who have come out of the great ordeal.'*"

hen I was in seminary, one of my favorite courses was a wildly intensive two-week summer class on the Book of Revelation. Team-taught by professors in preaching, worship, storytelling, and theater, the class met for twelve hours a day. We began each day in the chapel. Sitting in a circle, we started with morning prayer and then spent the next hour going around the circle and reading the entire Book of Revelation out loud.

The class immersed me in Revelation as I had never before experienced. Like many, my occasional exposure to the book across my life had come largely at the hands of those on the extreme fringes of Christianity who lifted out the more disturbing parts of Revelation, using them out of context in an attempt to terrify their hearers into salvation. (The mainline circles in which I grew up had been largely content to leave Revelation to the folks on the fringe.)

The class gave me my first experience of really meeting Revelation in its wholeness, of entering into the full sweep of it. It is a bizarre book, to be sure. Yet, in that seminary summer I learned that it is beautiful, too—that its dizzying words and signs and symbols and visions, which can strike us as so strange and confusing, actually work together to create something so powerful and poetic and hopeful that it's hard to find anything else in scripture that compares. The "something" that its writer created is not just a book; Revelation invites us into a space that engages our every sense in order to impress upon us how much God loves us and is continually and eternally working to bring about wholeness, restoration, and redemption—not only for us personally but for all of creation.

Part of what makes Revelation so challenging for us to read is that it doesn't unfold in the way that most stories do—in a linear, chronological format where one event naturally leads to the next. Time shifts back and forth in the book. Past and future intertwine with the present in ways that are not easy to separate out. John writes of events that may seem far off but are actually intended to transform our present lives. The effect can be discombobulating. It becomes difficult to find our footing as the chapters unfold.

This is part of the genius and grace of the book. In disrupting our attachment to linear time, Revelation gives us two gifts. Its first gift to us is that it asks us to let go of the belief that we can know and understand everything about God. The confusion it stirs can become a powerful starting place for prayer, for humility, for asking God to show us something unexpected rather than assuming we know it all.

Revelation's second gift is that it offers us a glimpse of the kind of time that God lives in. Although God entered fully into linear time in the person of Jesus, God also dwells in a kind of time that is beyond our grasp: time that isn't linear, that doesn't depend on chronology, that doesn't unfold in a forward progression that can be traced, that cannot really be described as time as we think of it.

There's a wonderful notion that comes to us from Ireland and its neighbors that helps me have a sense of what the writer of Revelation is going after with all this temporal bending and intertwining. From ancient times,

Celtic folk have had a sense of what they call *thin places*—spaces where the veil between worlds becomes permeable, and heaven and earth meet. It's not that God somehow magically becomes more *there* in these places than in other places; rather, something about thin places enables a veil within us to fall away: to see, to hear, to pay attention, to become present to the God who is always present to us.

Thin places exist in the physical landscape—think of pilgrimage sites such as Iona or Santiago or Jerusalem. Thin places occur also in the turning of the year, in particular times that call us to be especially aware of and open to the God who lives within time and lives beyond time in such strange and wondrous ways.

This day we celebrate today—the Feast of All Saints—has historically been one of these thin places in the wheel of the Christian year. With roots in a Celtic festival that fell at a time when the gates between the worlds were thought to become open and past and present met, All Saints' Day was created as a day to recognize the beloved faithful who have gone before us, and who are never far away from us.

Saints are those who are able to glimpse the wholeness that God is continually working to bring about—the restoration and redemption that Revelation depicts with such power. Saints are those who, having glimpsed this wholeness, give their lives to inhabiting this wholeness, becoming bearers of it, pointing toward it and proclaiming it and embodying it with their prayers and actions and entire lives. Having accomplished this in their lifetime, and having "made it through the great ordeal," as John describes in the reading from Revelation for this day, saints are those who now have more than a glimpse—who now see with fullness, with completeness, and who are still somehow at work to support and encourage us as we live into the redemption that God is bringing about.

The Feast of All Saints invites us to remember that the beloved faithful who have gone before us are still part of our Christian community. Death does not release the saints from being in relationship with us. This day offers us a thin place, a space in which to acknowledge the threads of connection that persist, and to give thanks for the communion that abides. This day calls us to remember that they, and we, belong to a God who is not bound by time. We belong to a God for whom and in whom the past and present and future intermingle and intertwine, offering doorways through which we can receive encouragement and strength so that we may work toward the world that, somehow, God has already brought about in that place beyond time—a place that John describes at the end of Revelation 7:

> They will hunger no more, and thirst no more;
> the sun will not strike them,
> nor any scorching heat;
> for the Lamb at the center of the throne will be their shepherd,
> and he will guide them to springs of the water of life,
> and God will wipe away every tear from their eyes. (16-17, NRSV)

As we move through this day, how might we open ourselves to the God who lives both within and beyond time? How would it be to ask for a glimpse of the wholeness that God is working to bring about within us and through us? What vision or dream is God stirring in us? How will we call upon the strength of the saints to encourage and inspire us?

All Hallows Blessing

Who live
in the spaces
between our breathing

in the corner
of our vision

in the hollows
of our bones

in the chambers
of our heart:

nowhere can they
be touched
yet still

how they move us,
how they move
in us,

made from the
tissue of memory
like the veil
between the worlds

that stirs at
the merest breath
this night
and then is
at rest.

WISDOM 3: 1-9
ROMANS 5: 5-11
JOHN 6: 37-40

"The souls of the just are in the hand of God"

I was baptized in a graveyard. In it, my parents, grandparents, great-grandparents and great-great-grandparents are buried. Standing in the center of it is St. Colmcille's Church, where members of my family have worshipped since 1834, located in the village of Aughnacliffe, County Longford.

The day of my baptism was the fourth day of November. It was a good day, a Sunday, and a good place, this graveyard was, to go under the water (however small the portion) because St. Paul says:

> *"All of us, who were baptized into Christ Jesus, were baptized into his death. By baptism into his death, we were buried together with him, so that just as Christ was raised from the dead by the glory of the father, we too might live in newness of life"*
> ROMANS 6:3 – 4

Great words indeed, good food for thought today, as we focus on All Souls, on the second day of November.

November is rightly aligned in the Western world with endings, and darkness, and death. It was Samhain season in olden times, meaning the end of summer, when the crops were gathered, the hatches were hasped, firewood was stored, and the cattle came down from the hills. At this time we think of God's holy harvest of all human beings gathered from the fields of His earth. The leaves fall from the trees and sometimes the dry ones spin in an eerie silence that tickles the imagination. Samhain was a time when, thousands of years ago, people felt that the dead were near. The veil that hung between the living and the dead became awfully thin and easily penetrated. It is good that we have our Christian sense of Samhain with the celebration of All Souls Day. Other religions have their times of connecting with the dead in thought and ritual. But just as Thanksgiving Day, a wonderful harvest day in the U.S.A., is not just for one day of gratitude, so All Souls is not for one day, but a memorial day for all days, a reminder to not forget those who are gone before us. The Biblical verse (2 Macc. 12:46) is a good reminder: "It is a holy and wholesome thought to pray for the dead that they may be released from their sins."

God be praised for the human spirit. I have always rejoiced in the fact that human beings, in general, deal with the dead with respect, ritual, and memorial. The name of the village where I was baptized, Aughnacliffe, means "field of stones". It is true that stones, going back to Moses and the tablets, are enduring material. The Ten Commandments were not written on loose-leaf. The stones of Aughnacliffe, five in all, form a dolmen to honor the dead. This dolmen is made up of three big stones holding up one end of a huge top stone and one standing alone holding up the other end. The top stone is estimated to weigh twenty tons, and it rests on the standing stone, six feet in height, on a point that is the size of my fist. It has been resting there, unmoved, for 4000 years. Who could ever calculate the effort, the human ingenuity, and the reverence for the dead that is expressed in this ageless monument?

It is an extraordinary example of human beings honoring those who are gone and their own need to express it in a lasting way. Today, the dolmen of Aughnacliffe is not unknown in the glance of Google at our planet. But great arrangements of huge stones that constitute dolmens or portal tombs are found in many countries, especially in Europe. Western Europe has the oldest dolmens on the planet, and Ireland has 163. But Korea has the most in the world. They are found in many places from India to Israel. And each one of them announces that the people who erected them and those who wanted them erected were writing hope for the continuation of human life. They didn't write this hope in letters; the permanence of the stones themselves comprised the words of hope.

All Souls Day celebrates that message of hope. The human heart does not surrender to death, and has not, through all the fog and blinding obstacles of an earlier half-conscious Odyssey. That urgent quest continued until Jesus emerged from his tomb and walked on the earth at the dawn of the day. Easter, the greatest day in human history, gives All Souls Day its awesome core of truth against all the odds and ends of reality.

Only God could count the bits of bone and dust that lie in our punctured earth, unmarked and unknown. Thinking of this, my mind goes to secondary school and Joseph Addison's essay on the graveyard at Westminster Abbey. I still remember the words "promiscuous heap of matter" after more than 60 years.

"Upon my going into the church, I entertained myself with the digging of a grave; and saw in every shovelful of it that was thrown up, the fragment of a bone or skull intermixt with a kind of fresh mouldering earth, that some time or other had a place in the composition of a human body. Upon this, I began to consider with myself what innumerable multitudes of people lay confused together under the pavement of that ancient cathedral; how men and women, friends and enemies, priests and soldiers, monks and prebendaries, were crumbled amongst one another, and blended together in the same common mass; how beauty, strength, and youth, with old age, weakness and deformity, lay undistinguished in the same promiscuous heap of matter." Addison does not say that all the bits count in God's big basket of Human Harvest. But they do. They count in the universal celebration of All Souls.

On February 28, 1973, I read the prayers at the grave of my uncle Matthew Creegan in Calvary Cemetery in Queens, NY. There he lies with more than three million buried bodies inside the gates of Calvary. That number is more than the number today (2.248 million) of living people above the ground in the whole of Queens. There are thirty cemeteries that are open in Queens and fifty-five closed and full. Manhattan, in 2013, has a population of 1.6 million, and it is increasing every year. It is a city where babies can be born but no body can be buried. It's a place where the mythical boatman of death, Charon, would be very busy rowing across the East River to Queens. It reminds us that it is a great idea to have a day for All Souls.

The importance of All Souls Day was greatly enhanced by Pope Benedict XV, who led the Roman Catholic Church from 1914-1921, even though All Souls Day had its start 1100 years before his pontificate. He was very conscious of the horrendous four-year slaughter of human beings in the First World War. Ten million people died. No such killing had ever been seen on this planet up to that time. All Souls. All those souls. Each with a name. He created the opportunity for his priests to offer Mass three times on that day.

In All Souls Mass for November 2, 2014, the first reading, Wisdom, chapter 3:1, announces that "the souls of the just are in the hand of God and no torment shall touch them." In the lines preceding these words, Wisdom assures us that "God formed human beings to be imperishable; the image of his own nature God made them. But by the envy of the devil, death entered the world." But Wisdom continues: "The souls of the just ....are in peace. God tried them and found them worthy of Himself." Like the bread and wine from the wheat and the grapes that go through the mill and the wine press to be worthy of the breaking and the sharing; to be worthy of the transformation into the Body and Blood of Christ, we too go through the mill of life's pressure into what God can find "worthy of Himself". Death, more than any other reality, forces us to cling to hope.

The great Jesuit priest, Karl Rahner, who was acknowledged as the greatest theologian of the last century, has this to say about the dead: "Though invisible to us, our dead are not absent. They are living near us, transfigured into light and power and love." The dead are near. It is we who are away. We need to be home in the heart that remembers. I knew a man in a popular family food store in South Philadelphia who served hoagies to the people in his neighborhood for a lifetime. Over the years, as people died, he faithfully went to the viewings, said his prayer, and took a card back to the store to be placed in the special stack on his shelf. Every day Michael played out his stack of cards, and each name got his glance and his remembrance. Every day, he did his bit, as we all should do, to honor All Souls.

CHRIST THE KING

FR. GREG BOYLE, SJ

EZEK. 34:11-12, 15-17
1 COR. 15:20-26, 28
MATT. 25:31-46

"Whatever you did for one of the least brothers of mine, you did for me."

I never preach about Kings on the feast of Christ the King. I don't think Jesus would approve if I did. The readings, after all, aren't very regal. Instead, they are about what Martin Luther King called "the Least, the Lost and the Last." We are called to "search them out," and so fully identify, with an exquisite mutuality, with the stranger, the hungry and the incarcerated. We are invited, as Pope Francis would say, "to the outskirts," and by so standing at the margins, we join Jesus in erasing them. We plant ourselves in solidarity with the demonized so that the demonizing will stop. We situate ourselves exactly with the "disposable" so that the day will come when we stop throwing people away. "The Least, the Lost and the Last" are the only royalty in which Jesus has any interest.

For 25 years, I've run Homeboy Industries, the largest gang intervention, rehab and re-entry program in the world. It's a tough sell, but a good bet. I suppose if we were a decaying Hollywood sign, instead of a sign of hope to gang members, Los Angeles wouldn't let us crumble. If we were a center for abandoned puppies, instead of a place of second chances, we'd never worry about closing. When the gospel connects with our hearts and we find ourselves on the "outskirts", those on the margins wonder what we're doing there. They aren't accustomed to our accompaniment. I knew a homie named William who was shot on 33. Word reached me the following day and I showed up in his hospital room. He sees me and brightens. "What ya get me for Christmas?" "Nothing," I tell him, "but it looks like God gave you a proper-ass gift."

He's startled by this announcement. "Yeah? What?"

"A second chance at life, cabrón!"

"Oh, yeah…that," William says, all things dawning on him now. "Yeah, the doctor said the bullet destroyed *one-fourth* of my lungs. That's almost *half!*"

I congratulate him on his mastery of fractions.

Since he's in the neighborhood of stuff "dawning" on him, he says, "Hey, G. Who ya visiting here?"

"I'm sorry?" I say, not catching it.

"I mean…who'd ya come to see at the hospital?"

"*You*, menso…*you!*"

"Nuh-uh," William says with unbridled disbelief.

I have no idea what he thought. Perhaps that I was wandering the halls when I came upon him, or I was visiting other hospitalized parishioners. "The least ones" have to get used to your being there.

Louie was a big 'ol tattooed gang member who did a lot of time in prison. He said to me once, "I was disguised as that guy." When he finished his 18-month training program with us, he asked to speak at our morning meeting. 300 of us were packed in the lobby for our daily ritual and he looked out at this crowd of other tattooed faces. "All of you are diamonds…covered in dust. You can wipe your dust off here."

We had located a job for him as he transitioned from life with us to the "real world." He texted me one Saturday. "Hey G. My fridge just died. Can you help?"

I text back. "Sears. 4 pm." He responds immediately. "Got it. Beers. 4 pm." As the homies say, "Louie's got jokes."

I see him in the appliance section of Sears at the appointed hour. He's carrying on with two salespeople, gregarious and playful. He sees me and beelines it to give me a bear hug in aisle 9, lifting me off the ground. "Have they called security on your ass yet?", I ask him.

"Nope, but it's just a matter of time."

We secure his refrigerator, on a payment plan, to be delivered to his humble apartment. I drive him home.

Before he gets out of the car, though, he says, "Can I tell ya somethin? Lately...I've been havin' one-on-ones...with...you know...God." Now he gets quiet and still. "And...the Dude shows up." Now he turns and looks at me, and his eyes moisten. "I mean...why would He do that?" Now he's crying. "I mean...after all the shit I've done...why would He do that?" God, seeking out the Least, is a tough sell...even to the Least.

In the end, the measure of our compassion with the "Least, the Lost and the Last" lies not in our service of those on the margins, but in our willingness to see ourselves in kinship with them. Jesus doesn't speak of how grand it is to feed the hungry or visit folks in jail. His identity with them is total. I am the jailed one. I am the hungry one. It speaks of a kinship so mutually rich that even the dividing line of "service provider/service recipient" is erased.

Martha has had a tough life. Abandoned, tortured, and abused as a child, she, predictably, transmitted her pain, long before she got around to transforming it. Gangs, drugs, and prison filled nearly two decades of her life. And she carries that particularly heartbreaking pain of, in her addiction, giving birth and having the child taken away and raised by strangers. She works for me and is solid in her recovery now. But the shame and disgrace, the principal suffering of the poor, still weighs heavily. We talk in my office one day, about, well, stuff and she just begins to sob. She folds her arms on the front of my desk and rests her weary, weeping head there. I touch her shoulder and ask, "Why are you crying?" She looks up and blurts, "I wish you were God." This makes me chuckle, "Why?" When Martha can form the words through her sobbing, she says, "I think… you'd let me into heaven." Now it's my turn to cry. I reach across the expanse of my desk, and I grab both her hands and pull her in close. "Kiddo, I swear to you…if I get to heaven and you're not there…I'm not stayin'."

Martha has changed my life forever. Knowing her has altered the course of my days, re-shaped my heart and returned me to myself. Both of us… diamonds…covered in dust. She has not taught me that I am somebody, but that I am everybody. And so is she. Exquisite mutuality. Kinship. It is what's left, when the margins get erased.

Kingship makes Jesus yawn. Now, kinship…that's another story.

THEMATIC CROSS REFERENCE

Adversity: 231, 261

Anger: 169

Anxiety: 23, 123, 175

Attachment: 215

Baptism: 51, 199, 277

Beatitudes: 155, 269

Barriers: 77

Community: 37, 101, 139, 161, 185, 221
235, 245, 255

Compassion: 315, 203, 277

Conversion: 265

Courage: 193

Darkness: 57, 151

Death: 81, 87, 175, 303, 309

Desert: 57

Discernment: 19

Discipleship: 151,181,189,193,207,221,
269

Divorce: 165

Ego: 215, 235, 241, 277

Emptiness: 119

Eucharist: 33, 45, 91, 221, 227 299

Evangelism: 181, 185, 261

Faith: 77, 81, 181, 231, 261, 281, 285

Family: 37

Fear: 115

Forgiveness: 111,139, 169, 175, 249. 293

Freedom: 19

Gifts: 285

Glory: 133

Grace: 281

Gratitude: 199, 265

Grief: 19, 227

Healing: 77

Hope: 41, 309

Hospice: 87

Hospitality: 115, 199, 221

Incarnation: 293

Immigrants: 273

Inclusion: 209

Indwelling: 235, 269

Intimacy: 137

Journey: 147

Justice: 231, 253

Kingdom: 105, 155

Kingship: 315

Lament: 57

Laws: 209

Light: 147, 161

Loss: 123

Love: 169, 203, 209, 255, 273

Marginalized: 73, 155, 245, 315

Marriage: 165

Mercy: 209, 249, 281

Ministry: 73

Mystery: 293

Patience: 29

Persistence: 231, 261

Poor: 161, 189, 273

Possessions: 151

Poverty: 119

Power: 95

Praise: 33

Prayer: 169

Preparedness: 7, 13

Reconciliation: 165

Relationship: 123, 147, 161, 249, 255

Remembrance: 91

Renewal: 51

Repent: 57

Resurrection: 81, 105, 101

Revelation: 303

Saints: 13, 303

Salvation: 175, 241, 253, 265

Service: 73, 215, 299

Sin: 63, 185, 249

Solitude: 227

Spirit: 129, 137, 139

Surrender: 95, 175

Temptation: 63

Threshold: 69

Time: 29, 303

Transfiguration: 69

Transition: 147

Transformation: 37, 41, 57, 129, 241

Trinity: 293

Trust: 29

Wilderness: 63

Woundedness: 73

THE CONRTIBUTORS

REV. WILLIAM J. BAUSCH is a parish priest of the diocese of Trenton, New Jersey. He is the award-winning author of numerous books on parish ministry, the sacraments, Church history, storytelling, and homiletics. His book, *Traditions, Tensions, Transitions in Ministry* received an honorable mention in 1983 from the Catholic Press Association; *Storytelling: Faith and Imagination* was awarded second place in 1985 for best pastoral work; *The Total Parish Manual* won first place in 1995; *Brave New Church* first place in 2002; and *Once Upon a Gospel* won third place in 2009.

He was awarded the President's Award in 1996 from the National Federation of Priests' Councils for Parish Leadership, the Catholic Library Association's Aggiornamento Award for Notable Contribution to Parish Life in 2004 and the Walter J. Burghardt, S. J. Preaching award in 2008 for his contribution to Catholic preaching. He has lectured and given workshops at such colleges and universities as Notre Dame; Sacred Heart in Fairfield, Connecticut; Boston College; Charles Carroll in Cleveland; and in most U.S. dioceses as well as abroad. His latest book is *Encounters*, a book of homilies.

First and foremost, however, though retired from the pastorate, he remains happily engaged in his first love: being a parish priest active in assisting at three parishes, writing, and giving lectures and retreats.

ROB BELL was named one of Time Magazine's 100 Most Influential People in the World in 2011. Rob Bell is the author of a number of books, including *Velvet Elvis*, *Drops Like Stars*, and the *New York Times* bestsellers *Love Wins* and *What We Talk About When We Talk About God*. The founding pastor of Mars Hill, an innovative church in Grand Rapids, Michigan, his Nooma short film series has been viewed by over thirty million people around the world. His sold-out speaking tours of clubs and theaters have repeatedly taken him around the English-speaking world and in 2013 he launched CraftLab, a leadership event designed to help executives, writers, artists, and activists develop and create compelling new content. He and his wife Kristen live with their three children in Southern California. For more information on Rob go to: www.robbell.com.

REV. JOEL BLUNK is Associate Pastor at the State College Presbyterian Church in Pennsylvania, where he has led the Fellowship in Senior High (FISH) youth group since

1994. Beginning in 2012, Joel launched a new outreach ministry known as the *Wheel-House* (www.scpresby.org/), which seeks to help people find that place where their "deep gladness and the world's deep hunger meet." Professionally, Joel has enjoyed being an athlete, coach, singer/songwriter, pastor, and spiritual director. His focus is now devoted to men's groups, rite of passage experiences for youth and young adults, helping older adults embrace the second half of life, and tending to the sacred threads that weave one's soul. He enjoys basketball, playing guitar, hiking with his wife Kristen, and playing disc golf with his three sons. He is a graduate of Duke University and Vanderbilt Divinity School. His music is available on iTunes.

FR. GREGORY BOYLE, SJ was born in Los Angeles and is one of eight children. He entered the Society of Jesus (Jesuits) in 1972 and was ordained a priest in 1984. He received his BA in English from Gonzaga University, an MA in English from Loyola Marymount University, and advanced theology degrees from the Weston School of Theology and the Jesuit School of Theology at Berkeley.

He has taught at Loyola High School in Los Angeles, was chaplain in the Islas Marias Penal Colony in Mexico and at Folsom Prison, and worked with Christian Base Communities in Cochabamba, Bolivia. He was appointed pastor of Dolores Mission Church in the Boyle Heights neighborhood of East Los Angeles in 1986, where he served through 1992. Homeboy Industries was born in 1988 and is now the largest gang intervention, rehabilitation, and re-entry program in the United States. (www.homeboyindustries.org)

Fr. Boyle is the author of the *New York Times* bestselling book *Tattoos on the Heart: The Power of Boundless Compassion*. His debut book has been honored by SCIBA (Southern California Indie Booksellers Association), Pen USA, *Publishers Weekly*, and Goodreads Choice Awards.

Fr. Boyle has received numerous honorary degrees, awards, and recognitions, including the Civic Medal of Honor, the California Peace Prize, Humanitarian of the Year from *Bon Appetit Magazine*, and in 2011 was inducted into the California Hall of Fame.

Fr. Boyle has served on the U.S. Attorney General's (DOJ) National Task Force on Children Exposed to Violence, the Office of Juvenile Justice and Delinquency Prevention's (OJJDP) National Gang Center Advisory Board, the State Commission for Juvenile Justice and Delinquency Prevention, and the Loyola Law School Center for Juvenile Law and Policy (CJLP) Advisory Board.

SISTER SIMONE CAMPBELL, SSS has served as Executive Director of NETWORK since 2004. She is a religious leader, attorney, and poet with extensive experience in public policy and advocacy for systemic change. In Washington, she lobbies on issues of peace-building, immigration reform, healthcare, and economic justice. Around the country, she is a noted speaker and educator on these public policy issues.

During the 2010 congressional debate about healthcare reform, she wrote the famous "nuns' letter" supporting the reform bill and got 59 leaders of Catholic Sisters, including LCWR, to sign on. This action was cited by many as critically important in passing the Affordable Care Act. She was thanked by President Obama and invited to the ceremony celebrating its being signed into law.

In 2012, she was also instrumental in organizing the "Nuns on the Bus" tour of nine states to oppose the "Ryan Budget" approved by the House of Representatives. This budget would decimate programs meant to help people in need. "Nuns on the Bus" received an avalanche of attention across the nation from religious communities, elected officials and the media. She recently led a new cross-country Nuns on the Bus trip (May 28 through June 18, 2013) focused on comprehensive immigration reform.

Simone has often been featured in the national and international media, including recent appearances on *60 Minutes, The Colbert Report*, and *The Daily Show with Jon Stewart*.

She has received numerous awards, including the "Defender of Democracy Award" from the international Parliamentarians for Global Action and "Health Care Heroes Award" from Families USA. In addition, she has been the keynote or featured speaker at numerous large gatherings, including the 2012 Democratic National Convention.

Prior to coming to NETWORK, Simone served as the Executive Director of JERICHO, the California interfaith public policy organization that works, like NETWORK, to protect the interests of people living in poverty. Simone also participated in a delegation of religious leaders to Iraq in December 2002, just prior to the war, and was later (while at NETWORK) part of a Catholic Relief Services delegation to Lebanon and Syria to study the Iraqi refugee situation there.

REV. DR. DAVID A. DAVIS is currently the senior pastor of the Nassau Presbyterian Church in Princeton, New Jersey. He has served that congregation since 2000. David earned his Ph.D. in Homiletics from Princeton Theological Seminary. He is currently the Chairperson of the Board of Trustees for the Presbyterian Foundation. His academic work has focused on preaching as a corporate act and the active role of the listener in the preaching event. Before arriving in Princeton, he served for fourteen years as the pastor of the First Presbyterian Church, Blackwood, NJ. David is married to Cathy Cook, a Presbyterian Minister who is Associate Dean of Student Life at Princeton Seminary. They have two children, Hannah and Ben.

David is a regular contributor to the *Huffington Post* and various journals in the discipline of preaching and has had published of a collection of his sermons. The book is titled *A Kingdom You Can Taste: Sermons for the Church Year.*

You can follow David's weekly homilies at: www.nassauchurch.org/worship/sermons.php

MSGR. MICHAEL DOYLE was born on a farm in Rossduff, County Longford, Ireland. Ordained a Catholic priest in Wexford, Ireland, he came to the Diocese of Camden in 1959, where he taught high school and assisted in various parishes. In 1974, Msgr. Doyle was appointed pastor of Sacred Heart Parish, where he continues to serve.

Fr. Doyle earned a Master's Degree in Education from Villanova University in 1962 and received an honorary Doctorate in Humanities from Villanova in May 2007. He has a lifelong commitment to peace and justice. In 1971, he participated in the "Camden 28" peace action against the Vietnam War at the Federal Building in Camden and was arrested. He was acquitted two years later in a trail where he acted as his own defense. Anthony Giacchino directed and produced a documentary about the "Camden 28" in 2007.

He has been the subject of television programs such as *60 Minutes'* "Michael Doyle's Camden" in 1983 and CBS's *Sunday Morning,* December 1995, and of newspaper articles such as *The Philadelphia Inquirer's* series on inspiring preachers, 1996.

During his tenure at Sacred Heart, he has established a free medical clinic serving those without medical benefits; founded the Heart of Camden Housing, which renovates abandoned houses and assists low-income families to become homeowners, and helped to establish Camden Churches Organized for People, CCOP, a church-based community organizing effort. He has written numerous magazine and newspaper articles and pens a monthly "letter" that is mailed to thousands on his mailing list. A collection of his letters was published in March 2003 in a book called *It's a Terrible Day, Thanks Be to God.*

ROBERT ELLSBERG was born in 1955 and raised in Los Angeles. He graduated from Harvard College with a degree in religion and literature and later earned a Masters in Theology from the Harvard Divinity School. From 1975 to 1980 he interrupted his college studies to join the Catholic Worker community in New York City, serving from 1976 to 1978 as managing editor of *The Catholic Worker* newspaper. He worked with Dorothy

Day for the last five years of her life, an experience that prompted his conversion to Catholicism and shaped his subsequent life. His first book was an anthology of Dorothy Day's writings. More recently, he edited her diaries, *The Duty of Delight*, and her selected letters, *All the Way to Heaven*.

Since 1987, he has served as editor-in-chief of Orbis Books, the publishing arm of the Maryknoll Society, where he has overseen the publication of over 1000 titles. In 2006, he also became the publisher of Orbis.

Ellsberg is the author of a number of bestselling books, including *All Saints: Daily Reflections on Saints, Prophets, and Witnesses for Our Time*, *Blessed Among All Women*, and *The Saints' Guide to Happiness*.

MICHELLE FRANCL-DONNAY is a professor of chemistry and a writer. Her reflections on the joys and struggles of attempting to live a contemplative life in the midst of the everyday chaos that being a wife, mother of teenagers, and teacher brings appear regularly at the Philadelphia Archdiocese's *CatholicPhilly.com*. She is an occasional contributor to *Give Us This Day* and *Liguorian Magazine*, and a regular columnist for the science journal *Nature Chemistry*. Her essays have appeared in several print collections, including *Professing and Parenting* and *The Open Laboratory* 2009, and online at *dotMagis* (www.ignatianspirituality.com/author/francl-donnay/) and *This Ignatian Life* (ignatianlife.org/author/mfranci/). Michelle gives the occasional retreat and blogs about prayer, God, and laundry at *Quantum Theology* (quantumtheology.blogspot.com).

FR. JAMES J. GREENFIELD, OSFS, is an Oblate of St. Francis de Sales and has worked in a variety of educational roles at the university level, and also as director of a number of Salesian programs for his community prior to his present ministry as its provincial superior of the Wilmington-Philadelphia Province, a position he has served since January 2008. He now lives with his local Oblate community in Wilmington, DE.

Fr. Greenfield followed his undergraduate degree in politics from DeSales University with master's degrees in divinity and counseling from DeSales School of Theology and George Washington University, respectively. He later returned to GW to earn his doctorate in human development.

Fr. Greenfield serves as chairman of the board at Salesianum School and Nativity Preparatory School, both in Wilmington, DE, and the Washington Theological Union in D.C. He is also a trustee on the boards of Father Judge High School and DeSales University. He was selected by the leaders of religious communities of men in the United States to serve as president-elect of the Congregation of Major Superiors of Men (CMSM) and will become its president in August 2014.

Working many years in Washington, D.C., Fr. Greenfield has served in a number of parishes for weekend ministry, where he greatly enjoys preaching and celebrating Mass. He has traveled throughout the various regions of his province leading parish missions, retreats, and days of recollection. He is a certified pastoral counselor and author of a number of articles on religious life, seminary formation and the intersection of spirituality and human development. He enjoys running, practicing the piano, and spending time with his nieces and nephews.

REV. PAUL A. HOLMES, S.T.D., was ordained a priest for the Archdiocese of Newark in 1981 and is now Distinguished University Professor of Servant Leadership at Seton Hall University. In 1992, Father Holmes helped inaugurate Clergy Consultation and Treatment Service, an interdisciplinary outpatient treatment program for priests at St. Vincent's Hospital in Harrison, New York, and has recently returned to serve once again as the program's Spiritual Director.

Father Holmes was invited to be the first occupant of the Carl J. Peter Chair of Preaching at the North American College in Rome. He has published articles in numerous journals and was invited to create *This Sunday's Scripture*, the first homily service of Twenty-Third Publications. He has also offered a number of "Authentic Preaching" practicums to deacons and priests from around the English-speaking world. In collaboration with the National Leadership Roundtable on Church Management, he has developed the Toolbox for Pastoral Management, offered twice a year, teaching new pastors the administrative skills needed to lead a vibrant Catholic parish in the 21st century.

FR. DANIEL P. HORAN, OFM, is a Franciscan Friar of Holy Name Province, a columnist at *America* magazine, and the author of several books, including *The Last Words of Jesus: A Meditation on Love and Suffering* (2013), *Francis of Assisi and the Future of Faith: Exploring Franciscan Spirituality and Theology in the Modern World* (2012), and *Dating God: Live and Love in the Way of St. Francis* (2012). In addition to his award-winning popular writing, Fr. Dan has published dozens of articles in scholarly journals including *Theological Studies*, *New Blackfriars*, *Worship*, *Cistercian Studies Quarterly*, and *The Merton Annual*, among others. He has previously taught in the Department of Religious Studies at Siena College and the Department of Theology at St. Bonaventure University. A frequently sought-after speaker, Fr. Dan has lectured, directed retreats, and led workshops around the United States and in Europe. He is currently completing a Ph.D. in Systematic

Theology at Boston College. Additionally, Fr. Dan is currently a member of the Board of Directors of the International Thomas Merton Society. His blog is www.datingod.org, and you can follow him on: Facebook www.facebook.com/DanHoranOFM and Twitter @DanHoranOFM. For more information, visit www.DanHoran.com.

MICHAEL LEACH is publisher emeritus and editor-at-large of Orbis Books. A leader in Catholic publishing for more than 30 years, he has edited and published more than two thousand books. His authors include Nobel Prize winners, National Book Award winners, and hundreds of Catholic Book Award winners. He has served as president of the Catholic Book Publishers Association and the ecumenical Religion Publishers Group. Before joining Orbis as director and publisher in 1997, Michael was president of the Crossroad/Continuum Publishing Group in New York City. In 2007, the Catholic Book Publishers Association honored him with a Lifetime Achievement Award. Dubbed "the dean of Catholic book publishing" by *U.S. Catholic* magazine, he has also authored or edited several books of his own, including the bestsellers *Why Stay Catholic?* and *I Like Being Catholic, A Maryknoll Book of Prayer, The People's Catechism,* and *I Like Being Married.* He is a columnist for the *National Catholic Reporter* (ncronline.org/authors/michael-leach). A popular speaker at Catholic conferences nationwide, Mike lives in Connecticut with his wife of forty-four years, Vickie.

FR. JAMES MARTIN, SJ, is a Jesuit priest, author, and editor-at-large of *America*, the national Catholic magazine. Father Martin is the author of several books, including *The Jesuit Guide to (Almost) Everything*, which was a *New York Times* bestseller and won a Christopher Award in 2010. His memoir *My Life with the Saints*, which also received a Christopher Award, and his book *Between Heaven and Mirth: Why Joy, Humor and Laughter are at the Heart of the Spiritual Life*, were both named among "Best Books of the Year" by *Publishers Weekly*. His newest book is *Jesus: A Pilgrimage*. His books have been translated into Spanish, German, Chinese, Portuguese, Korean, Polish, Lithuanian, and Slovenian.

Father Martin entered the Jesuits in 1988, after graduating from the Wharton School of Business and working at General Electric for six years. During his Jesuit training, he worked in a homeless shelter and with the seriously ill in Boston; at a hospice run by the Missionaries of Charity in Kingston, Jamaica; with street-gang members and with the unemployed in Chicago; as a prison chaplain in Boston; and, for two years, in Nairobi, Kenya, with the Jesuit Refugee Service, where he helped East African refugees start small businesses. He received his Master's Degree in Divinity (M.Div.) and in Theology (Th.M.) from the Weston Jesuit School of Theology in Cambridge, Mass. and was ordained a priest in 1999. Since his ordination he has received honorary degrees from several colleges and universities.

Father Martin has written for a variety of publications, both religious and secular, including *The New York Times*, *The Wall Street Journal*, *The Boston Globe*, *Slate*, and *The Huffington Post*, and has appeared on all the major networks, including venues as diverse as CNN, BBC, the History Channel, and Vatican Radio. He has also been featured on such programs as NPR's *Fresh Air with Terry Gross*, PBS's *NewsHour*, Fox TV's *The O'Reilly Factor*, and Comedy Central's *The Colbert Report*. Father Martin blogs regularly for *America* magazine's "In All Things," posts to a public Facebook page (FrJamesMartin) and tweets under @JamesMartinSJ.

DEACON GREG KANDRA is the Multimedia Editor of Catholic Near East Welfare Association (CNEWA), a pontifical society founded by Pope Pius XI in 1926. He oversees all online content for the agency and edits its award-winning quarterly magazine, *ONE*. Deacon Greg is also the author of the popular blog "The Deacon's Bench," carried on the spiritual website *Patheos*.

Before joining CNEWA, Deacon Greg spent nearly three decades in broadcast journalism, most of that time at CBS News, where he was a writer and producer for a variety of programs, including *48 Hours*, *60 Minutes II*, *Sunday Morning* and *The CBS Evening News with Katie Couric*. He was also the founding editor of "Couric & Co.," Katie Couric's blog at *CBSNews.com*. In addition to his work with CBS News, from 2000 to 2004 he also served as a writer and producer on the live finales of the hit reality series *Survivor*.

In 2002, he co-wrote the acclaimed CBS documentary "9/11," hosted by Robert DeNiro, which told the story of firefighters on September 11, 2001. The film showed the only footage shot inside the World Trade Center that day, and featured the last images of Fr. Mychal Judge, moments before he became the first official fatality of the attacks.

In print, Deacon Greg's radio essays were featured in Dan Rather's best-selling book *Deadlines and Datelines*. His spiritual writing has been published in *America*, *U.S. Catholic*, *Catholic Digest*, *Reality* and *The Brooklyn Tablet*. He contributes homiletic reflections to *Connect!*, the award-winning parish resource published by Liturgical Publications, and writes spiritual reflections for the monthly prayer guide *Give Us This Day*.

Deacon Greg has received every major award in broadcasting, including two Emmys, two Peabody Awards and four awards from the Writer's Guild of America. He has been honored three times by the Catholic Press Association.

A Maryland native, Deacon Greg graduated from the University of Maryland with a B.A. in English. He was ordained a deacon for the Diocese of Brooklyn in 2007. He and his wife live in Forest Hills, New York, where he serves at Our Lady Queen of Martyrs parish.

You can follow Deacon Greg on his blog at www.patheos.com/blogs/deaconsbench

DEACON JIM KNIPPER is a Roman Catholic deacon serving the Diocese of Trenton, N.J. When not serving his faith community at St. Paul's in Princeton, he is CEO of J. Knipper and Company, Inc., and a principal of Clear Faith Publishing LLC and editor/contributor of this book.

In 1981, Jim graduated from the University of Scranton with a degree in Chemistry, and in 1984 he received a Master's in Business in the Pharmaceutical Industry from Fairleigh Dickinson University. He is currently pursuing his Masters in Theology from Georgian Court University.

He is a member of the Board of Trustees for Georgian Court University, the only Catholic University in the Trenton Diocese, and a former member of the Board of Trustees for the University of Scranton, one of the 28 Jesuit colleges and universities in the United States.

Deacon Jim lives with his wife, Teresa, in Princeton and Cape May, NJ, and is father of four sons.

You can follow him and his homilies on his blog site: teachbelief.blogspot.com, Facebook page: www.facebook.com/teachbelief, Twitter @jjknipper

FR. RICHARD G. MALLOY, SJ, aka "Mugs," was born at Temple University Hospital in Philadelphia, and earned a doctorate in Cultural Anthropology from Temple (He didn't go very far in life!) His dissertation was an ethnographic study of Puerto Rican leaders in Camden, NJ.

After being educated by the Sisters of Mercy in grade school, he went on to the Jesuit high school in Philadelphia, St. Joseph's Prep. He attended Lafayette College in Easton, PA, and then entered the Jesuit Novitiate in Wernersville, PA. While in Jesuit formation, he spent two years teaching high school in Osorno, Chile, and one year in pastoral work in Santiago.

For 15 years (1988-2003), Fr. Malloy lived and worked at Holy Name Church in Camden, NJ, as a member of the Jesuit Urban Service Team (JUST). From 1994 to 2008, he also taught at St. Joseph's University in Philadelphia.

In September 2010, he was sent to the University of Scranton, where he serves as the Vice President for University Mission and Ministry, working with campus ministry, community outreach, service learning, and international service trips. He teaches cultural anthropology, lives in a freshman dorm (anthropological fieldwork!), and plays his guitar to awaken students who fall asleep in class or during his homilies.

Fishing is his passion in life, and he prays for the day when he will catch a 10 lb. trout or a 47 inch Muskie. He is convinced that such a catch, the Eagles winning the Super Bowl, or the Phillies beating the Yankees in the World Series would all be sure signs that the second coming of Jesus is at hand.

You can follow Fr. Malloy on his blog: jesuitjottings.blogspot.com and Twitter @FrMalloy.

BROTHER MICKEY O'NEILL MCGRATH, OSFS, an Oblate of St. Francis de Sales, is an award-winning artist, author, and storyteller who lives and works in Camden, NJ. He is a popular presenter and frequent keynote speaker at conferences, parishes, and retreat centers throughout the United States and Canada. Using his own paintings and the stories which inspired them, Bro. Mickey makes deep and often humorous connections between art, social justice, and religious faith around a wide variety of themes and subjects.

Bro. Mickey also paints on commission for parishes and schools, and his most recent commissions can be viewed on his website. He has created illustrations and/or written articles for many of today's leading Catholic publishers, including *America Magazine*, *Commonweal*, and *St. Anthony Messenger*. In 2010, his painting "Christ the Teacher" was presented to Pope Benedict XVI. God only knows where it is now.

Mickey's first and foremost love, however, is books, in all aspects: illustrating, writing, publishing, and promoting. In 2013, *Saved By Beauty: A Spiritual Journey with Dorothy Day*, was the recipient of two first place awards from the Association of Catholic Publishers and the Catholic Press Association.   Bro. Mickey sees his work as being at the service of Catholic social teaching. To that end, he has created posters for the United States Conference of Catholic Bishops to promote immigration reform and home missions and has licensed his work to Catholic textbook publishers. He is a recipient of the Thea Bowman Black Catholic Education Award in recognition of his work on Sr. Thea Bowman, his great spiritual mentor and inspiration.

Mickey also offers workshops on the creation of mandalas and other forms of artistic meditation. Since 1987 he has been a summer faculty member at the Grunewald Guild in Leavenworth, Washington, an interfaith art guild where he is officially designated a "Guild Master."

Bro. Mickey currently lives and works in Camden, NJ. You can visit his website at www.bromickeymcgrath.com.

REV. CAROL HOWARD MERRITT has been a pastor for 14 years, serving growing Presbyterian churches in the swamps of Cajun Louisiana, a bayside village in Rhode Island, and in an urban neighborhood in D.C. She is the award-winning author of *Tribal Church* (Alban 2007) and *Reframing Hope* (Alban 2010). She has contributed to numerous books, websites, magazines, and journals. Her blog, TribalChurch.org, is hosted by the Christian Century. Carol is a sought-after speaker and a host of Unco (short for Unconference). She co-hosts God Complex Radio, a podcast with Derrick Weston. Carol lives in Chattanooga, TN with her daughter and husband. You can follow her on: Twitter @CarolHoward Facebook: www.facebook.com/carolhowardmerritt.

REV. PENNY A. NASH serves as Associate Rector at Bruton Parish Episcopal Church in Williamsburg, Virginia, where she is engaged in ministry with children, youth, young adults, and families. After completing her priestly formation and M.Div. (with a Certificate in Anglican Studies) from the Candler School of Theology at Emory University, she was ordained in 2008 in the Diocese of Atlanta. She loves working in downtown Colonial Williamsburg, where she parks next to a horse and serves communion to people dressed in 18th century costume. Penny has written meditations for Forward Movement publications, contributed to a collection of essays called *Letters to Me: Conversations with a Younger Self*, and serves as a Celebrity Blogger in the annual *Lent Madness* online devotional (www.lentmadness.org). An amateur photographer, she posts daily prayers, reflections, and visual meditations at "One Cannot Have Too Large a Party" (www.penelopepiscopal.blogspot.com) and is an avid user of social media to build community and spread the Gospel. Follow her on: Twitter @penelopepiscopl and Facebook: www.facebook.com/penny.nash.733

MSGR. WALTER E. NOLAN is a retired Catholic priest within the Diocese of Trenton, N.J. He received a BS degree in Pharmacy from Fordham University, a Masters Degree in Divinity from Pope John University in Massachusetts, and a Masters Degree in Pastoral Counseling from Iona College. He served as Associate Pastor of St. Gregory's, Chaplain and Athletic Moderator of Notre Dame High School, Chaplain at Rider University, Director of Priest's Personnel for the Diocese, and served the Catholic community of Princeton as pastor of St. Paul Church for fourteen years before retirement. He continues to host the *Trenton Diocese Catholic Corner* radio and TV show.

CHRISTINE VALTERS PAINTNER, PH.D. is the online Abbess at www.AbbeyoftheArts.com, a global monastery without walls and an online gathering place for the Holy Disorder of Dancing Monks. She is the author of seven books on contemplation and creativity, including *The Artist's Rule: Nurturing Your Creative Soul with Monastic Wisdom* and *Eyes of the Heart: Photography as a Christian Contemplative Practice*. Christine is a teacher, pilgrimage guide, spiritual director, and Benedictine oblate, and she lives out her commitment as a monk in the world with her husband John in Galway, Ireland.

JAN RICHARDSON is an artist, writer, and ordained minister in the United Methodist Church. She serves as director of The Wellspring Studio, LLC, and travels widely as a retreat leader and conference speaker. Known for her distinctive intertwining of word and image, Jan's work has attracted an international audience drawn to the welcoming and imaginative spaces that she creates in her books (including *Night Visions* and *In the Sanctuary of Women*), blogs, and public events.

Jan serves as the Visiting Artist at First United Methodist Church of Winter Park, Florida, is on the faculty of the Grünewald Guild in Washington State, and belongs to Saint Brigid of Kildare Monastery, a community that draws from Methodist and Benedictine traditions. She makes her home in Florida with her husband and frequent collaborator, the singer/songwriter Garrison Doles. Visit her primary website at janrichardson.com.

FR. RICHARD ROHR, OFM is a globally recognized ecumenical teacher bearing witness to the universal awakening within Christian mysticism and the Perennial Tradition. He is a Franciscan priest of the New Mexico Province and founder of the Center for Action and Contemplation (CAC) in Albuquerque, New Mexico. Fr. Richard's teaching is grounded in the Franciscan alternative orthodoxy—practices of contemplation and lived kenosis (self-emptying), expressing itself in radical compassion, particularly for the socially marginalized.

Fr. Richard is author of numerous books, including *Everything Belongs*, *Adam's Return*, *The Naked Now*, *Breathing Under Water*, *Falling Upward*, and *Immortal Diamond: The Search for Our True Self*.

CAC is home to the Rohr Institute, where Fr. Richard is Academic Dean of the Living School for Action and Contemplation. Drawing upon Christianity's place within the Perennial Tradition, the mission of the Rohr Institute is to produce compassionate and powerfully learned individuals who will work for positive change in the world based on awareness of our common union with God and all beings. Learn more about Fr. Richard and CAC at cac.org.

MARY ELIZABETH SPERRY holds a Master's Degree in Liturgical Studies from the Catholic University of America and a Master's Degree in Political Science from the University of California, Los Angeles. She has worked for the United States Conference of Catholic Bishops since 1994. She is the author of *Bible Top Tens* (Our Sunday Visitor), *Ten: How the Commandments Can Change Your Life* (Franciscan Media), and *Scripture in the Parish: A Guide for Ministers* (Liturgical Press). Her articles have appeared in *Liguorian Magazine, Emmanuel, Today's Parish* and other publications. She has spoken in the Dioceses and Archdioceses of Baltimore, Los Angeles, Dallas, Harrisburg, and Orange and has given talks and retreats in numerous parishes. She has been interviewed about the Bible on National Public Radio, CBS Radio, *Catholic Community of Faith, The Drew Mariani Show*, and *Seize the Day*.

FRAN ROSSI SZPYLCZYN is a writer and public speaker with a focus on how spirituality intersects with daily life. By day she is the Pastoral Associate for Administration at the Church of the Immaculate Conception in Glenville, NY. Fran worships at St. Edward the Confessor in Clifton Park, NY, where she is involved in liturgical ministry and catechesis. In May of 2013, she received her MA in Pastoral Studies from St. Bernard's School of Theology. Her work has been published in *The Evangelist* (www.evangelist.org), the newspaper of the Roman Catholic Diocese of Albany (www.rcda.org), in the *Albany Times Union* (www.timesunion.com) and in the *National Catholic Reporter* (www.ncronline.org). She lives in Clifton Park, NY with her husband, Mark, and step-daughter, Erica. You can explore her work at her personal blog, *There Will Be Bread* (breadhere.wordpress.com). Fran also hosts blogs for her two parishes, which can be found at *The Parish Blog of St. Edward the Confessor* (stedwardsblog.wordpress.com) and *Pastoral Postings* (pastoralpostings.wordpress.com) Follow Fran on: Twitter @FranSzpylczyn and Facebook: www.facebook.com/fran.szpylczyn.

PATRICK J. WENRICK graduated with an M.Div. in Mission Specialization from Catholic Theological Union in 1982 and was ordained a priest in October of the same year. Since that time he has been in various ministries within the Church, including being a Vocation Director and Assistant Pastor of two churches in NJ, as well as an Assistant Rector of a religious community. In 1997 he graduated from LaSalle University with a Master's Degree in Pastoral Counseling and went to work first as a therapist and later as Program Director for a drug and alcohol outpatient facility in Bucks County, Pennsylvania. While Program Director he also taught World Religions as an adjunct faculty member at Bucks County Community College. In 1998 he also established his own clinical practice in New Jersey and was licensed in the state as a professional counselor.

In July 2003, Rev. Wenrick married his lovely wife Susan in Princeton, NJ, and together they moved to the Tampa area with their daughter, Allyson. He continues to witness marriages, perform baptisms, and to be available for visiting the sick and dying in hospitals and nursing homes. A gifted preacher, Rev. Wenrick and his wife also continue to tend to the poor and needy of the community through donations of food and clothing, and by assisting with other needs. He has been a member of CITI Ministries and the International Council of Community Churches since 2004.

While in Tampa he has served as Director of an Allied Health Career School, and a tutorial program for licensed practical nurses who wish to become registered nurses. He also has served as a chaplain with a hospice in Lakeland, FL. He has given numerous workshops and talks on life-span development, mid-life spirituality, and loss resolution issues. He has weaved a healthy spiritual-psychological approach to the issues that confront contemporary society.

THE CHARITIES

BETHESDA PROJECT began in 1979 when Father Domenic Rossi and members of his prayer group from Daylesford Abbey in Paoli, Pennsylvania, reached out to a group of women experiencing homelessness in Center City, Philadelphia. Committed to caring for the women as they would members of their own family, the group rented a former rooming house. The women had a new home there, and the prayer group provided the caring support that they needed to help them cope with mental illness. In 1982, Bethesda Project bought its first permanent house.

By 1984, Bethesda Project began to branch out by adding professional staff to its ongoing volunteer efforts and opening several shelters for homeless men. Now operating as an interfaith, nonprofit organization, Bethesda Project serves more than 2,500 homeless and formerly homeless men and women each year at 14 sites throughout Philadelphia. Its facilities offer a continuum of care ranging from low-demand drop-in centers, shelters, and safe havens to permanent supportive residences and semi-independent, low-income housing.

With the image of a caring family as our model, we find our greatest strength is in building long-term, trusting relationships with the most vulnerable among the homeless. Now, more than 30 years since our beginning, Bethesda Project remains committed to our initial calling—to find and care for the abandoned poor and to be family with those who have none.

For more information about Bethesda Project:
Website: www.bethesdaproject.org
Facebook: www.facebook.com/BethesdaProject

DRESS FOR SUCCESS Mercer County promotes the economic independence of disadvantaged women by providing professional attire, a network of support, and the career development tools to help them thrive in work and in life.

Founded in 2007, Dress for Success Mercer County has served more than 2,000 women throughout central New Jersey. They are an independent 501(c)(3) nonprofit organization and an affiliate of Dress for Success Worldwide, a global nonprofit corporation that has supported more than 700,000 women in need in 130 cities around the world since 1997. While they are known for providing business attire to disadvantaged women entering or returning to the workplace, it is their employment retention programs that are the cornerstone of their program model. Finding work is only one step in a woman's journey towards economic independence; remaining employed and building a rewarding career are essential if a woman is to become self-sufficient.

Dress for Success Mercer County's innovative continuum of job-readiness programming offers the tools to transition out of a life of dependency, into the workplace, and on to a successful career. Their clients come to us from a diverse group of non-profit and government agencies.

For more information about Dress for Success Mercer County:
Website: www.dressforsuccess.org/mercercounty
Facebook: www.facebook.com/DressForSuccessMercer
Twitter @dfsmercer

HOMEFRONT began over 22 years ago when Connie Mercer was taken by a pediatrician friend to the bleak welfare motels then dotting the highway leading into Trenton, NJ, where homeless families, some with three or four children, were crowded into single rooms. They had no food, no way to get food, and no way to prepare it even if they had it. There was no place for the children to play except the cracked parking lot. At day's end, Connie's friend turned and said to her, "There are hungry, homeless children in your community. Fix it."

Since that day, HomeFront set out to do just that, first by providing hot meals and organizing volunteers to get food to these families. And since that day, with the help of well-trained staff and dedicated volunteers, HomeFront has grown to a multi-site organization with a comprehensive slate of programs. Their mission is to end homelessness in Central New Jersey, with a particular focus on family homelessness. In the past year alone, almost 7,000 heads of households walked through their front doors looking for help. On any given night, they provide emergency shelter, transitional housing and permanent affordable housing to over 450 individuals, two-thirds of them children.

In addition to shelter, food, and other necessities, they make sure their clients have whatever support they need to become—and remain—stable, from educational assistance to employment skills, parenting help and other life skills. They remain focused on the emotional and physical needs of homeless children, as they believe that children born into poverty and homelessness should not face these conditions as a life sentence.

HomeFront utilizes all segments of the community to accomplish its mission of providing comprehensive programs that enable formerly homeless families to become independent, contributing members of the community. They have established wonderful collaborations with a wide range of congregations, corporations, and organizations, who assist in their mission of returning families to independence. More than 1,200 volunteers work with them each year.

For more information about HomeFront:
Website: www.homefrontnj.org
Facebook: www.facebook.com/HomeFrontNJ

NEWBORNS IN NEED, INC. is a 501(c)3 charity organized to take care of needy babies. Their volunteers provide care necessities such as blankets, sleepers, diapers, hats, and booties to agencies and hospitals serving premature, ill, or impoverished newborns. Newborns In Need distributes items free of charge to babies in the United States. Founded upon Christian principles of love and acceptance, NIN has provided essential items without charge to those in need since 1992. They are also there for the saddest need of all, providing bereavement items for the one who left the family too soon.

Chapters serve their own communities by contacting local agencies, hospitals, and shelters and provide items wherever needed. Volunteers meet monthly to cut, sew, knit, crochet, pack, and organize these care items throughout their geographic area. Made up of hand-made and store-bought items, these donations are delivered each month to waiting recipients.

Here in New Jersey, there is only one Essential Needs Chapter of NIN, in Burlington County, founded in April, 2011, and one Diaper Bank Chapter in Union County, founded in 2012. Although they are located in a specific area, they do not hesitate to cross county boundaries to provide gift bags to those in need. In Burlington County, they work closely with the Virtua Center for Women in Lumberton, who distributes gift bags to their needy clients. Individuals may also request assistance privately.

By providing these "Newborns in Need" with these necessary items in order to see them through their first few weeks of life, they are contributing to the welfare of not only the baby, but the whole family. Babies do not choose the circumstances of their birth, but they do deserve a safe place to sleep and clothing and blankets to keep them warm.

For more information about Newborns in Need, Burlington County:
Website: www.newbornsinneed.org
Facebook: www.facebook.com/pages/Burlington-County-Newborns-in-
    Need/101486969952529

ACKNOWLEDGEMENTS

*O*ne *could assume that once* you get to the second book, the work becomes easier. I am not sure about that, but I do know that the following people were invaluable in making this project come together. So my sincere thanks and blessings to them:

— Joelle Chase whose knows so well the voice of our spiritual friend.

— Dave Clarfield who provides the critical eye that yielded a well proofed manuscript.

— Steve Clarfield who taught me what great things can come from the 'no's' of life.

— Doug Cordes who continues to add great style to the work of our Contributors.

— Maureen Edore who adds the necessary order in my life.

— Meredith Gould who has always been a valued sounding board from the very first thought of this book series.

— Mike Krupa whose experience in executing quality print production yields an incredible book.

— Mickey McGrath, whose gift and grace of his art brings to life the words that have been written.

— To Linda, Nancy, Joanne, Mike, Frank, Joe and all the employees at J. Knipper and Company whose unending support allows me the time and space to work on my passion.

— For my sons, Tim, Jon, Peter and Jacob, for your constant love and support.

And, of course, to all of the Homilists for the Homeless in this volume. Your talented words have created a volume of wisdom that I know will touch each reader in a way that will bring them closer to the one they call God. And in doing so, together we do our part in feeding the hungry, clothing the naked and caring for the sick.